Newington, New Hampshire Families *in the* Eighteenth Century

Henry Winthrop Hardon

HERITAGE BOOKS
2020

HERITAGE BOOKS
AN IMPRINT OF HERITAGE BOOKS, INC.

Books, CDs, and more—Worldwide

For our listing of thousands of titles see our website
at
www.HeritageBooks.com

Published 2020 by
HERITAGE BOOKS, INC.
Publishing Division
5810 Ruatan Street
Berwyn Heights, Md. 20740

Copyright © 1991 Heritage Books, Inc.

All rights reserved. No part of this book may be reproduced or transmitted in any form or by any means, electronic or mechanical, including photocopying, recording or by any information storage and retrieval system without written permission from the author, except for the inclusion of brief quotations in a review.

International Standard Book Number
Paperbound: 978-1-55613-540-8

PREFACE

Henry Winthrop Hardon (1861-1934) was born in Boston and was a successful lawyer in New York City until his death. However, it is through his avocation of genealogy that he is best remembered today. The New Hampshire Historical Society has six published and twenty-eight unpublished genealogies by him, on such families as Cole, Huckins, Lord, Peverly and Roberts. Because of their high standards of scholarship and extensive use of primary sources, Hardon's works continue to be used extensively.

As Hardon explains in his "Introduction," the basis for *Newington Families* was Rev. Joseph Adams' record of marriages and baptisms, dating from 1716 to 1783. These Hardon rearranged by family, and then made numerous additions, from such sources as the *New England Historical and Genealogical Register*, various volumes of the *New Hampshire State Papers* and published genealogies. For some families the entries are brief - perhaps just a few marriages or baptisms. But for many, the treatment is so lengthy that it amounts to a genealogy in itself. Among these are the families of Adams, Ayres, Bickford, Fabyan, Furber, Nutter, Peavey, Pickering, Place, Shackford, Trickey and Walker.

The Town of Newington borders on the north and west of Portsmouth, in the southeast part of New Hampshire. Originally a part of Dover called Bloody Point, it was separated as a town in its own right in 1713. Being so close to the earliest settlements in New Hampshire, Newington is an important town for anyone doing research into 17th and 18th-century New Hampshire. However, no published history of Newington includes genealogies.

The New Hampshire Historical Society is pleased to make its original manuscript of *Newington Families* available to a wider audience. We hope that by publications such as this, we will continue our mission of communicating the values of New Hampshire history to everyone.

William Copeley
Librarian
N.H. Historical Society

INTRODUCTION

There is no town history of Newington. A sketch with special reference to the old church is to be found in the *Register*, vol. 58, p. 24. Scattered references to Newington families are to be found in Miss Thompson's *Landmarks of Ancient Dover*.

Having had frequent occasion to consult the printed copies of Rev. Joseph Adams' record of baptisms and marriages, 1716-1783, it occurred to me that I should save myself and subsequent searchers uncertainty and loss of time, if I arranged his records in family groups, which I have now done. The arrangement has disclosed some errors in his record and suggests ommissions. It is not to be assumed that a clergyman, however painstaking, is not subject to the lapses of memory common to mankind. Some of the errors I have noted. Some of the ommissions I have been able to supply. Both errors and ommissions may have been due, in part, to lack of care in the copyist who prepared the record for publication. This is clearly true of the earlier copy published in the *Register*. I cannot speak definitely of the copy which I have followed, for I have not examined the original. I assume that for practical purposes, it is accurate enough.

I have amplified the family records in some cases by references to printed matter or other records. I have not, however, sought to bring the account of any family down to date, but merely to present a view of the families in Newington during Mr. Adam's pastorate.

The reader may assume that dates of baptisms and marriages found in the following pages are for the period of Mr. Adams' pastorate derived from his record unless another source is indicated in the text.

Henry W. Hardon

7 Day Street, New York, April 13, 1924.

NEWINGTON, NEW HAMPSHIRE FAMILIES in the EIGHTEENTH CENTURY

ABBOTT

Capt. JOHN^3 ABBOTT (Walter$^{2-1}$) (*Descendants of George Abbott*, p. 1033, Libby's *Gen. Dict. of Maine and N.H.*), m. 24 July 1718, probably as his second wife, MARY HEPWORTH, formerly of Ireland (*Register*, vol. 23, p. 395).

HENRY ABBOTT, m. 24 Oct. 1750, ELIZABETH SIMPSON, both of Portsmouth.

ADAMS

1. Rev. JOSEPH^4 ADAMS (Joseph$^{3-2}$, Henry^1), of Newington, 1715, clergyman, A.B. Harvard 1710, b. at Braintree, Mass., 4 Jan. 1688/9,$^+$ d. 20 May 1783, m. (1) 10 Oct. 1720 (*Register*, vol. 24, p. 14), ELIZABETH (KNIGHT) JANVIN,

---

+*Henry Adams and His Descendants*, 1898. The compiler apparently did not have the benefit of the record kept by Rev. Joseph^4 Adams.

John Adams, afterwards President, met his cousin Rev. Joseph^4 in Portsmouth in 1771 and says in his diary: "How I used to love him! He is broken to pieces with rheumatism and gout now. To what cause is his ruin ascribed?"

dau. of John and Bridget (Sloper) (Stackpole's *Durham*, vol. 2, p. 244) and widow of John, b. at Portsmouth, d. 10 Feb. 1757, m. (2) 3 Jan. 1760, ELIZABETH BRACKETT.

The will of John Knight dated 29 Nov. 1720, proved 7 June 1721, mentions his wife, Bridget, and daughter, Elizabeth Adams, (*N.H. State Pap.*, vol. 32, p. 125).

Children by first wife, born at Newington:

    i. ELIZABETH^5, bapt. 22 Oct. 1721, d. 13 Oct. 1722/3.

2   ii. JOSEPH, bapt. 20 Jan. 1723, b. 17 Jan. 1723.

    iii. HANNAH, bapt. 4 Apr. 1725, m. Rev. GRAY, of Boston.

3   iv. EBENEZER, bapt. 11 Sept. 1726, b. 4 Sept. 1726.

4   v. BENJAMIN, bapt. 19 Jan. 1728/9, b. 18 Jan. 1728/9.

2. JOSEPH^5 ADAMS (Joseph$^{4-2}$, Henry^1), of Newington and Barnstead, 1792, physician, A.B. (Harvard, 1745), bapt. 20 Jan. 1723, d. 22 Mar. 1801, m. JOHANNA GILMAN, dau. of Maj. Ezekiel and Sarah (Dudley) (*Gilman Genealogy*, p. 235).

Children, baptized at Newington:

5   i. EZEKIEL GILMAN^6, bapt. 26 Nov. 1747.

6   ii. JOSEPH, bapt. 16 June 1751.

7   iii. EBENEZER, bapt. 24 June 1753.

    iv. DUDLEY GILMAN, bapt. 18 Jan. 1756, m. 8 Apr. 1790, SARAH WALKER, dau. of David Walker, b. at Portsmouth.

    Child:

    1) Elizabeth, m. Ebenezer Adams 6-i.

    v. WILLIAM, bapt. 5 Mar. 1758.

    vi. JOHN, of Newington, bapt. 25 Feb. 1759, d. 27 Aug. 1831 (*Register*, vol. 73, p. 197) m. 1787, ABIGAIL^5 COLMAN (2-iii), dau. of Phineas^4 and Abigail (Huntress), *q.v.*

    vii. ELIZABETH, bapt. 6 Sept. 1761, m. 1784, as his second wife, JOHN^3 JANVRIN (1-i-1), son of John^2 and Elizabeth (Stickney), *q.v.*

    viii. ABIGAIL, bapt. 19 Aug. 1764, m. 24 Nov. 1796, WILLIAM^3 JANVRIN (1-i-2), son of John^2 and Elizabeth (Stickney), *q.v.*

    ix. BENJAMIN, bapt. 21 May 1767, s. *s.p.*, m. ELIZABETH RAND, dau. of David.

    x. NATHANIEL, bapt. 31 Mar. 1770, m. OLIVE^6 HODGSON (7-iii), dau. of Charles^5 and Hannah (Dennett), *q.v..*

    xi. POLLY, bapt. 19 Mar. 1786 (*Newington Church Records*).

3. EBENEZER^5 ADAMS (Joseph$^{4-2}$, Henry^1), of Newington, bapt. 11 Sept. 1726, d. Nov. 1764, m. 13 Jan. 1757, LOIS DOWNING, b. 1729, d. 16 Sept. 1820.

Children, baptized at Newington:

8   i. SAMUEL^6, bapt. 12 Mar. 1758.

ii. JOHANNA GILMAN.

iii. ELIZABETH, b. 1760, d. 6 Jan. 1844 (*Register*, vol. 73, p. 199), m. 8 Dec. 1779, her cousin, Capt. JOSEPH^6 ADAMS, (6) son of Dr. Joseph^5 and Joanna (Gilman), *q.v.*

4. Deac. BENJAMIN^5 ADAMS (Joseph$^{4\text{-}2}$, Henry^1), of Newington, town officer, member of the Convention which adopted the Federal Constitution, soldier in the Revolution (Capt. Smith's Company), bapt. 19 Jan. 1729, 24 Mar. 1803, m. (1) 6 June 1751, ABIGAIL^4 PICKERING (3-vi), dau. of Lt. James^3 and Mary (Nutter) *q.v.*, m. (2) 22 Apr. 1784, SUSANNA BROWN, b. 26 May 1755, d. 20 Jan. 1824 (*Register*, vol. 73, p. 196). He had his father's homestead at Newington.

Children by first wife, baptized at Newington:

  i. Capt. JAMES^6, of Rochester, bapt. 8 Mar. 1752, m. June 1778, MARY COLE, dau. of Capt. Amos and Elizabeth (Wallingford), b. at Berwick, Me., 22 Aug. 1756.

  ii. ELIZABETH, bapt. 20 Oct. 1754, d. 10 Feb. 1757.

  iii. NATHANIEL WEBB, bapt. 23 Mar. 1756, d. 23 Apr. 1831, m. at Rochester, 12 Feb. 1783, ELIZABETH COLE, b. at Rochester 16 June 1762, d. 29 Oct. 1848 (*Register*, vol. 73, p. 201).

  iv. RUTH WEBB, bapt. 4 June 1758, d. 21 Dec. 1825, m. 20 Apr. 1777 JOHN^5 SHACKFORD (9-iii), son of Capt. Samuel^4 and Elizabeth (Ring), *q.v.*

  v. MARY, bapt. 24 Aug. 1760, m. Hon. JAMES SMITH, of Portsmouth.

  vi. ABIGAIL, bapt. 4 Nov. 1770, d. 7 Aug. 1823, m. Capt. GEORGE NUTTER (17-iii), son of Matthias^5 and Martha (Perkins), *q.v.*

  vii. BENJAMIN, bapt. 7 Nov. 1772, d. 1 May 1838, m. ELIZABETH TALPEY.

  viii. THOMAS, of Portsmouth and Boston, bapt. 27 June 1779, m. MARY^6 PICKERING, dau. of William Pepperell^5 (6-ii) and Mary (Nelson), *q.v.*

5. EZEKIEL GILMAN^6 ADAMS (Joseph$^{5\text{-}2}$, Henry^1), of Barnstead and Gilmanton, joiner, bapt. 26 Nov. 1747, d. 24 May 1831, m. (1) 24 Dec. 1771, MARY^5 HOYT (3-x), dau. of John^4 and Lydia (Miller), *q.v.*, m. (2) 17 Nov. 1801, DRUSILLA EWER, dau. of Capt. Ewer, b. 1780, d. Apr. 1877.

Children by first wife, baptized at Newington:

  i. WILLIAM^7, of Barnstead, bapt. 17 July 1774, d. 1842, m. HANNAH JACOBS.

  ii. MARY, bapt. 26 May 1776, m. JONATHAN ROSS.

  iii. NANCY, bapt. 2 Nov. 1777, d. 23 Dec. 1866, m. 24 May 1801, SAMUEL FABIAN^6 HOYT (4-iii), son of Dennis^5 and Elizabeth (Fabian), *q.v.*

  iv. EZEKIEL, d. in infancy.

- v. ELIZABETH, bapt. 25 Sept. 1783, d. 31 Dec. 1825, m. CHARLES[6] HODGDON (7-iv), son of Charles[5] and Hannah (Dennett), *q.v.*
- vi. JOHN, of Barnstead and Gilmanton, privateersman, b. 31 July 1787, d. Nov. 1814, m. 29 Apr. 1806, SARAH AYRES[6] HODGDON (9-iv), dau. of Benjamin[5] and Rosamond (Colman), *q.v.*

Children by his second wife, the first three born at Barnstead, the others at Gilmanton:
- vii. RUFUS, b. 1 Oct. 1802, d. 1825.
- viii. RHODA, b. 6 July 1804, m. 1823, NATHAN MORRILL.
- ix. JEREMIAH WILSON, b. 13 Oct. 1806, d. in New York, Apr. 1827/8.
- x. ABIGAIL, b. 1 Oct. 1808, d. 15 May 1846, m. MOSES[6] WINGATE, son of John[5] and Sarah (Garland) (*Wingate Family*, p. 108), of Madbury, Troy, N.Y., and Bangor, Me., b. at Madbury 7 July 1789, d. 1861.
- xi. EZEKIEL GILMAN, of Amesbury, Mass., b. 21 Oct. 1810, d. at Franklin, N.Y. Dec. 1877, m. JANE ADAMS.
- xiii. DRUSILLA, b. 2 Oct. 1813, m. (1) 4 June 1832, GEORGE P. ROBINSON, m. (2) Mar. 1865, J. L. LINCOLN, of Minneapolis, Minn.
- xiii. SARAH B., b. 24 Nov. 1815, d. 3 Dec. 1844, m. FRANKLIN WHITTIER.

6. Capt. JOSEPH[6] ADAMS (Joseph[5-2], Henry[1]), of Newington, bapt. 16 June 1751, m. 8 Dec. 1779, his cousin, ELIZABETH[6] ADAMS (3-iii), dau. of Ebenezer[5] and Lois (Downing), *q.v.*

Children, baptized at Newington:
- i. EBENEZER[7], of Newington, blacksmith, soldier in the War or 1812, bapt. 4 June 1780, d. 1827, m. Nov. 1809, ABIGAIL[7] ADAMS, dau. of Dudley Gilman[6] (2-iv) and Sarah (Walker), *q.v.*
- ii. JOSEPH, bapt. 22 Oct. 1782, d. unm. 1850.
- iii. NATHANIEL, of Durham.
- iv. MARY, bapt. 19 Mar. 1786, m. ----- DOWNING.
- v. JOHN, privateersman, d. unm. 1812.
- vi. LOIS, m. 25 July 1816, GEORGE[6] PEVERLY, son of William[5] and Johanna (Vicker), of Newington, farmer, b. about 1792, d. 24 Dec. 1856 (town records).
- vii. ELIZABETH, b. 1800, d. 11 Feb. 1881, m. (1) 1815, JOSEPH[5] LYFORD, son of Jonathan[4] and Anna (Stevens) (*Francis Lyford Family*, p. 43), of Livermore, Me., b. at Barnstead, d. 1899, m. (2) ----- HILL, of Kent's Hill, Me.

7. EBENEZER[6] ADAMS (Joseph[5-2], Henry[1]), of Newington and Barnstead, farmer, soldier in the Revolution, bapt. 24 June 1753, d. 1832, m. 20 Apr. 1779, LYDIA[6] HOYT (3-iv-1), dau. of John[5] and Sarah (Furber), *q.v.*

Children, the first two baptized at Newington, the others born at Barnstead:
  i. JOHN HOYT[7], of Newburyport, Mass., and Dover, N.H., hat manufacturer, soldier in the War of 1812, bapt. 7 Jan. 1781, d. at Methuen, Mass., 14 Sept. 1846, m. 26 Nov. 1801, REBECCA W. ANDERSON, b. at Newburyport, Mass., 2 Jan. 1784, d. 29 June 1846.
  ii. JOHANNA GILMAN, bapt. 22 Oct. 1782, d. at Loudon in 1860, m. DUDLEY PEASE.
  iii. Capt. EBENEZER, of Barnstead, b. 5 June 1784, d. June 1820, m. 1808, SARAH COOLBROTH.
  iv. NANCY, b. 11 May 1786, d. Apr. 1866, m. ELISHA MORRILL, of Barnstead.
  v. ELIZABETH, b. 9 May 1790, d. *s.p.*, m. SOLOMAN EMERSON, of Barnstead.
  vi. SARAH, b. 18 June 1792, d. 28 May 1830, m. 12 May 1816, Capt. AZARIAH[5] CAVERLY, son of Lt. John[4] and Elizabeth (Boody) (*Caverly Family*, p. 81), of Strafford, farmer, militia officer, b. at Barrington, 28 Dec. 1792, d. 14 Dec. 1843.
  vii. HANSON HOYT, of Kittery, Me., b. 7 Nov. 1794, d. 22 July 1851, m. 4 Aug. 1817, NANCY W. NORTON, b. 1798, d. 6 Dec. 1866.
  viii. JAMES, of Barnstead, b. 19 July 1798, d. 25 May 1868, m. (1) 19 Nov. 1820, ELIZABETH BELLAMY, m. (2) 12 Nov. 1840, HANNAH W. VARNEY, d. 17 Jan. 1891.

8. SAMUEL[6] ADAMS (Ebenezer[5], Joseph[4-2], Henry[1]), of Newington, town clerk, A.B. (Harvard), bapt. 12 Mar. 1758, d. 24, Apr. 1821, m. 19 May 1782, LYDIA[5] COLMAN (4-i), dau. of Joseph[4] and Abigail, *q.v.*

Children, born at Newington (*Henry Adams Family*, p. 406):
  i. SAMUEL[7], of Newington, mariner, b. 3 Aug. 1783, d. unm. 27 Apr. 1808.
  ii. EPHRAIM C., of Newington, mason, b. 10 Feb. 1785, d. 15 Dec. 1827, m. 26 July 1805, TEMPERENCE FURBER.
  iii. WILLIAM C., of Newington, blacksmith, soldier in the War of 1812, b. 3 Apr. 1787, d. 1868, m. ----- CHESLEY.
  iv. OLIVE C., b. 1 Mar. 1789, d. 3 June 1850, m. 1816, JOSEPH COLMAN.
  v. ELISHA H., of Talladega, Ala., b. 11 July 1791, d. unm.?
  vi. EBENEZER, of Bangor, Me., 1828, b. 15 Feb. 1795, d. 1884, m. (1) 17 Apr. 1819, MARTHA HARRIS, d. 15 Nov. 1834, m. (2) 1835, REBECCA (HARRIS) FERNALD, sister of his deceased wife.
  vii. GEORGE, of Eastport, Me., b. 1 Mar. 1797, d. 15 Dec. 1880, m. 21 Mar. 1824, MARY HIGGINS.
  viii. LYDIA, b. 15 Aug. 1799, d. 18 Nov. 1836, m. Jan. 1827, THEODORE FERNALD.

    ix. RUFUS, of Portsmouth, mason, b. 3 Dec. 1801, d. 1858, m. MEHITABLE WHITE, b. at Newcastle, Me., 1809, d. 1846.
    x. ELIZA ANN, b. 10 Sept. 1804, d. 29 Sept. 1820.
    xi. OLIVER, of Bangor, Me., carpenter, b. 10 Apr. 1807, d. 7 May 1842, HARRIET FERNALD.

ADAMS (unconnected)

ESTHER ADAMS, dau. of Charles, m. 10 Mar. 1717, THOMAS BICKFORD.

ELIZABETH^3 ADAMS (Mathew^2, John^1) (Stackpole's *Durham*, vol. 2, p. 5), m. 21 Apr. 1749, JEREMIAH BURNHAM, both of Durham.

Rev. JOHN^3 ADAMS (Mathew^2, John^1) (Stackpole's *Durham*, vol. 2, p. 6), m. 13 Oct. 1752, SARAH WHEELER, both of Durham.

MURIEL^3 ADAMS (Mathew^2, John^1) (Stackpole's *Durham*, vol. 2, p. 5), m. 6 Aug. 1754, WINTHROP BURNHAM, both of Durham.

ELEANOR^4 ADAMS (John$^{3-2}$, Christopher^1) (Stackpole's *Kittery*, p. 272), m. 31 Aug. 1764, THOMAS PETTIGREW, both of Kittery.

JOSEPH^4 ADAMS (John$^{3-2}$, Christopher^1) (Stackpole's *Kittery*, p. 273), m. 13 May 1768, MARY DENNETT, both of Kittery.

BENJAMIN ADAMS, d. at Rochester (80 *Reg.* 306), 20 Sept. 1816, *aet.* 39.

ELIZABETH ADAMS, d. at Rochester (80 *Reg.* 306), 28 June 1837, wid. of Benjamin, *aet.* 58.

ALCOCK

1. Sgt. JOHN^1 ALCOCK, of York, Me., 1640, planter, died about 1675, leaving a widow, ELIZABETH (Stackpole's *Kittery*, p. 275).
   Children (*ibid.*):
2 i. JOSEPH^2, b. 1634.
   ii. Capt. JOB, of Portsmouth, 1693, member of the council, associate judge of the Superior Court, d.*s.p.* 1714, apparently had a wife, DOROTHY, for 16 Jan. 1692/3. Capt. John Alcock and Mrs. Dorothy Alcock from the York Church were admitted to the church at Portsmouth (*North Church Rec.*). His will dated 2 Dec. 1712, proved 27 Jan. 1716/7,

mentions his "cousins" (nephews), John Snell and Joseph Banks, and contains gifts to Robert Walker and his wife, Abial Hill, Abigail Walker, Mary Wellwright (?Wheelwright), Hannah Littlefield and Samuel and Joseph Alcock, Ebenezer Hill and Robert Walker, executors (*N.H. State Pap.*, vol. 31, p. 696).

   iii. SAMUEL, Samuel signed the submission of 1652.
   iv. HANNAH, m. GEORGE SNELL.
      Children:
      1) Samuel^3
      2) John
   v. MARY, m. JOHN TWISDEN, of York, Me.
   vi. ELIZABETH, m. RICHARD BANKS, of York, Me.
      Children:
      1) Joseph^3
   vii. SARAH, m. (1) JOHN GIDDINGS, of Gloucester, Mass., m. (2) HENRY HERRICK, of Beverly, Mass.
   viii. LYDIA, m. Rev. SHUBAEL DUMMER, of York, Me., clergyman.

2. JOSEPH^2 ALCOCK (John^1), of Kittery, Me., b. 1634, d. 1676, m. ABIGAIL^2 PAUL, dau. of Daniel^1 and Elizabeth (Stackpole's *Kittery*, p. 643), b. at Kittery, Me., who m. (2) ROBERT ROWSLEY, of Portsmouth.

Children, born at Kittery, Me.:

3   i. JOHN^3, b. 1659.
4   ii. SAMUEL, b. 1665.

3. JOHN^3 ALCOCK (Joseph^2, John^1), of Kittery, Me., shipwright, eldest son^4, b. 1659, d. 1693, m. JOHANNA AMEREDETH, dau. of John and Johanna (Shapleigh), d. 1693, administration on her estate to her mother, 28 Nov. 1693.

His will proved 30 Aug. 1693, gives all his estate to his widow (*Maine Wills*, p. 39).

The will of John Amerideth, cooper, "late of Dartmouth in England and now of Kittery," dated 26 Jan. 1690, proved 16 June 1691, mentions his widow, Joan, and his son and daughter, John and Joanna Alcock, and their children, Joseph, Joanna, Abigail, and Mary (*Main Wills*, p. 94).

Children, born at Kittery, Me.:

5   i. JOSEPH^4
    ii. JOHANNA, m. 1 Aug. 1706, WILLIAM SENTLE, of Boston.
       Child:
       1) John^5, b. 18 July 1707.
    iii. ABIGAIL
    iv. MARY

4. SAMUEL[3] ALCOCK (Joseph[2], John[1]), of Portsmouth, master mariner, b. 1665, d. 13 Oct. 1708 (*N.H. Gen. Rec.*, vol. 3, p. 152), m. ELIZABETH[3] CHADBURN, dau. of Humphrey[2] and Lucy (Treworgy) (Stackpole's *Kittery*, p. 322), b. at Kittery, Me., 1667, d. 1743.

Her will dated 4 July 1743, proved 28 Dec. 1743, gives all her estate to her grandson, Samuel Alcock, then under twenty-one, son of Elizabeth Newmarch, wife of John Newmarch (*N.H. State Pap.*, vol. 33, p. 169).

Children, born at Portsmouth:

  i. SAMUEL[4], of Portsmouth, mariner, b. 1690 ?, m. at Wells, 11 Oct. 1722, ELIZABETH WHEELWRIGHT, dau. of John and Mary, (*Old Eliot*, vol. 3, p. 177) who m. (2) 29 May 1726, (*Register*, vol. 25, p. 121) JOHN[2] NEWMARCH (Rev. John[1]) of Portsmouth, boatbuilder.[+] His widow renounced administration 21 Oct. 1723, in favor of her mother-in-law, Elizabeth Alcock (*id.*, p. 526).

  Children, born at Wells, Me.:

    1) Samuel[5], bapt. 5 June 1726, (*First Church rec.*)

  ii. MARY, m. ----- VAUGHAN.

In his will dated 17 Mar. 1704, proved 12 Feb. 1716/7, he mentions his wife, Elizabeth, only son, Samuel, "Kinsman" (first cousin once removed). Joseph Alcock (5) and children of his sister, Mary Vaughan (*N.H. State Pap.*, vol. 31, p. 525).

5. JOSEPH[4] ALCOCK (John[3], Joseph[2], John[1]), of Portsmouth, master mariner, m. KETURAH ROLLINS, dau. of Capt. Benjamin and Eunice (Stackpole's *Kittery*, p. 275).

Administration on his estate 13 Sept. 1726, to Keturah, his widow (*N.H. State Pap.*, vol. 32, p. 287). Her father was a mariner of Boston.

Children, born at Portsmouth:

6   i. JOSEPH[5], b. 26 Feb. 1716/7 (*Register*, vol. 23, p. 393).
   ii. JOHANNA, bapt. 5 May 1717 (*N.H. Gen. Rec.*, vol. 4, p. 101).
  iii. BENJAMIN, b. 3 Sept. 1719, d. 26 Feb. 1720 (*id.*, vol. 1, p. 19).
   iv. MARY, bapt. 4 Mar. 1721/2 (*id.*, vol. 5, p. 38).

+He had by his wife, Elizabeth (Wheelwright) Alcock at Portsmouth (*Register, Vol. 25*, p. 121):

1) Mary, b. 16 Nov. 1727.
2) John, b. 23 Aug. 1730.
3) Elizabeth, b. 10 Dec. 1731.
4) Easter, b. 24 Feb. 1733/4.

6. JOSEPH[5] ALCOCK (Joseph[4], John[3], Joseph[2], John[1]), of Portsmouth, merchant, b. 26 Feb. 1716/7, d. 14 Feb. 1795 (*Register*, vol. 10, p. 51), funeral 28 Feb. 1795 (*North Church Rec.*), m. 14 Sept. 1740, JANE[4] RING (i-iii), dau. of Deac. Seth[3] and Elizabeth (Libby), *q.v.*

His will dated 1795, mentions his son, Joseph, "if he be in the land of the living," grandchildren, Joseph and Jane Alcock, and daughter, Anna (*Rockingham Probate*).

Children, born at Portsmouth:
- i. JOSEPH[6], of Portsmouth, m. at Portsmouth, 8 Nov. 1797, ELIZABETH SEWARD (*North Church Rec.*).
    Children:
    1) Joseph[7]
    2) Jane
- ii. ANNA
- iii. MARY, b. about 1740, d. *s.p.*, m. NATHANIEL GRIFFITH, son of John and Deborah[3] (Lang) (*Robert Lang Family*, 3-v-9), of Portsmouth, goldsmith, b. about 1740, d. 26 Feb. 1771. Administration on his estate 24 Jan. 1775 to Mary, his widow, Joseph[5] Alcock, surety (*Rockingham Probate*).

ALLARD

HENRY[1] ALLARD, of Newington and Rochester, 1740, m. 23 Apr. 1730 SARAH ROLLINS (2-iii), daughter of Joseph[2] and Sarah Rollins, *q.v.*

She was admitted to the church at Rochester 22 July 1739 (*N.H. Gen. Rec.*, vol. 7, p. 90) and he 12 Oct. 1740 (*Ibid*).

Children, born at Newington:
- i. SARAH[2], bapt. 28 Mar. 1734.
- ii. SHADRACH, bapt. 30 Sept. 1736.
- iii. ELIZABETH, bapt. 30 Sept. 1736.

ALLARD (unconnected)

BETSEY ALLARD, d. 20 Jan. 1843, in the poor house *aet.* 75 yrs. (*Register*, vol. 73, p. 199).

ALLEN

JUDAH ALLEN, of Stratham, m. 7 July 1766, SARAH PHILBROOK, of Greenland.

AYRES

1. Capt. JOHN¹ AYRES,+ of Ipswich, Mass., 1648, Brookfield, Mass., 1672, b. 1625, d. 3 Aug. 1675, killed by the Indians (Whitmore's *Ayres Family*), m. 29 Apr. 1666, ANNA SYMONDS, dau. of Mark and Joanna.

Children, born at Ipswich, Mass. (*Ayres Family*, p. 10):

- 2   i. ? JOHN²
- 3   ii. SAMUEL
- 4   iii. THOMAS
-      iv. JOSEPH, of Ipswich and Brookfield, Mass.
- 5   v. EDWARD, b. 12 Feb. 1658.
- 6   vi. MARK, b. 14 Dec. 1661.
- 7   vii. NATHANIEL, b. 6 June 1670.
-      viii. SUSANNA, m. JAMES DAY, son of Robert.

MARY AYRES, m. 1660, Capt. WALTER² NEAL, at Portsmouth (*Piscataqua Pioneers*, p. 135).

2. JOHN² AYRES (John¹), of Ipswich, Mass., d. in Boston, 12, Aug. 1711, m. MARY -----.

Children (*Tremain Family*, vol. 2, p. 1233):

- i. A CHILD³, b. Sept. 1677.
- ii. ABIGAIL, b. 14 May 1680, m. JOSEPH MOULTON, of Portsmouth.
   Children born at Portsmouth:
   1) Joseph⁴, b. 29 Sept. 1710.
   2) John, b. 15, Dec. 1713.
   3) Alice, b. 4 June 1715.
- iii. RUTH, d. 24 Dec. 1685.

3. SAMUEL² AYRES (John¹), of Newbury and Rowley, Mass., m. 21 Mar. 1677, ABIGAIL FELLOWS, dau. of William.

Children (*Tremain Family*, vol. 2, p. 1234):

- i. MARY³, b. 13 Jan. 1678.
- ii. JOHN, b. 16 Mar. 1679.
- 8   iii. WILLIAM, b. 26 Jan. 1682.
-      iv. EPHRAIM, b. 13 Feb. 1687.
-      v. STEPHEN, b. 13 Mar. 1689.

+Whitmore's *Ayres Family* does not trace the descendants of Thomas², Edward², nor Mark² Ayres.

      vi. JABEZ, b. 27 Dec. 1690.
9   vii. SAMUEL
     viii. JOSEPH
       ix. EBENEZER
       x. EDWARD

4. THOMAS^2 AYRES (John^1), of Newbury and Ipswich, Mass., and Portsmouth, 1716, m. (1) 21 Mar. 1677/8, HANNAH ERRINGTON, m. ? (2) ELIZABETH -----.

Administration on his estate 5 Dec. 1722 to his sons, Abraham and Thomas, both of Portsmouth; Ephraim Dennett and John Downing, sureties (*N.H. State Pap.*, vol. 32, p. 157). Inventory £ 110/5-0.

Children, born at Portsmouth (*Ayres Family*, p. 14):

10   i. THOMAS^3, b. 25 Jan. 1678/79, d. in infancy.
     ii. HANNAH, b. 2 Aug. 1680, m. 6 Oct. 1711, as his second wife, EDWARD TOOGOOD (*N.H. Gen. Rec.*, vol. 5, p. 41, *Register*, vol. 23, p. 271), of Portsmouth, mason, d. 1737. He had a seat in the church in 1693 (*Brewster's Rambles*, p. 66). His will dated 14 May 1737, proved 6 June 1737, mentions his wife, Hannah, and daughter, Mary Cotton (*N.H. State Pap.*, vol. 32, p. 639).

Child, born at Portsmouth:

1) Mary^4, bapt. 19 Apr. 1713 (*N.H. Gen. Rec.*, vol. 4, p. 58), m. ----- Cotton, of Portsmouth.

    iii. REBECCA, b. 27 May 1682, d. before 1725, m. 17 Aug. 1712, JOSEPH^3 MOSES (*Register*, vol. 23, p. 271), son of Aaron^2 and Ruth (Sherburn) (*Moses Family*, pp. 102, 201), of Portsmouth, joiner, b. at Portsmouth, who m. (2) HANNAH ----- and m. (3) 10 Aug. 1759, ELEANOR (JACKSON) LANG, dau. of John^4, and wid. of Joseph.

Children (See *Moses Family*, p. 201):

1) Joseph, b. 9 Sept. 1713 (*Register*, vol. 23, p. 271)

    iv. A DAUGHTER (? SUSANNA), b. June 1686, m. (1) 19 May 1707, WILLIAM SCALES, of Rowley, Mass., Ipswich, Mass., Portsmouth, Falmouth, Me., North Yarmouth, Me., killed by the Indians 24 Apr. 1725, m. (2) Capt. CORNELIUS SOULE.

11   v. ABRAHAM, b. 18 June 1688.
     vi. SARAH, b. 29 Aug. 1690.
    vii. MEHITABLE, b. 5 Aug. 1697, m. ? 19 Apr. 1718, ABNER SENTER (*Register*, vol. 23, p. 395), of Ipswich, Mass.
   viii. THOMAS

5. EDWARD^2 AYRES (John^1), of Portsmouth, blacksmith, b. 12 Feb. 1658, d.
30 ----- 1723, m. (1) ALICE -----, b. 1665, d. 9 Feb. 1717/8 (*Register*, vol. 23, p.

394), m. (2) 2 Oct. 1718 (*Register*, vol. 23, p. 395), HANNAH (MARTYN) JOSE, dau. of Richard and Sarah (Tuttle) Martyn, and wid. of Richard[2] (Christopher[1] Jose), b. 1664, d. 12 Jan. 1718/9 (*Register*, vol. 23, p. 395, *Locke's Cemetery Inscriptions*), m. (3) 23 Feb. 1719/20 (*Register*, vol. 24, p. 13), MARGARET WILLIAMS.

Administration on his estate 23 Jan. 1723/4 to his sons (*sic*) John and John Cutt (*N.H. State Pap.*, vol. 32, p. 209).

He had a house and lot running from Water Street to the river bounded north by Penhallow and south by Warren which he conveyed to his son, John[3], in 1725 (*Rockingham Deeds*, vol. 136, p. 532).

Children, born at Portsmouth (*N.H. Deeds*, vol. 26, p. 546):

i. ELIZABETH[3], b. about 1678, m. (1) 30 Oct. 1701, Dr. CALEB GRIFFITH, of Portsmouth, m. (2) Nov. 1719, Lt. HENRY LYON, of York, Me., and Roxbury, Mass., m. (3) 23 Feb. 1720/1 (*N.H. Deeds*, vol. 26, p. 544), MOSES INGRAHAM, of Portsmouth and York, Me., tailor.

Administration on the estate of Caleb Griffith 24 May 1710, to Henry Lyon, of York, Me., and his wife, Elizabeth, wid. of Caleb; Edward Ayres, surety (*N. H. State Pap.*, vol. 31, p. 662).

Children by first husband, born at Portsmouth (*Tremain Family*, vol. 2, p. 1237):

1) Caleb[4], b. 8 Aug. 1702.
2) Edward, b. 1 Feb. 1703.
3) Joshua, b. 1 Feb. 1704.
4) Gershom, b. 23 Sept. 1704 (See *N.H. Deeds*, vol. 63, p. 239)

Child by third husband:

5) Edward

ii. ABIGAIL, b. 14 May 1680, m. 25 Nov. 1709 (*Register*, vol. 23, p. 394), JOSEPH[3] MOULTON, son of Joseph[2] (*Moulton Family*, p. 35), of Portsmouth, blacksmith.

Children, born at Portsmouth:

1) Joseph[4], b. 29 Sept. 1710 (*Register*, vol. 23, p. 394), m. Sarah -----.
2) John, b. 15 Dec. 1713 (*ibid.*).
3) Alice, b. 4 June 1715 (*ibid.*).

12 iii. JOHN, b. about 1685, bapt. in July 1708.

iv. SUSANNA, b. about 1690, bapt. 28 Nov. 1708 (*N.H. Gen. Rec.*, vol. 4, p. 53), m. 20 Sept 1715, JOHN[2] CUTT, son of John[1] and Sarah (Martyn) (*Cutt's Family*, p. 450; *Register*, vol. 23, p. 272; *id.*, vol. 26, p. 17), of Portsmouth, cooper, town officer, b. at Portsmouth, 20 Sept. 1681. For children, see *Cutts Family, loc. cit.*

v. MARY, bapt. with Phebe and John in the North Church in 1708 (*N.H. Gen Rec.*, vol. 4, p. 52), m. 10 Apr. 1710 (*Register*, vol. 58, p. 341) JOHN FOSTER, of Boston, blacksmith, d. by 1763.

vi. HANNAH, m. 16 July 1724 (*Register*, vol. 24, p. 18), NATHANIEL FELLOWS, of Portsmouth (?Ipswich), cooper, b. at Ipswich, Mass.

vii. PHEBE, b. about 1700, d. leaving a large estate, m. 15 Feb. 1721/2, JOSEPH[3] SHERBURN, (*Register*, vol. 59, p. 58, *id.*, vol. 24, p. 15), son of Henry[2] and Sarah (Wiggin), of Portsmouth, master mariner, merchant, b. at Portsmouth about 1694.

Only child, born at Portsmouth:

1) Phebe[4], m. Bradstreet Wiggin, son of Judge Andrew.

viii. EDWARD, d. *s.p.* (*Libby's Dictionary*, p. 70).

6. MARK[2] AYRES (John[1]), of Portsmouth and Newington, 1721, cordwainer, b. 14 Dec. 1661, m. SARAH -----, b. 1662 (tombstone), d. 12 Jan. 1727/8.

He and his wife had seats in the North Church 1693/4 (*N.H. Gen. Rec.*, vol. 3, p. 174).

Children (*Ayres Family*, p. 15):

i. ? MARK[3], b. ? 1682.

13   ii. GEORGE, b. ? 1690.

14   iii. THOMAS, bapt. in North Church, 10 Dec. 1693 (*N.H. Gen. Rec.*, vol. 3, p. 53).

7. Sgt. NATHANIEL[2] AYRES (John[1]), of Portsmouth and Boston, blacksmith, Sergeant, 1695, J.P., 1699, b. 6 June 1670, d. in Boston, 4 Dec. 1737, m. AMY (COWELL) FURBER, dau. of Edward and Agnes, and wid. of Jethro[3] (i-v), *q.v.* She was living in Boston in 1740, Court Files, No. 26470.

On June 22, 1693, they were admitted to the North Church at Portsmouth on dismissal from the North Church at Boston (*N.H. Gen. Rec.*, vol. 3, p. 52).

In 1699, he made the iron work to hold the bell for the new meeting house (*N.H. Court Papers*).

In 1700, he was surety on the bond of George Veasey, of Exeter, for the administration of the estate of George Wilson, of Exeter, deceased husband of Martha (*N.H. State Pap.*, vol. 31, p. 456).

Children (*Ayres Family*, p. 15):

i. AMY[3], m. 16 Jan. 1710/11, SAMUEL SWASEY.

ii. EDWARD, of Boston, shipwright, m. (1) 26 Apr. 1716, REBECCA MARSHALL, m. (2) 5 Nov. 1724, HANNAH EVELETH.

iii. ELNATHAN, of Boston, m. 4 July 1720, MARY JONES.

iv. NATHANIEL, of Boston, bapt. in North Church Portsmouth, 22 Apr. 1724 (*N.H. Gen. Rec.*, vol. 3, p. 53), m. 5 Nov. 1724, ELIZABETH KITTS.

8. WILLIAM[3] AYRES (Samuel[2], John[1]), of Portsmouth, saddler, b. about 1685, m. 24 Oct. 1706 (*N.H. Gen. Rec.*, vol. 4, p. 12), MARY HOPLEY, dau. of

Robert and Elizabeth (Tucker) Hopley, born at Portsmouth, who m. (2) 4 Oct. 1716, as his second wife, SAMPSON² DOE, son of Nicholas and Martha (Stackpole's *Durham*, vol. 2, p. 132) and m. (3) ----- STEVENS, of Portsmouth (*ibid.*).

In 1712, William Ayres, of Portsmouth, saddler, and Mary, his wife, conveyed their interest in common lands at Portsmouth allotted to Ursala Tucker, widow of John Tucker, late of Portsmouth, and in common lands allotted to Elizabeth Roberts, formerly Hopley, then wife of Thomas Roberts, of Dover (*N.H. Deeds*, vol. 8, p. 329). Mary Ayres, formerly Mary Hopley, was granddaughter of John Tucker (*id.*, vol. 9, p. 156; *id.*, vol. 23, p. 289; *id.*, vol. 21, p. 392).

Administration on his estate 28 Sept. 1716, to Mary, his widow (*N.H. State Pap.*, vol. 31, p. 791). Her will mentions her children by Doe (*Rockingham Probate*).

Children, born at Portsmouth (baptisms in North Church):

15   i. WILLIAM⁴, bapt. 1709 (*N.H. Gen. Rec.*, vol. 4, p. 54)
16   ii. HOPLEY, bapt. 1709 (*ibid.*), m. 14 Oct. 1730, MARY FROST, (*Register*, vol. 25, p. 117), b. at Newcastle.
      iii. MARY, bapt. 20 June 1714 (*N.H. Gen. Rec.*, vol. 4, p. 98).

9. SAMUEL³ AYRES (Samuel², John¹), of Newbury and Rowley, Mass., and Greenland, 1741, m. (1) 7 June 1715, ELEANOR RANDALL, d. 31 Oct. 1734, m. (2) (intentions 31 Dec. 1737), HANNAH GOLD.

Children by first wife (*Tremain Family*, vol. 2, p. 1236):

      i. MARTHA⁴, b. 2 Mar. 1718.
      ii. JOHN, b. 22 Nov. 1719, d. 20 Feb. 1721.
17   iii. JOHN, b. 17 Sept. 1721.
      iv. ELIZABETH, b. 6 Oct. 1723, d. 9 Oct. 1723.

10. THOMAS³ AYRES (Thomas², John¹), of Portsmouth, Newington, 1721, and Greenland, 1731, yeoman, b. 25 Jan. 1678/9, d. 1764, m. 13 Aug. 1713 (*N.H. Gen. Rec.*, vol. 5, p. 42), RUTH SHERBURN, dau. of Capt. John (*N.H. State Pap.*, vol. 32, p. 191) and Mary Hannah (Jackson) (*Register*, vol. 58, p. 393), b. at Portsmouth in 1695.

The will of John Sherburn dated 17 Dec. 1723, proved 16 Feb. 1730/1, mentions his daughter, Ruth Ayres (*N.H. State Pap.*, vol. 32, p. 191).

In 1742, Thomas³ Ayres was tenant at Greenland of Joshua Pierce (*id.*, vol. 33, p. 135).

In his will dated 3 June 1764, proved 25 July 1764, he names the following children except No. v., and his grandchildren Ruth, Mary, Elizabeth, and Priscilla Ayres (*N.H. Colonial Probate*, vol. 23, p. 262).

Children, the first one born at Portsmouth, the next two at Newington, the others at Greenland:

      i. RUTH⁴, bapt. 1 Aug. 1714 (*N.H. Gen Rec.*, vol. 4, p. 98), m. CALEB

ROLANS (?ROLLINS), of Stratham.
    ii. HANNAH, bapt. 2 June 1721, m. ----- NEAL.
    iii. MEHITABLE, bapt. 9 May 1725, m. ----- BECK.
    iv. MARY, bapt. 1731 (*Register*, vol. 29, p. 71), d. unm.
    v. OLIVE, bapt. 1735 (*id.*, p. 33), d. in infancy.
    vi. OLIVE, bapt. 1742 (*id.*, p. 35), m. ----- JOHNSON.
18 vii. THOMAS, bapt. 1743, of Portsmouth, husbandman.
19 viii. SAMUEL, of Greenland, 1766.
20 ix. JOHN
21 x. PELETIAH

11. ABRAHAM^3 AYRES (Thomas^2, John^1), of Portsmouth, b. 18 June 1688, covenant in the North Church, 11 Aug. 1711, d. living 1723, m. ? (1) ELIZABETH -----, m. (2) 18 Oct. 1716, MARY JACKSON (*Register*, vol. 23, p. 393), dau. of Samuel and Mary (Melcher) Jackson. She m. (2) JACOB LAVERS.

Child by first wife, baptized in North Church:
    i. ELIZABETH^4, bapt. 11 Aug. 1711 (*N.H. Gen. Rec.*, vol. 4, p. 101).
Child by second wife, baptized in North Church:
22 ii. ABRAHAM, bapt. 18 Feb. 1721/2 (*id.*, vol. 5, p. 38).

12. Capt. JOHN^3 AYRES (Edward^2, John^1), of Portsmouth, b. ? 1695, d. ? 1764, m. (1) 6 Jan. 1722/3 (*N.H. Gen Rec.*, vol. 5, p. 45, *Register*, vol. 24, p. 16), MARY HUNKING, b. at Portsmouth in 1704, d. 17 July 1754, m. (2) as early as 31 May 1758, DEBORAH (SHACKFORD) (SUMNER) WATERHOUSE, (3-iv), *q.v.*

In 1734 with John Pray, he was surety for Damaris Joce as administratrix of the estate of her husband, Richard (*N.H. State Pap.*, vol. 32, p. 41). In 1746 with Edward Cate, he was surety for Damaris Wheelwright and her husband, James, as administrators of the estate of Richard Joce, Gent., late of Portsmouth (*i.d.*, vol. 33, p. 389).

In 1739, he had the land and buildings formerly of his father, Edward^2, in Bridge Street running down to the (South Mill Pond) Creek (*i.d.*, vol. 32, p. 41). Administration on his estate 26 Sept. 1764 to his son, John (*N.H. Probate*, vol. 23, p. 293), Inventory £ 10, 111-6/10.

Thirteen children, born at Portsmouth (*Register*, vol. 67, p. 88):
    i. MARY^4, b. 10 July 1723, bapt. 8 Nov. 1724 (*Register*, vol. 81, p. 420).
    ii. EDWARD, b. 3 Nov. 1724, bapt. 8 Nov. 1724 (*ibid.*), d. 28 Nov. 1724.
23 iii. JOHN, b. 20 Aug. 1725.
    iv. ELIZABETH, b. 29 Aug. 1727, d. 7 Aug. 1728.
    v. WILLIAM, b. 4 Feb. 1729/30, d. Apr. 1730.
24 vi. NATHANIEL, b. 1 June 1731.
    vii. SARAH, b. 16 Oct. 1733, d. 12 Apr. 1734.
    viii. ALICE, b. 28 Sept. 1735.

25   ix. EDWARD, b. 17 Feb. 1736/7.
      x. HANNAH, b. 2 June 1740.
      xi. PHILIP, b. 26 Mar. 1742, d. 30 July 1742.
      xii. SARAH, b. 9 Aug. 1743.
      xiii. JANE, b. 5 Mar. 1745, d. 16 Sept. 1792.

13. GEORGE^3 AYRES (Mark^2, John^1), of Portsmouth, cordwainer, b. about 1690, m. 10 Dec. 1712 (*N.H. Gen. Rec.*, vol. 5, p. 41), ABIGAIL PERKINS, dau. of Jonathan and Sarah$^+$, b. at Hampton.

In 1748, with Jonathan Ayres, of Portsmouth, cordwainer, he was surety on the bond of Sarah Freese, as administration of the estate of Jonathan Freese, of Northampton (*N.H. State Pap.*, vol. 33, p. 555).

His will, dated 23 Mar. 1761, proved in May 1771, mentions his wife, Abigail, and children George, Jonathan, Perkins, Sarah, Abigail, Susanna, Margaret, Mary and Ann; Joseph Cotton, boatbuilding, and Theodore Moses, barber, both of Portsmouth, sureties (*Rockingham Probate*).

Children, born at Portsmouth as mentioned in his will (baptisms at North Church):

26   i. GEORGE^4, b. about 1713.
27   ii. JONATHAN, bapt. 11 Feb. 1721/2 (*id.*, vol. 5, p. 38), b. about 1715.
28   iii. PERKINS, b. about 1717.
      iv. A CHILD (?SARAH), bapt. 8 Sept. 1718 (*N.H. Gen. Rec.*, vol. 4, p. 102), m. (1) JONATHAN FREESE, son of Jacob and Rachel (Chase) (*Dow's Hampton*, p. 717), of Hampton, b. at Hampton, 27 Dec. 14??, d. 5 Apr. 1748, m. (2) PHILIP DOW.
      v. ABIGAIL, b. about 1719, d. unm.?
      vi. SUSANNA, bapt. 28 Feb. 1719/20 (*ibid.*), m. ? 25 Oct. 1749, as his second wife, MATTHIAS NUTTER (94), son of John^3, *q.v.*
      vii. MARGARET, b. about 1722, d. unm.?
      viii. MARY, b. about 1724, d. unm.?
      ix. ANN, b. about 1727, d. unm.?

14. THOMAS^3 AYRES (Mark^2, John^1), of Newington, clothier, bapt. 10 Dec. 1693, m. HANNAH -----.

Children, baptized at Greenland:
29   i. EDWARD^4, of Newington, bapt. 1716 (*Register*, vol. 28, p. 417), m. 1

+In 1744, Sarah Sanborn, of Hampton, conveyed her right in the estate of Jonathan Perkins, late of Hampton, to her son-in law, George Ayres, of Portsmouth, cordwainer (*N.H. Deeds*, vol. 25, p. 315).

Nov. 1742, MARY³ ROWE (i-i), dau. of Thomas² and Rachel (Pevey), q.v.

Children, baptized at Newington:
1) Ruth⁵, bapt. 14 Aug. 1743, m. ? 3 Dec. 1764, Samuel Abbott (Parson's *Rye*, p. 573).
2) Mary, bapt. 16 Sept. 1744.
3) Mehitable, bapt. 15 June 1746.

30   ii. THOMAS, bapt. 1718 (*id.*, p. 418).

iii. DEPENDENCE, of Newington, bapt. 11 Nov. 1750 (*id.*, p. 37), m. 9 Jan. 1772, ELIZABETH⁵ NUTTER (9-i), dau. of Joshua⁴ and Sarah (Richards), q.v.

Child, baptized at Newington:
1) William⁵, bapt. 29 Nov. 1772.

iv. STEPHEN, of Portsmouth, bapt. 1 Sept. 1751 (*ibid.*), m. 2 Sept. 1773, SARAH⁵ HODGDON, (6-ix), dau. of John⁴ and Mary (Decker), q.v.

Child, baptized at Newington:
1) Stephen⁵, bapt. 27 Sept. 1778.

19. GEORGE⁴ AYRES (George³, Mark², John¹), of Portsmouth, husbandman, b. ?1725.

Children, born at Portsmouth (baptisms in North Church):
i. THOMAS⁵, bapt. 24 Apr. 1748 (*N.H. Gen. Rec.*, vol. 5, p. 87).
ii. A CHILD, bapt. 1749 (*id.*, p. 88).

28   iii. PERKINS, bapt. 6 Oct. 1751 (*id.*, p. 90).

iv. ELIZABETH, bapt. 27 July 1753, (*id.*, p. 91).
v. ALICE, bapt. 17 Sept. 1758 (*id.*, p. 133).
vi. RUTH, bapt. 6 July 1760 (*id.*, p. 135).

_____ AYRES, b. at Gloucester, Mass., 1722, m. about 1744, RUTH⁴ COTTON, dau. of Thomas³ and Comfort (Bass) (*Register*, vol. 58, p. 298). Can this be Nathaniel⁴ who had a wife, Ruth?

GEO. AYRES, of Newington, yeoman, and wife, ANNA, 1767, convey lands, in Ports. (84-119).

JAMES AYRES, of Newington, cordwainer, 1768, conveys 50 acres in Newmarket.

20. PERKINS⁴ AYRES (George³, Mark², John¹), of Portsmouth, cordwainer, b. about 1717, m. before 2 Feb. 1755 (*Register*, vol. 82, p. 29), RUTH -----.

Administration on his estate 24 Sept. 1798 to Richard Salter (*Rockingham Probate*).

Children, born at Portsmouth (*Rockingham Deeds*, vol. 164, p. 280) (baptisms in South Church):

   i. RUTH⁵, b. 1764, d. 1855, m. WINTHROP AYRES, of Barnstead, b. 1763, d. 1849.
   ii. SARAH, m. SAMUEL LEAVITT, of Stratham.
   iii. MARY, b. 12 Aug. 1754, bapt. 18 Aug. 1754 (*Register*, vol. 80, p. 29), d. 29 Apr. 1851, m. GIDEON GARLAND (Stackpole's *Durham*, vol. 2, p. 200), of Durham.

   Children, born at Durham (*ibid.*):
   1) John⁶, b. 15 July 1781, m. 28 July 1804, Comfort Durgin.
   2) James, of Durham, b. 21 Aug. 1782, m. 1805, Polly Mills.
   3) Hannah (twin), b. 13 Apr. 1784, m. Nathan Wiggin.
   4) Elizabeth (twin), b. 13 Apr. 1784, m. 1806, Samuel Ferrin.
   5) Samuel, b. 27 Nov. 1792, m. Clara Edgerly.
   6) Mary, b. 7 May 1795, m. 27 Feb. 1812, James Langley.
   7) Nathaniel, b. May 1805, d. 19 Dec. 1893, m. 4 May 1828, Harriet Pickering.

23. JOHN⁴ AYRES (Capt. John³, Edward², John¹), of Portsmouth, blacksmith, b. 20 Aug. 1725.

Administration on his estate 8 Mar. 1770, to Henry Sherburne (*N.H. Probate*, vol. 26, p. 255) Inventory £ 81/9-2.

Children, born at Portsmouth (baptisms in North Church):

   i. ELIZABETH, bapt. 16 Sept. 1750 (*N.H. Gen. Rec.*, vol. 5, p. 89), d. in infancy.
   ii. MARY, bapt. 17 Dec. 1752 (*id.*, p. 91).
   iii. SUSANNA, bapt. 5 May 1754 (*id.*, p. 129).
31 iv. JEREMIAH, bapt. 30 Nov. 1755 (*id.*, p. 131).
   v. ABIGAIL, bapt. 18 Sept. 1757 (*id.*, p. 132).
   vi. ELIZABETH, bapt. 11 Apr. 1762 (*id.*, p. 137).
   vii. SARAH, bapt. 23 Oct. 1763 (*id.*, p. 139).

24. NATHANIEL⁴ AYRES (John³, Edward², John¹), of Portsmouth, b. 1 June 1731, m. 23 Nov. 1750, RUTH SHAPLEIGH (Parson's *Rye*, p. 573), b. at Gosport.

Children, born at Portsmouth (baptisms in North Church):

   i. HONOR⁵, bapt. 26 Sept. 1756 (*N.H. Gen. Rec.*, vol. 5, p. 131).
   ii. MARY, bapt. 29 Jan. 1759 (*id.*, p. 134).

25. EDWARD⁴ AYRES (John³, Edward², John¹), of Portsmouth, b. 17 Feb. 1736/7, d. 19 May 1792, m. ELIZABETH SHERBURN, dau. of ----- and Elizabeth (Morison) (*N.H. Wills*, vol. 22, p. 297), b. 1740, d. 29 Aug. 1821 (tombstone).

Children, born at Portsmouth (baptisms in North Church):

i. SARAH⁵, bapt. 1 Mar. 1761 (*N.H. Gen. Rec.*, vol. 5, p. 135), d. unm. 12 Jan. 1827 (tombstone, North Church) at Portsmouth.
32 ii. JOHN, bapt. 8 July 1764 (*id.*, p. 140).
  iii. ELIZABETH, bapt. 2 Nov. 1766 (*id.*, p. 185).
  iv. MARY, bapt. 5 Mar. 1769 (*id.*, p. 188).
  v. HANNAH, bapt. 27 Dec. 1772 (*id.*, vol. 6, p. 44).

27. JONATHAN⁴ AYRES (George³, Mark², John¹), of Portsmouth, cordwainer, merchant, bapt. 11 Feb. 1721/2, d. at Canterbury, 14 Dec. 1801, m. ALICE SHERBURN, dau. of Edward.

He had a house and lot on Board Street running through to Jeffrey Street (*Rockingham Deeds*, vol. 163, p. 334).

Children, born at Portsmouth (Lyford's *Canterbury*, vol. 2, p. 9, *Rockingham Deeds*, vol. 178, p. 97) (baptisms in North Church):

  i. JOSEPH⁵, of Canterbury, cordwainer, inn holder, b. 15 Aug. 1745, d. 28 Apr. 1812, m. (1) 14 Dec. 1767, SARAH BICKFORD, d. 10 Oct. 1768, m. (2) 11 Oct. 1770, MIRIAM⁵, FROST, dau. of Charles⁴ and Jane (Pepperell) (Stackpole's *Kittery*, p. 417), b. at Kittery, Me., 9 May 1743, d. 20 Dec. 1834.

  Children by first wife, born at Portsmouth (Lyford's *Canterbury*, p. --, *N.H. Gen. and Fam. Hist*, vol. --, p. --):

  1) Joseph Sherburn⁶, of Portsmouth, painter, merchant, b. 30 Sept. 1768, m. at Portsmouth, 6 Jan. 1793 (town rec.), Nancy Pitman.
  2) Daughter
  3) Daughter

  Children by second wife, born at Portsmouth:

  4) Jonathan, of Canterbury, farmer, member of the legislature, J.P., b. 14 Sept. 1771, d. 5 Sept. 1834, m. (1) 1806, Hannah Haines, dau. of Samuel and Hannah (Johnson), b. at Canterbury, 30 May 1780, d. 7 Dec. 1823, m. (2) 19 Dec. 1825, Susanna (Stevens) Hackett, dau. of Deac. Jesse and wid. of Asa, b. 23 July 1789, d. 26 Aug. 1882.
  5) Polly, b. 26 Feb. 1774, d. Sept. 1774.
  6) Sarah, b. 8 Nov. 1775, d. 26 Dec. 1775.
  7) Statira Manning, b. 24 May 1779.
  8) Eliza, b. 2 May 1782.
  9) Abigail, b. 20 June 1778.
  10) Miriam, b. 26 May 1787.

  ii. A CHILD, bapt. May 1747 (*N.H. Gen. Rec.*, vol. 5, p. 86).
  iii. ALICE, bapt. 2 July 1749 (*N.H. Gen. Rec.*, vol. 5, p. 88), m. GEORGE RICHARDS, of Portsmouth, clergyman.
  iv. STATIRA, b. 1753, d. 8 June 1807, *aet.* 54, m. THOMAS MANNING, son of Thomas and his first wife, Mary (*Manning Family*, p. 795), of

Portsmouth, master mariner, merchant, commander of the privateer, *General Sullivan*, b. at ? Portsmouth, 1747, d. 24 Mar. 1819.

Children, baptized at Portsmouth (*Register*, vol. 82, p. 47):

1) Statira^6, bapt. 6 Apr. 1777, d. in infancy.
2) Statira, bapt. 1 July 1781, d. 5 June 1820, m. as his first wife, James H. Pierrepont, of Brooklyn, N.Y., physician.
3) Elizabeth Bennett^6, bapt. 1 June 1783, m. Andrew W. Bell, master mariner.
4) Mary Pierce, bapt. 6 Nov. 1785, m. James Kennard, of Portsmouth.
5) Thomas Augustus, of Portsmouth, mariner, bapt. 3 June 1787, d. unm. 1821.
6) Alice Sherburn, bapt. 27 Sept. 1789, m. 21 Oct. 1821 (*Register*, vol. 83, p. 25), as his second wife, James H. Pierrepont, surviving husband of her sister, Statira, *q.v.*
7) William, bapt. 13 Aug. 1791, d. in infancy.
8) Sarah Ann, bapt. 30 Sept. 1792, d. 2 Mar. 1877, m. 29 June 1823, as his second wife, Andrew^3 Halliburton, son of George^2 and Ann (Avery) (*Fales Family*, p. 187), of Portsmouth, merchant, president of the Portsmouth Bank, b. at Horton, N.S., 4 Sept. 1771, d. May 1846.
9) Edward Sherburn, Portsmouth, merchant, bapt. 19 July 1795, d. *s.p.*, 16 June 1821, m. 25 June 1820, (*Register*, vol. 83, p. 25), Mary Ann Shaw, who m. (2) 26 Feb. 1822 (*ibid.*), Thomas Stanhope English, of Boston.

v. ABIGAIL, bapt. 30 Nov. 1755 (*id.*, p. 131), m. JOHN SALTER, of Portsmouth, master mariner.

Children, born at Portsmouth (*Rockingham Deeds*, vol. 178, p. 97):

1) Henry^6, of Portsmouth, mariner.
2) Edward, of Portsmouth, mariner.
3) Sarah Ann, m. ----- Holmes.
4) Lucy Maria
5) Abigail
6) Eliza, d. unm.

vi. SARAH, bapt. 15 Jan. 1758 (*id*, p. 133), d. unm. 12 Apr. 1829 (tombstone).

vii. JONATHAN, of Northfield, 1799, cordwainer, b. 25 Sept. 1759, bapt. 30 Sept. 1759 (*i.d.*, p. 136), d. 19 Nov. 1839, m. 18 Feb. 1785, DOROTHY DEERING, dau. of Ebenezer^6 and Mary (Frost) (Stackpole's *Kittery*, p. 342), b. at Kittery, Me., 27 Mar. 1762, d. 16 Mar. 1846.

Children, the first six born at Portsmouth, the others at Northfield (Cross' *Northfield*, part 2, p. 16; Lyford's *Canterbury*, p. --):

1) Mary B.^{6}, b. 25 May 1786, d. 24 Nov. 1796.
2) Phebe, b. 15 Dec. 1787, d. 5 Jan. 1804.

3) Andrew Deering, of Greensboro, Vt., 1848, b. 17 Nov. 1789, d. 23 July 1853, m. 1821, Mary F. Kent.
4) Sarah Peperell, b. 13 July 1792, d. *s.p.*, 24 Sept. 1875, m. 1831, John Sanborn (*Sanborn Family*, p. --), of Franklin.
5) John Simes, of Greensboro, Vt., 1836, and Glover, Vt., b. 1 Sept. 1794, d. 24 Aug. 1882, m. 15 Feb. 1818, Mary Cross, dau. of Jesse, b. at Northfield.
6) Charles Deering, of Greensboro, Vt., merchant, b. 16 Nov. 1796, d. 6 Jan. 1883, m. Olive Johnson, b. at Gilmanton.
7) Elihu Deering, of Nichollville, N.Y., merchant, b. 21 May 1799, d. 6 Oct. 1872, m. 2 Mar. 1826, Apphia Clarke.
8) Martin P., of Ohio, b. 10 May 1801, d. 20 Aug. 1878, m. Hannah Johnson.
9) William D., of New York City, b. 27 June 1803, d. unm. 20 Mar. 1834.
10) Statira, b. 16 Dec. 1806, d. unm. 18 May 1888.

viii. MARY ANN, m. ----- CONVERSE.
ix. HENRY, said to have gone to England.
x. EDWARD, said to have gone to England.
xi. PHEBE, b. 1767, d. unm. in Aug. 1787 *aet.* 20 years (*N.H. Gazette*, of 18 Aug. 1787).

S. B.

S. B. m. 10 Nov. 1748, B. C.

BABB

JOSHUA BABB, m. 12 Dec. 1720, DEBORAH BICKFORD.

MARY BABB, m. 16 Apr. 1721, JEREMIAH HODGDON.

SAMPSON BABB, JR., m. 29 Apr. 1725, DOROTHY HOYT, of Newington (*Register*, vol. 24, p. 357).

WILLIAM BABB, of Portsmouth, m. 7 Dec. 1732, DORCAS HAYNES, of York.

SARAH BABB, bapt. 2 Sept. 1732, dau. of Sampson and Dorothy.

BALDWIN

1. Capt. THOMAS BALDWIN, of Newington.
Children, born at Newington:
    i. RUTH, bapt. 26 Sept. 1740.
    ii. THOMAS, bapt. 16 Apr. 1742.

BANFIELD

HUGH BANFIELD, m. 9 Aug. 1722, HANNAH WELLS, of Portsmouth.

BARKER

ANNA BARKER, m. 4 May 1744, WILLIAM THOMPSON.

BARTLETT

DORCAS^6 BARTLETT, (Nathan$^{5-4}$, John^3, Richard$^{2-1}$), (Stackpole's *Kittery*, p. 285), b. 9 Jan. 1758, m. 20 June 1776, NATHAN COFFIN, *q.v.*

BEAR (BEAN?)

JERUSHA BEAR (BEAN), m. 19 Oct. 1760, ANDREW CARTER, of Durham.

BENSON

1. JAMES BENSON, of Newington, m. 8 Apr. 1725, SUSANNA ROWE.
Child, born at Newington:
    i. WILLIAM^2, bapt. 1 Nov. 1741.

1. JOHN BENSON, of Newington, m. SARAH -----.
Children, born at Newington:
    i. JAMES^2, bapt. 7 Aug. 1758.
    ii. JOHANNA, bapt. 18 May 1760.

1. JOSEPH BENSON, of Newington, m. 1 June 1759, MARY YEATON.
Child, born at Newington:
    i. ANNA PARKER^2, bapt. 18 May 1760.

BENSON (unconnected)

JAMES² BENSON, (Henry¹), of Kittery, m. 20 Mar. 1719, DEBORAH ROLLINS (Stackpole's *Kittery*, p. 293).

JOHN BENSON, m. 18 June 1724, HANNAH BROWN, both of Portsmouth (*Register*, vol. 24, p. 147).

HENRY BENSON, of Portsmouth, m. 4 Apr. 1736, MARY QUINT, of Newington (*id.*, vol. 26, p. 376).

SUSANNA BENSON, m. 10 Dec. 1741, SAMUEL ROWE, both of Portsmouth (*id.*, vol. 27, p. 9).

HANNAH BENSON, 1748, renewed covenant.

NOAH BENSON, bapt. 2 Oct. 1755, son of Mary.

BERRY

JAMES BERRY, of Dublin, Ire., m. 18 Oct. 1716, MEHITABLE LEACH, of Portsmouth (*Register*, vol. 23, p. 393).

WILLIAM BERRY, of Scarboro, m. 2 Dec. 1728, MARY LIBBY, of Portsmouth.

BENJAMIN BERRY, m. 25 Oct. 1739, MIRIAM BICKFORD.

BICKFORD

1. JOHN² BICKFORD (John¹), of Newington (Long Point), b. about 1662 (Stackpole's *Durham*, vol. 2, p. 17), (estate settled 1715), m. SUSANNAH² FURBER (1-iv), b. at Bloody Point, 5 May 1664, d. 1732, dau. of William¹ and Susanna Furber.

Her will dated 8 Nov. 1731, proved 13 Nov. 1732, names only her daughter, Anna Walker, widow (*N.H. State Pap.*, vol. 32, p. 425).

Children, born at Newington (Stackpole, *loc. cit.*):

 i. BRIDGET³, b. 30 July 1685, m. (1) ROGER² COUCH, of Kittery, Me., son of Joseph and Joanna (Deering) Couch (Stackpole's *Kittery*, p. 329), m. (2) 17 Aug. 1720, ROGER MITCHELL, of Kittery, Me.

2 ii. JETHRO, b. 15 Nov. 1689.

 iii. JOHN, b. 16 Mar. 1691/2.

iv. MARY, b. 13 Aug. 1693, m. 24 Oct. 1717, as his second wife, JOHN^2 WALKER, of Kittery, Me., b. at Kittery, 1694, d. 3 June 1745, son of William (Stackpole's *Kittery*, p. 785, where are their children).

v. JOSEPH, of Bristol, Eng., mariner, b. 13 July 1695.

vi. ANNA, b. 18 Sept. 1698, m. (1) 4 Oct. 1724, SAMUEL WALKER, m. (2) 31 July 1727, MOSES^4 FURBER (4), son of William^3 and Sarah Furber, *q.v.*

vii. PERCY, b. 9 Mar. 1701/2, m. 23 Feb. 1725, HANNAH MILLER.

viii. LEMUEL (twin), of Rochester, b. 6 Mar. 1703/4, m. TEMPERENCE^3 DOWNING (2-v), daughter of Col. John^2 and Elizabeth (Harrison) Downing, *q.v.*

Child (mentioned in the will of John^4 Downing):
1) John^4

ix. ELNATHAN (twin), of Kennebunkport, Me., b. 6 Mar. 1703/4, d. 22 Mar. 1748, m. MARY -----.

x. DODAVAH, b. 20 Aug. 1709, m. (int. 13 Oct. 1730), WINIFRED^3 CHICK, b. at Kittery, Me., dau. of Richard^2 and Martha (Lord) Chick (Stackpole's *Kittery*, p. 319).

Child, born at Newington:
1) Percy^4, bapt. 11 Jan. 1732.

2. JETHRO^3 BICKFORD (John$^{2-1}$), of Newington, b. 15 Nov. 1689, m. HANNAH^2 DOWNING (1-iii), dau. of Capt. John Downing, *q.v.*

Children, born at Newington:

i. JOHN^4, bapt. 4 Dec. 1715.

ii. SUSANNA, bapt. 28 Apr. 1717.

iii. BRIDGET, bapt. 24 May 1719.

iv. RICHARD, of Rochester, bapt. 26 Feb. 1721, m. SARAH -----.

v. DEPENDENCE, bapt. 14 Apr. 1723, m. OLIVE -----.

vi. ELIZABETH, bapt. 23 Mar. 1725, m. 10 Apr. 1755, SAMUEL HAM.

vii. LEMUEL, bapt. 12 Mar. 1727.

viii. JETHRO, bapt. 22 Sept. 1728.

ix. ALICE, bapt. 10 Mar. 1734.

1. BENJAMIN^1 BICKFORD, of Newington, planter, one of the original members of the church there, m. SARAH -----.

Children, as mentioned in his will dated 4 Apr. 1724, proved 2 June 1725 (*N.H. State Pap.*, vol. 32, p. 217):

2   i. BENJAMIN^2, b. ?1695.

3   ii. THOMAS, executor, b. 1690.

4   iii. JOHN, b. ?1700.

5   iv. JOSEPH, b. ?1715.

v. MARY, m. 8 Dec. 1707, JOSHUA CROCKETT (Stackpole's *Durham*, vol. 2, p. 26).

vi. ABIGAIL, m. 16 Aug. 1716, ZEBULON^4 DAVIS (3), son of John^3 and Jane (Rowe), *q.v.*

vii. ELIZABETH, m. 20 Feb. 1718, JOHN^4 DAVIS (4), son of John^3 and Jane (Rowe), *q.v.*

viii. DEBORAH, m. 28 Nov. 1720, JOHN BABB.

BENJ. BICKFORD, d. at Salem, Mass., 1773, *aet.* 62 (*N.H. Gazette*, June 4, 1773).

2. BENJAMIN^2 BICKFORD (Benjamin^1), of Newington, m. 23 Oct. 1718, DEBORAH BICKFORD.

Children, baptized at Newington:

6   i. SAMUEL^3, bapt. 16 June 1721.

ii. SARAH, bapt. 12 May 1722.

iii. ABIGAIL, bapt. 10 Dec. 1723.

7   iv. BENJAMIN, bapt. 17 Oct. 1725.

8   v. ANDREW, bapt. 26 Aug. 1727.

9   vi. SOLOMON, b. about 1734 (Stackpole's *Durham*, vol. 2, p. 26).

10   vii. JOHN, of Northwood, m. 4 Apr. 1754, MARY TRICKEY, wid. of Capt. Thomas (7), *q.v.*

viii. DEBORAH

ix. HANNAH, m. ? 7 Mar. 1758, NICHOLAS^4 PICKERING (11), son of Thomas^3 and Mary (Downing), *q.v.*

3. THOMAS^2 BICKFORD (Benjamin^1), of Newington, b. ?1690, m. at Greenland, 26 July 1711, SARAH SIMPSON.

Children, born at Newington (Stackpole's *Durham*, vol. 2, p. 27):

i. JOHN^3, covenant 10 Sept. 1753.

ii. EBENEZER, of Durham, covenant 10 Oct. 1741, m. 1 Feb. 1741, ANN QUINT, *q.v.*

Children, baptized at Newington:

1) George^4, bapt. 18 Oct. 1741, of Durham, N.H., and New Durham, Me., and Parsonsfield, Me. (Stackpole's*Durham*, vol. 2, p. 27), m. (1) ----- -----, m. (2) Ann Granville, m. (3) Sarah (Gilman) Thomas. He had a son, Ebenezer, bapt. at Newington, 21 Mar. 1741.

2) Anna, bapt. 30 Sept. 1744.

3) Eleanor, bapt. 4 Feb. 1745/6.

4) Samuel, bapt. 14 Sept. 1747.

iii. JONATHAN, covenant 18 Oct. 1741, m. 8 Nov. 1743, LYDIA BROWN.

Child, baptized at Newington:

1) Sarah[4], bapt. 29 Apr. 1745.

iv. JOSHUA, of Durham, covenant 18 Oct. 1741, m. 30 Mar. 1742, MARY WESTCOMBE, dau. of John and Elizabeth[3] (Lang) (*John Lang Family*, 1-i-2), b. at Portsmouth, who m. (2) 21 May 1758, PAUL WILLEY, of Durham.

v. THOMAS, b. ? 1725, bapt. 12 Dec. 1736, communion, 24 June 1744.

vi. BENJAMIN, b. ? 1727, bapt. 12 Dec. 1736.

vii. JOSEPH, b. ? 1729, bapt. 12 Dec. 1736.

viii. SAMUEL, b. ? 1731, bapt. 12 Dec. 1736.

ix. ICHABOD, of Newington, bapt. 12 Dec. 1736, d. 1800, m. (1) 18 July 1762, REBECCA BICKFORD, m. (2) ELIZABETH -----, b. 1752, d. 8 Dec. 1843, *aet.* 91 yrs. (*Register*, vol. 73, p. 199), if this is indeed his widow. His will dated 23 Sept. 1800, proved 15 Oct. 1800, mentions his children.

Children, as mentioned in the will:
1) Nathan[4]
2) Thomas
3) John
4) Joseph
5) Ichabod
6) Sarah
7) Eleanor

x. SARAH, bapt. 12 Dec. 1736, b. ? 1728, m. 28 Nov. 1749, JOSEPH PEARL, son of John and Mary, of Rochester, b. at Dover, 30 Mar. 1721.

xi. ELEANOR, bapt. 12 Dec. 1736, m. 4 June 1752, GIDEON[3] WALKER (1-viii), son of Lawrence[2] and Deliverance (Gaskin), *q.v.*

4. JOHN[2] BICKFORD (Benjamin[1]), of Newington and Rochester, m. 25 Feb. 1725, SARAH HODGDON (*Hodsdon-Hodgdon Family*, p. --).

Children, his first two baptized at Oyster River, the fourth at Rochester, the others at Newington:

i. SARAH[3], bapt. 24 Dec. 1727.

ii. ALEXANDER, bapt. 31 Mar. 1727/8.

iii. ABIGAIL, bapt. 3 Aug. 1729.

iv. ANNA

v. SARAH, b. ? 1733, bapt. 10 Sept. 1743.

vi. QUINT, b. ? 1735, bapt. 10 Sept. 1743.

vii. MARGARET, b. ? 1737, bapt. 10 Sept. 1743.

5. JOSEPH[2] BICKFORD (Benjamin[1]), of Newington, m. MARGARET -----.
Children, baptized at Newington:

i. LYDIA³, bapt. 9 May 1741.
ii. DANIEL, bapt. 23 May 1742.
iii. DENNIS, bapt. 23 May 1742.

9. SOLOMON³ BICKFORD (Benjamin²⁻¹), of Northwood, Nottingham, Lee and Northwood, b. about 1734 (Stackpole's *Durham*, vol. 2, p. 26), d. 3 Feb. 1830, m. SUSAN FOX, b. at Nottingham, 1736, d. 27 Oct. 1817.

Children, born at Nottingham (Cogswell's *Nottingham*, pp. 641-2):

i. JOHN⁴, of Nottingham, soldier in the Revolution, b. 29 Dec. 1759, d. 24 Nov. 1842.

Children, the first two born at -----, the others at Northwood:
1) John⁵

ii. DEBORAH, b. 5 July 1762, d. unm. 16 Feb. 1845.

iii. SOLOMON, of Northwood, b. 25 June 1764, d. 23 Aug. 1826, m. 17 Nov. 1788, ELIZABETH DEARBORN, dau. of Edward, b. at Dover, 5 Nov. 1768, d. 31 Mar. 1847.

Children, born at Northwood:
1) Sarah⁵, b. 25 June 1789.
2) Mary, b. 17 Nov. 1790.
3) Jeremiah, b. 5 June 1804, d. 18 Feb. 1875, m. 8 Aug. 1844, Huldah Lane.
4) Eliza (triplet), b. 22 Feb. 1807.
5) Joseph G. (triplet), b. 24 Feb. 1807, d. 14 July 1820.
6) A Child (triplet), b. and d. 24 Feb. 1807.

iv. GIDEON, of Northwood, b. 24 Nov. 1766, d. 1858, m. 24 May 1793, SARAH⁶ COVE, dau. of Jonathan⁵ and his first wife, Sarah (Sweatt) (Cogswell's *Nottingham*, p. 207; *Gove Book*, p. 80), b. at Nottingham, 20 Mar. 1771, d. 1858.

Children, born at Northwood:
1) Jonathan⁵
2) Sarah
3) William Smith
4) Olive Ann

v. BENJAMIN, of Northwood, b. 24 Aug. 1769, m. (1) MIRIAM DOW, b. at Epping, d. 1834, m. (2) July 1837, FRANCES (NOBLE) BLAKE, dau. of Rev. Oliver and ----- (Weld), wid. of Jonathan.

Children, by first wife, b. at Northwood:
1) Dudley⁵, d. unm. 7 Apr. 1824.
2) Samuel, of Belmont, b. 14 July 1802, m. Belinda Towle, b. at Gilmanton.
3) James, of Northwood, b. 3 Dec. 1807, m. 13 June 1832, Lydia Watson, b. at Pittsfield, 31 Dec. 1804.

4) George, b. 2 Dec. 1809, d. unm. ? Aug. 1833.
vi. SUSAN, b. 25 July 1771, m. BENJAMIN DURGIN, of Barnstead.
vii. JESSE (twin), of Northwood, b. 5 Oct. 1775, d. 4 Mar. 1852, m. 10 Feb. 1807, MARY^6 GOVE, dau. of Jonathan^5 and his second wife, Ruth (Philbrick) (Cogswell's *Nottingham*, p. 207, *Gove Book*, p. 81), b. at Nottingham, 16 Feb. 1779, d. 6 Feb. 1834.

Child, born at Northwood:
1) Bradbury G.^{5}, of Norwood, b. 30 Sept. 1811, m. 1 Dec. 1837, Abigail Franch, b. at Barnstead.

viii. Deac. ASA (twin), of Northwood, b. 5 Oct. 1775, m. (1) ELIZA WHITE, m. (2) ----- NUTTER, b. at Barnstead.

Children by first wife, born at Northwood:
1) Harriet^5, m. ----- -----, of Haverhill, Mass.
2) Jesse, of Lawrence, Mass.
3) Asa, of Northwood, m. Miriam F. Dow, dau. of Phineas, who m. (2) ----- Coffin, of Concord.

ix. HANNAH, b. 2 Nov. 1780, m. JOHN PEASE, of Sandwich.

BICKFORD (unconnected)

THOMAS BICKFORD, m. 10 Mar. 1717, ESTHER ADAMS.

HANNAH BICKFORD, m. 27 July 1721, JOHN CARTER.

THOMAS BICKFORD, of Portsmouth, m. 4 Oct. 1727, ESTHER FURBER.

MIRIAM BICKFORD, m. 25 Oct. 1739, BENJAMIN BERRY.

JOHN BICKFORD, son of Richard, bapt. 28 Sept. 1746.

ELIZABETH BICKFORD, m. 21 Apr. 1749, EBENEZER YOUNG, both of Dover.

SUSANNA BICKFORD, m. 3 May 1753, ROBERT MASON, of Newmarket.

ABNER BICKFORD, m. 3 Nov. 1754, SARAH BICKFORD, both of Durham.

SARAH BICKFORD, m. 3 Nov. 1754, ABNER BICKFORD, both of Durham.

DANIEL BICKFORD, m. 7 Aug. 1755, ELIZABETH HODGDON, both of Portsmouth.

HANNAH BICKFORD, m. 7 Mar. 1757, NICHOLAS PICKERING.

JOHN BICKFORD, son of Nicholas and Susanna, bapt. 5 July 1761.

WINTHROP BICKFORD, m. 16 May 1780, ESTHER LANGLEY, both of Durham.

ALICE BICKFORD, m. 3 July 1782, STEPHEN JONES.

BETTY BICKFORD, widow, d. 15 Sept. 1824, *aet.* 90 (*Register*, vol. 73, p. 196).

INDEPENDENCE BICKFORD, d. 9 Sept. 1842, *aet.* 75 (*id.*, p. 199).

MOSES BICKFORD, b. 1766, d. at Barnstead, 1859.

NANCY BICKFORD, b. 1776, wife of Moses preceding, d. at Barnstead, 1860.

ABIGAIL BICKFORD, b. 1765, wife of Moses, d. at Barnstead, 1835.

JOHN BICKFORD, b. 1768, d. at Barnstead, 1851.

BLY

WILLIAM BLY, renewed covenant, 15 Nov. 1761.

BOYD

GEORGE BOYD, of Boston, m. 31 Aug. 1730, and ABIGAIL HOYT.

GEORGE BOYD, son of George and Abigail, bapt. 23 Apr. 1732.

Capt. GEORGE BOYD, d. 31 Mar. 1773, *aet.* 66, at Portsmouth (*Gen. Mag.*, vol. 1, p. 17).

JOSEPH BOYD, m. 24 July 1776, ELIZABETH STOODLEY, both of Portsmouth.

BOYNTON

JOHN BOYNTON, of Wiscasset, m. 17 Oct. 1765, TEMPERANCE HODGDON.

BRACKETT

JOHN[4] BRACKETT (Joshua[3], Thomas[2-1]), of Greenland, m. 10 Dec. 1724, ELIZABETH PICKERING.

ELIZABETH BRACKETT, of Greenland, m. 3 Jan. 1760, Rev. JOSEPH ADAMS.

JOSHUA[5] BRACKETT (James[4], Joshua[3], Thomas[2-1]), m. 22 Nov. 1781, ALICE PICKERING.

BRASBRIDGE

1. **WILLIAM[2] BRASBRIDGE** (William[1]), of Newington, m. MARTHA[3] WALKER (i-vi), dau. of Edward[2] and Deliverance (Gaskin), *q.v.*

William Brasbridge, son of William, renewed his covenant 12 Apr. 1767.

Children, born at Newington:
  i. JOHN[2], bapt. 28 Oct. 1770.
  ii. CATHERINE, bapt. 28 Oct. 1770.
  iii. ELIZABETH, bapt. 28 Oct. 1770.
  iv. GEORGE, bapt. 16 Aug. 1772.

1. **EDWARD[2] BRASBRIDGE** (?William[1]), of Newington, m. ROSAMOND -----.

Children, born at Newington:
  i. JOHN[2], bapt. 29 Dec. 1771.
  ii. ROSAMOND, bapt. 7 Sept. 1774, d. unm. 7 Sept. 1836 (*Register*, vol. 72, p. 198).
  iii. JAMES, bapt. 29 Aug. 1774.
  iv. SARAH, bapt. 29 Aug. 1774.

BRASBRIDGE (unconnected)

HANNAH BRASBRIDGE, bapt. 12 Aug. 1781.

OLIVE BRASBRIDGE, widow, d. 21 May 1824 (*Register*, vol. 73, p. 1967.

BREWER

JACOB BREWER, m. 2 June 1770, LYDIA WEBBER, both of Kittery.

BREWSTER

ABIGAIL BREWSTER, of Portsmouth, m. 2 Sept. 1750, LEADER NELSON.

SAMUEL BREWSTER, of Barrington, m. 30 Jan. 1758, SARAH NORWOOD.

BROWN

HANNAH BROWN, m. 18 June 1724, JOHN BENSON, both of Portsmouth (*Register*, vol. 24, p. 173).

MADELINE BROWN, m. 11 May 1736, HUDSON PEVEY.

LYDIA BROWN, of Portsmouth, m. 8 Nov. 1743, JONATHAN BICKFORD.

ABIAH BROWN, m. 25 Sept. 1746, JEREMIAH DOW, both of Hampton.

ELIZABETH BROWN, of Hampton, m. 27 Jan. 1770, DANIEL HOYT.

BENJAMIN BROWN, m. 6 Oct. 1773, ABIGAIL GERRISH, both of Madbury.

JOSEPH BROWN, of Barnstead, m. 7 Oct. 1778, ELIZABETH NUTTER.

BURLEIGH

ELEANOR BURLEIGH, m. 10 July 1758, BENJAMIN LANG, both of Rye.

BURNHAM

1. NATHANIEL[4] BURNHAM (James[3], Samuel[2], Robert[1]), of Newington, m. MEHITABLE COLBATH (Stackpole's *Durham*, vol. 2, p. 43).
    Children, born at Newington:
    i. SUSANNA[5], bapt. 25 Jan. 1740/1.
    ii. JOSEPH, bapt. 11 Nov. 1744.
    iii. ENOCH, bapt. 7 Oct. 1746.

    iv. AMOS, bapt. 7 Oct. 1746.
    v. A SON, bapt. after 26 Aug. 1750.

BURNHAM (unconnected)

JEREMIAH BURNHAM, m. 21 Apr. 1749, ELIZABETH ADAMS, both of Durham.

WINTHROP BURNHAM, m. 6 Aug. 1754, MURIEL ADAMS, both of Durham.

BUSBEE

RICHARD BUSBEE, m. 15 May 1730, MABEL LITTLEFIELD, both of Wells.

B. C.

B. C., m. 10 Nov. 1748, S. B.

CALDWELL

JAMES CALDWELL, of Londonderry, m. 23 Oct. 1724, LETTICE MURDOCH.

CANNEY

DEBORAH CANNEY, m. 18 Apr. 1730, SAMUEL ROWE.

CARLTON

THEODORE CARLTON, of Exeter, m. 1 Sept. 1768, MARY HOYT.

CARTER

1. JOHN CARTER, of Newington, 1713 (*Register*, vol. 58, p. 249), b. ? 1660. Children:
2   i. RICHARD, b. ? 1695.
3   ii. JOHN
    iii. ELIZABETH, m. 21 Mar. 1717, WILLIAM WITHAM.

One of the oldest families in Newington (*Landmarks*, p. 39). Perhaps from Salisbury, Mass. Richard Carter was living in Newington near Pine Point, before 1648. No will or adm. to 1749. See also *Libby Gen. Dic.*

2. RICHARD CARTER (John), of Newington, b. 1695?, m. 12 Feb. 1719, SARAH PEAVEY.
Children, baptized at Newington:
   i. MARY, b. ? 1721, bapt. 20 Sept. 1724.
   ii. DEBORAH, bapt. 20 Sept. 1724.
   iii. SARAH, bapt. 20 Sept. 1724.
   iv. HEPSIBAH, bapt. 14 Mar. 1725.

Richard Carter was of Greenland sometime prior to 1723 (*N.H. State Pap.*, vol. 32, p. 200). No mention of any others in this family in *State Pap.*, vols. 31-33.

3. JOHN CARTER (John), of Newington, m. 27 July 1721, HANNAH BICKFORD.
Children, baptized at Newington:
4   i. RICHARD, bapt. 14 Mar. 1725.
   ii. ELIZABETH, bapt. 14 Aug. 1726.
   iii. SAMUEL, bapt. 26 Oct. 1740.

4. RICHARD CARTER (John, John), of Newington, bapt. 14 Mar. 1725, m. ELIZABETH -----.
Children, baptized at Newington:
   i. A SON, bapt. 9 Nov. 1740.
   ii. A SON, bapt. 9 Nov. 1740.

CARTER (unconnected)

MARY CARTER, m. 1 Feb. 1757, JOSEPH ROLLINS.

ANDREW CARTER, of Durham, m. 19 Oct. 1760, ELIZABETH BEAN ?

CAVERLY

ELIZABETH CAVERLY, of Portsmouth, m. Aug. 1715, THOMAS WILKINSON, of London, Eng. (*Register*, vol. 23, p. 272).

WILLIAM CAVERLY, m. 13 Oct. 1748, MARGARET HUGH, both of Portsmouth.

CHANDLER

ELIZABETH CHANDLER, of Kittery, m. 20 Jan. 1774, DIAMOND FERNALD.

CHAPMAN

JOHN CHAPMAN, of Newmarket, m. 19 Sept. 1762, SUSANNA MESERVE, of Durham.

CHASE

JOHN CHASE, m. 17 Aug. 1775, HANNAH DENNETT, both of Kittery.

CHICK

LUCY CHICK, m. 17 June 1766, JOHN HILL, both of Kittery.

CHUTE (CRISTE?)

ELIZABETH CHUTE, dau. of James, bapt. 22 July 1744.

JAMES CHUTE, son of James, bapt. 11 Feb. 1745/6.

JOHN CHUTE, son of John, bapt. 24 Apr. 1748.

PETER CHUTE, son of James, bapt. 17 June 1750.

CLARK

WILLIAM CLARK, son of Andrew and Mary, bapt. 7 Dec. 1735.

MARY CLARK, dau. of Andrew and Mary, bapt. 7 Dec. 1735.

JOHN CLARK, m. 26 Nov. 1747, ABIGAIL PEVERLY, both of Portsmouth (*Peverly Family*, p. 11).

JOSIAH CLARK, m. 14 Jan. 1748, MARY MOSES, both of Portsmouth.

SATCHEL CLARK, of Stratham, m. 8 Jan. 1755, ELIZABETH ROLLINS.

COFFIN

NATHAN⁵ COFFIN (Edmund⁴, Nathaniel³, Tristram²⁻¹) (Stackpole's *Kittery*, p. 324), m. 20 June 1776, DORCAS BARTLETT, both of Kittery.

COLBY

SPENCER COLBY, of Newbury, m. 23 Aug. 1747, LYDIA WATERHOUSE.

COLEMAN

11. **JOHN WOODMAN⁵ COLEMAN** (Deac. John⁴, Eleazur³, Tobias², Thomas¹), of Dover and Newington, yeoman, d. 8 May 1821, m. PHEBE -----.

In 1816, he bought of his brother, Eleazur, the farm in Newington, formerly of his father and devised it to his son, John Woodman.

Children, born at ----- (*Coleman Notes*, No. 1, p. 7):

  i. JOHN WOODMAN⁶, of Durham.

    Children, b. at Durham (*Coleman Notes, loc. cit.*):

      1) Joseph⁷, (lost at sea), m. Dorothy Card, dau. of Thomas (soldier in the War of 1812) and Phebe (Trefethen) Card.

      2) James

      3) Oliver Woodman, m. Mehitable Clark, b. at ?Strafford.

      4) Calvin, b. May 1800, d. 24 Oct. 1864, m. 5 Oct. 1823, Phebe Card, dau. of Thomas and Phebe (Trefethen) Card.

  ii. ANNA, m. ----- LOCKE, of Gilmanton.

  ii. ALICE (Stackpole's *Durham*, vol. 2, p. 393).

  iii. JAMES, ? m. POLLY MESERVE (Stackpole's *Durham*?, vol. 2, p. 289).

  iv. MEHITABLE, m. ----- MESERVE.

  v. KATHARINE, m. ----- TUTTLE.

  vi. MARY

  vii. CALVIN, b. May 1800.

  viii. OLIVER

  ix. JOSEPH

COLLINS

WILLIAM COLLINS, son of John and Sarah, b. 8 Sept. 1711, at Portsmouth (*Register*, vol. 25, p. 117).

Capt. WILLIAM COLLINS, of Portsmouth, m. 9 Oct. 1735, DEBORAH LEIGHTON.

COLMAN

1. **ELEAZUR³ COLMAN** (Tobias², Thomas¹⁺), of Newington, m. (1) MARY LANGSTAFF (*Coleman Notes*, No. 1, p. 5), dau. of Henry, m. (2) 1 Mar. 1717, ANNA NUTTER.

Children, baptized at Newington:
- 2   i. PHINEAS⁴, bapt. 22 Aug. 1719.
- 3   ii. ELEAZUR, bapt. 22 Aug. 1719.
-    iii. MARY, bapt. 30 Apr. 1721, m. 21 (31?) Jan. 1742, SAMUEL² HUNTRESS (1), son of George¹ and Mary, *q.v.*
-    iv. JAMES, bapt. 14 Mar. 1725.
-    v. ANNA, bapt. 29 May 1726, m. 20 June 1745, BENJAMIN⁵ MATHES, son of Frances⁴ and Lydia (Drew) (Stackpole's *Durham*, vol. 2, p. 264), of Canterbury, b. at Oyster River about 1724.
- 4   vi. JOSEPH, b. 15 July 1727, bapt. 27 July 1728.
- 5   vii. JOHN, bapt. 16 Apr. 1730.
-    viii. ROSAMOND, bapt. 20 Jan. 1734, m. 27 Dec. 1753, JOSHUA TRICKEY (9), son of John³ and Mary (Witham), *q.v.*
-    ix. SARAH, bapt. 26 Oct. 1735, m. 21 Oct. 1756, ENOCH TOPPAN, of Newbury.
-    x. LYDIA, bapt. 4 June 1738, d. 16 Feb. 1832 (*Register*, vol. 73, p. 197), m. Maj. EPHRAIM⁴ PICKERING (10), son of Joshua³ and Deborah (Smithson), *q.v.*

2. **PHINEAS⁴ COLMAN** (Eleazur³), of Newington, bapt. 22 Aug. 1719, m. 22 Apr. 1739, ABIGAIL³ HUNTRESS, (1-iii), dau. of Samuel² and Abigail (Ham), *q.v.*

Children, baptized at Newington:
- 6   i. PHINEAS⁵, bapt. 30 Dec. 1739.
-    ii. MARY, bapt. 7 June 1741, m. WILLIAM⁵ FURBER (13), son of Moses⁴ and Anna (Bickford) (Walker), *q.v.*
-    iii. ABIGAIL, b. 14 July 1743, m. JOHN⁶ ADAMS (2-vi), son of Dr. Joseph⁵ and Johanna (Gilman), *q.v.*
-    iv. ELIZABETH, bapt. 12 Jan. 1745/6, m. 17 July 1771, ENOCH⁵ HOYT (3-xi), son of John⁴ and Lydia (Miller), *q.v.*
-    v. ROSAMOND, bapt. 31 July 1748, d. 3 Nov. 1841, m. 8 Apr. 1776, BENJAMIN⁵ HODGDON (6-vii), son of John⁴ and Mary (Decker), *q.v.*

+For the first two generations see *Coleman Notes*, No. 1, Bk. 2-5.

vi. LYDIA, bapt. 15 Jan. 1755.

3. ELEAZUR⁴ COLMAN (Eleazur³), of Newington, bapt. 22 Aug. 1719, m. 20 Sept. 1739, KEZIAH⁵ LEIGHTON (i-vi), dau of Thomas⁴ and Deborah, *q.v.*
Children, baptized at Newington:
7   i. WILLIAM⁵, bapt. 20 Dec. 1741.
    ii. TEMPERENCE, bapt. 21 June 1747.
    iii. ELEAZUR, bapt. 15 Jan. 1748/9.

Eleazur Colman m. 1 Jan. 1756/7, Dorothy Fernald, dau. of Ebenezer and Patience (Mendum), b. at Kittery, Me., 25 Feb. 1738/9 (Stackpole's *Kittery*, p. 380).

4. JOSEPH⁴ COLMAN (Eleazur³), of Newington, bapt. 27 July 1728, m. ABIGAIL DOWNING (Coleman Notes, No. 1, p. 6).
Children, baptized at Newington:
    i. LYDIA⁵, bapt. 29 Mar. 1761, d. 1847, m. 19 May 1782, SAMUEL⁶ ADAMS (12), son of Ebenezer⁵ and Lois (Downing), *q.v.*
10   ii. JOSEPH, bapt. 10 July 1763, d. 4 May 1853 (*Register*, vol. 73, p. 202).
    iii. OLIVE, bapt. 28 Apr. 1765.

5. Deac. JOHN⁴ COLMAN (Eleazur³), of Newington, bapt. 16 Apr. 1730, d. 18 Oct. 1807, m. MARY⁵ WOODMAN, dau. of John⁴ and Mary³ (Fabyan), b. at Durham, 14 Feb. 1734, d. 9 Sept. 1819.

His will, dated 1805, mentions his children as below, except Nos. iv. and vii.; his granddaughter, Alice Coleman Furber; and the four children of his son, Benjamin, as below stated (*Rockingham Probate*). He gave all his real estate to his son, Eleazur.

Children, baptized at Newington:
    i. ALICE⁵, bapt. 30 May 1756, m. 18 June 1780, Gen. RICHARD⁶ FURBER (9-iii), son of Richard⁵ and Elizabeth (Downing), *q.v.*
11   ii. JOHN WOODMAN, bapt. 30 Dec. 1757.
12   iii. BENJAMIN, of Newington, bapt. 19 Aug. 1759, d. 11 July 1800, m. 2 Jan. 1791, HANNAH⁵ SHACKFORD (9-ix), dau. of Capt. Samuel⁴ and Elizabeth (Ring), *q.v.*
    Children, born at Newington (baptisms in Newington Church Rec.):
    1) Samuel Shackford⁶, b. 21 Dec. 1793, d. 9 Jan. 1830, m. 26 Sept. 1816, Mehitable Burnham.
    2) Timothy Palmer, b. 15 Oct. 1794, d. unm.
    3) Alice, b. 12 Aug. 1798, bapt. 13 July 1800, m. at Portsmouth, 28 June 1821 (town rec.) James⁵ Huntress, son of Samuel⁴ and Elizabeth (Slade), of Portsmouth, drayman, b. at Newington 1800.

      4) Benjamin, b. 31 Aug. 1800, bapt. 13 July 1800, d. unm.
- iv. MARY, bapt. 30 Aug. 1761. She is not named in her father's will.
- v. ELIZABETH, bapt. 28 Apr. 1765, m. ----- COLBATH.
- vi. ANNA, bapt. 20 Sept. 1772, m. BENJAMIN MOSES.
- vii. MEHITABLE, bapt. 20 Sept. 1772. She is not named in her father's will.

13 viii. ELEAZUR, of Newington, bapt. 28 Sept. 1777, d. 11 Oct. 1830 (*Register*, vol. 73, p. 197).

6. PHINEAS^5 **COLMAN** (Phineas^4, Eleazur^3), of Newington, yeoman, b. 12 Dec. 1739, bapt. 30 Dec. 1739, d. 15 Aug. 1783, m. 24 Feb. 1774, SARAH WHIDDEN, dau. of Samuel and Hannah (Langdon), b. at Greenland, 1752, d. 9 Sept. 1821 (tombstone).

Children, baptized at Newington:

14 i. JAMES^6, bapt. 25 Dec. 1774.
- ii. HANNAH, bapt. 5 Mar. 1776.

15 iii. JOSEPH (twin), bapt. 27 May 1778.
16 iv. SAMUEL (twin), bapt. 27 May 1778.
17 v. ENOCH TOPPAN, bapt. 20 Aug. 1780.
18 vi. PHINEAS, bapt. 22 Sept. 1782.

COLMAN (unconnected)

MARGARET COLMAN, wife of E. COLMAN, d. 25 Dec. 1832, *aet.* 47 (*Register*, vol. 73, p. 197)

COOK

PETER COOK, of Somersworth, m. 21 Nov. 1748, ABIGAIL ROLLINS.

COOLBROTH

1. GEORGE^1 **COOLBROTH**, of Newington, yeoman, b. in Ulster, Ireland, about 1690 (*Mass. Genealogy*, p. 2454), m. MARY -----.

Children, baptized except the first one, at Newington:

- i. GEORGE^2, of Newington, husbandman, b. about 1712, d. 1738, m. 28 Feb. 1734, ELIZABETH^4 HOYT (1-iv), *q.v.*, dau. of William^3 and Elizabeth (Haley) (Nelson) Hoyt.

    Administration on his estate was granted 30 Aug. 1738 to his father (*N.H. State Pap.*, vol. 32, p. 722).

    Child, baptized at Newington:
      1) Lemuel^3, bapt. 19 Oct. 1735.

- ii. JAMES, bapt. 19 Sept. 1725.

  iii. PITMAN, bapt. 19 Sept. 1725.
  iv. WILLIAM, bapt. 19 Sept. 1725.
  v. JOSEPH, bapt. 19 Sept. 1725.
  vi. BENJAMIN, bapt. 19 Sept. 1725.
  vii. SUSANNA, bapt. 19 Sept. 1725.
  viii. MEHITABLE, bapt. 19 Sept. 1725.

2. JAMES² COOLBROTH (George¹), of Newington, b. about 1714, bapt. 19 Sept. 1725, m. OLIVE⁵ LEIGHTON (1-i), *q.v.*, dau. of Thomas⁴ and Deborah Leighton.

Children, baptized at Newington:

7 i. LEIGHTON³, bapt. 1 Dec. 1739.
8 ii. HUNKING, bapt. 17 Feb. 1743/4.
  iii. DEBORAH, bapt. 9 Oct. 1746.
9 iv. WINTHROP, bapt. 1751.
  v. AMY, bapt. 9 July 1758.

3. PITMAN² COOLBROTH (George¹), of Newington, b. about 1718, bapt. 19 Sept. 1725, m. JANE⁵ HODGDON (6-i), *q.v.*, dau. of John⁴ and Mary (Decker) Hodgdon.

Children, baptized at Newington:

  i. MARY, bapt. 5 May 1754, d. in infancy.
  ii. ELIZABETH, bapt. 5 May 1754.
  iii. A DAUGHTER, bapt. 3 Oct. 1756.
  iv. GEORGE, bapt. 22 Mar. 1761. He was living, 1850, in the family of Robert⁶ and Jane Colbath⁷ (Sherburn) Peverly, at Portsmouth (U.S. Census).
  v. ELIZABETH, bapt. 13 Nov. 1763.
  vi. JOHN, of Barnstead, bapt. 20 July 1766.
  vii. WILLIAM, bapt. 21 Aug. 1768.
  viii. MARY, bapt. 7 June 1772.

7. LEIGHTON³ COOLBATH (James², George¹), of Newington, bapt. 1 Dec. 1739, m. 3 Dec. 1761, DEBORAH⁶ LEIGHTON (4-i), *q.v.*, dau. of Thomas⁵ and Mary (Smithson) Leighton.

Child, baptized at Newington:

  i. LEMUEL⁴, bapt. 10 Oct. 1762.

8. HUNKING³ COOLBATH (James², George¹), bapt. 17 Feb. 1743/4, m. 4 Mar. 1776, SUSANNA⁴ KNIGHT (2-iii), *q.v.*, dau. of Nicholas³ and Sarah (Thompson) Knight.

9. **WINTHROP³ COOLBROTH**⁺(James², George¹), of Barnstead, bapt. 16 June 1751.

COOLBROTH (unconnected)

ELIZABETH COOLBROTH, m. 2 May 1725, JOSEPH RICHARDS, both of Portsmouth (*Register*, vol. 24, p. 357).

SUSANNA COOLBROTH, of Portsmouth, m. 1 Oct. 1730, THOMAS FOLLETT, b. in the Island of Jersey (*Register*, vol. 25, p. 117).

MARY COOLBROTH, admitted to communion, 26 Sept. 1736.

ALICE COOLBROTH, renewed covenant, 29 Dec. 1771.

DEPENDENCE COOLBROTH, m. 25 Nov. 1773, ELEANOR WALKER. He was of Barnstead, 1792. He d. 1838, *aet.* 90; she 1833, *aet.* 81.

LOIS COOLBROTH, m. 17 Sept. 1777, JOHN PEVEY.

GEORGE COOLBATH, m. 24 Oct. 1780, MARIANNA COOLBATH.

MARIANNA COOLBATH, m. 24 Oct. 1780, GEORGE COOLBATH.

ALICE COOLBROTH, m. 28 June 1781, WILLIAM VINCENT.

TEMPERENCE COOLBROTH, m. 5 Feb. 1782, EBENEZER NUTTER.

SARAH W. COOLBROTH, m. about 1790, JOSEPH⁵ EDGERLY, son of Moses⁴ and Polly (Thompson) Edgerly, b. at Newmarket, 1769 (*Register*, vol. 34, p. 285).

COTTON

ABIGAIL⁵ COTTON (John⁴) (*Register*, vol. 58, p. 341), of Portsmouth, m. 18 Feb. 1773, EBENEZER SULLIVAN, of Berwick.

⁺He was great-grandfather of Henry Wilson, born Coolbroth, Vice-President of the United States (*Thompson's Landmarks*, p. 32).

CRAWFORD

ELIZABETH CRAWFORD, m. 2 Apr. 1736, THOMAS GLEER?.

CRISTE (See CHUTE)

CROCKER

JOHN CROCKER, m. 25 Apr. 1758, BETHIAH GREEN, both of Kittery.

CROCKETT

JOSHUA CROCKETT, 1713, living at Newington (*Register*, vol. 58, p. 249).

DEBORAH CROCKETT, communion, 11 Mar. 1716.

MARY CROCKETT, m. 16 Apr. 1717, SAMUEL THOMPSON.

JOHN^3 CROCKETT (Joshua^2, Thomas^1) (Stackpole's *Kittery*, p. 330), of Falmouth, Me., 1748, shipwright, m. 16 May 1718, MARY KNIGHT, dau. of Nathan and Mary, of Scarborough, Me.

SARAH^2 (TRICKEY) CROCKETT, dau. of Thomas^1 and wife of Joshua^2 Crockett (Stackpole's *Kittery*, p. 331), covenant, 6 Oct. 1726.

JOSHUA CROCKETT, covenant, 7 Feb. 1741/2.

JOSHUA CROCKETT and wife, **ELIZABETH^4** (NUTTER) (4-iv), dau. of Henry^3 and Mary (Shackford), communion, 6 June 1742.

CRUMELL

JACOB^4 CRUMELL (Joshua^3, John^2, Philip^1) (Stackpole's *Durham*, vol. 2, p. 82), of Durham, m. 16 Dec. 1762, ABIGAIL DAM.

DAM

1. Deac. JOHN^3 DAM (John$^{2-1}$), (*Register*, vol. 65, p. 213), of Newington (Bloody Point), b. there 23 Feb. 1667/8, living in 1734 (*Libby*), m. (1) JANE ROWE, dau. of Richard, m. (2) 4 Nov. 1732, ELIZABETH (HALEY) (NELSON) (HOYT) HILLIARD, dau. of Andrew and Deborah (Wilson), and widow of JOHN NELSON (first husband), WILLIAM HOYT (second husband), and NICHOLAS

HILLIARD (third husband), b. at York, Me., d. in Feb. 1765, *aet.* 99 yrs. (*N.H. Gazette*, of 8 Mar. 1765).

Children by first wife, born at Newington (*Register, loc. cit.*):

3   i. ZEBULON^4, b. about 1693.
4   ii. JOHN, b. about 1695.
5   iii. RICHARD, b. 26 Aug. 1699.
     iv. ELNATHAN, b. 27 Apr. 1706, m. at Greenland, 1 Nov. 1736, MARY ROLLINS.
     v. ALICE, b. about 1708, m. 5 May 1720, SAMUEL^3 ROLLINS (6), son of Joseph^2 and Sarah, *q.v.*
     vi. ELIZA (probably)
     vii. SUSANNA

2. Deac. MOSES^3 DAM (John$^{2-1}$), of Newington, b. 14 Oct. 1673, m. 22 July 1714 (*N.H. Gen. Rec.*, vol. 5, p. 42), ABIGAIL^2 HUNTRESS, dau. of George^1 and Mary, b. at Bloody Point.

Children, baptized at Newington:
     i. ABIGAIL^4, bapt. 22 Jan. 1716, m. 7 Mar. 1735 (*N.H. Gen. Rec.*, vol. 3, p. 138), SOLOMON LOUD, of Portsmouth.
     ii. JOHN, bapt. 5 May 1717.
6   iii. ELIPHALET, bapt. 20 Dec. 1719.
     iv. SOLOMON, bapt. 12 May 1722.
     v. THEOPHILUS, bapt. 6 Dec. 1724.
     vi. GEORGE, bapt. 8 Jan. 1727.
     vii. WILLIAM, bapt. 20 July 1729.
     viii. JABEZ, bapt. 4 Apr. 1731.
     ix. MARY, bapt. 17 Feb. 1734.

3. ZEBULON^4 DAM (John$^{3-1}$), of Newington and Rochester, b. about 1693, m. 16 Aug. 1716, ABIGAIL^2 BICKFORD (1-vi), dau. of Benjamin^1 and Sarah, b. at Bloody Point about 1695.

Children, baptized at Newington:
     i. SARAH^5, bapt. 13 July 1718.
     ii. ABNER, of Rochester, bapt. 17 Aug. 1723, m. MARY DANA.
     iii. KETURAH, bapt. 17 Aug. 1723, m. PAUL JENNESS, of Rochester.
     iv. A DAUGHTER, bapt. 16 Oct. 1734.
     v. JOSEPH, b. 19 Sept. 1739.
     vi. MARY, b. 19 Sept. 1739.
     vii. ZEBULON, b. 1740, m. MARY -----.

4. JOHN^4 DAM (John$^{3-1}$), of Newington, b. about 1695, d. Jan. 1768/9, m. (1) 20 Feb. 1718, ELIZABETH BICKFORD (1-vii), dau. of Benjamin^1 and Sarah, *q.v.*,

m. (2) 2 Nov. 1732, ELIZABETH HILLIARD.
He had the ancestral farm on Dame's Point.
Children by first wife, baptized at Newington:
7   i. JOSEPH[5], bapt. 26 Sept. 1719.
- ii. MOSES, of Newington and Lee, bapt. 12 May 1722, m. 1743, ANNA HUNKING, dau. of Capt. Mark (Stackpole's *Durham*, vol. 2, p. 88).
8   iii. ISSACHAR, bapt. 12 May 1722.
- iv. JOHN, of Wiscasset, Me., bapt. 18 Oct. 1724.
- v. ELNATHAN, of Newington, bapt. 28 Aug. 1726, m. MARY[3] ROLLINS (2-iv), dau. of Joseph[2], *q.v.*
  Child baptized at Newington:
  1) Eleazer[6], bapt. 9 Sept. 1747.
- vi. ELIZABETH, bapt. 1 June 1728, m. 20 May 1758, JOSEPH TRICKEY, son of Thomas and Mary, *q.v.*

Children by second wife, baptized at Newington:
9   vii. THEODORE, bapt. 7 Oct. 1733.
- viii. MARY, bapt. 5 Sept. 1736.
- ix. OLIVE, bapt. 5 Sept. 1736, m. 12 July 1759, SAMUEL[4] EDGERLY, son of John[3] and Elizabeth (Wakeham) (Stackpole's *Durham*, vol. ii, p. 172).
- x. ALICE, b. 1733, m. 17 July 1751, JOSEPH[4] PLACE (9), son of John M.[3] and Eunice (Rowe), *q.v.*
- xi. ESTHER, b. 1736, m. 18 Dec. 1755, JAMES[5] NUTTER (14-v), son of James[4] and Abigail (Furber), *q.v.*

5. RICHARD[4] DAM (John[3-1]), of Newington, b. 26 Aug. 1699, d. 13 May 1776, m. 24 Jan. 1724, ELIZABETH[5] LEIGHTON (1-iii), dau. of Thomas[4] and Deborah, *q.v.*

Children, baptized at Newington:
- i. MARY[5], bapt. 28 Feb. 1725.
- ii. JONATHAN, of Rochester, town clerk, bapt. 11 Apr. 1726, m. MERCY H. VARNEY.
- iii. MARTHA, bapt. 18 Aug. 1728.
- iv. BENJAMIN, of Newington, bapt. 9 Aug. 1730, m. JANE SIMPSON.
- v. JABEZ, of Rochester, bapt. 23 Sept. 1733, d. 14 Nov. 1813 (*Register*, vol. 80, p. 307), m. MERIBAH[5] EMERY, dau. of Simon[4] and Martha (Lord) (Stackpole's *Kittery*, p. 368), b. at Kittery, Me., 20 Mar. 1740, d. 24 Feb. 1838.
- vi. SAMUEL, bapt. 8 Apr. 1736.
- vii. TIMOTHY, of Newington, bapt. 5 July 1752, m. 12 Mar. 1767, ELIZABETH[4] PICKERING (5-viii), dau. of Thomas[2] and Mary[2] (Janvrin), *q.v.*

Child, baptized at Newington:
1) Richard[6], bapt. 6 May 1768.
viii. JOHN, of Durham, bapt. 5 July 1752, m. 22 Oct. 1767, ELIZABETH[5] FURBER (5-viii), dau. of Deac. Moses[4] and Anna (Bickford) (Walker), *q.v.*
ix. ABIGAIL, bapt. 5 July 1752.
x. ELIZABETH, bapt. 5 July 1752.

6. **ELIPHALET[4] DAM** (Moses[3], John[2-1]), of Newington, bapt. 20 Dec. 1719, d. 1783, m. ABIGAIL[4] NUTTER (3-v), dau. of Hatevil[3] and Leah (Furber), *q.v.*
Children, baptized at Newington:
i. ABIGAIL[5], bapt. 5 May 1747, d. in infancy.
ii. MARY, bapt. 5 May 1747.
iii. ABIGAIL, bapt. 30 Oct. 1748, d. in infancy.
iv. TEMPERANCE, bapt. 16 June 1751.
v. SARAH, bapt. 24 June 1753, m. ? at Portsmouth, 2 Sept. 1784 (town rec.), SETH[4] HUNTRESS (5-vi), son of Jonathan[3] and Mary (Walker), *q.v.*
vi. ELIZABETH, bapt. 18 Jan. 1756, m. 21 June 1779, JOHN[5] NUTTER (8-v), son of Maj. John[4] and Anna (Symmes), *q.v.*
vii. MOSES, bapt. 19 Apr. 1758.
viii. NANCY, bapt. 30 Nov. 1760.
ix. JOSEPH PATTESON, bapt. 22 Nov. 1761.
x. SUSANNA, bapt. 30 Oct. 1764.
xi. ABIGAIL, bapt. 9 Oct. 1769.
xii. STEPHEN FIELD, bapt. 9 Oct. 1769.
xiii. JOHANNA, bapt. 9 Oct. 1769.

7. **JOSEPH[5] DAM** (John[4-1]), of Newington, yeoman, bapt. 26 Sept. 1719, d. Apr. 1807, m. MEHITABLE HALL.

His will, dated 2 Apr. 1800, proved 4 May 1807, mentions his sons George and John; daughters Mary, Esther Nutter, and Bethiah Trickey; grandsons James and Joseph (sons of deceased son, Joseph); and grandchildren Joseph, Mehitable, Hannah and Mary (children of his deceased son, Samuel); and Samuel's wife, Hannah (*Rockingham Probate*).

Children, born at Newington (See also *Register*, vol. 65, p. 215):
i. MARY[6], b. 10 Nov. 1740, d. unm.
ii. JOSEPH, of Barnstead, b. 24 Mar. 1743, d. before 2 Apr. 1800, m. PATIENCE[6] CHADBOURNE, dau. of James[5] and Bridget (Knight) (Stackpole's *Kittery*, p. 313).
Administration on his estate was granted in 1774 to his widow, Patience; Gideon Walker, surety (*Rockingham Probate*).

Children, baptized at Newington:
- 1) James Chadburn[7], b. 25 Aug. 1770, bapt. 7 Sept. 1770.
- 2) Joseph, b. 20 Nov. 1772, bapt. 13 Dec. 1772.

iii. RICHARD
iv. GEORGE, b. 26 June 1748.
v. JOHN, of Newington, b. 20 Oct. 1750. He had his father's farm.
vi. ESTHER, b. 28 June 1752, m. 11 Jan. 1781, HATEVIL[5] NUTTER (16-viii), son of Hatevil[4] and Hannah (Decker), *q.v.*
vii. BETHIAH, b. 19 Feb. 1755 (*Register*, vol. 65, p. 215), m. 3 June 1778, JOHN[5] TRICKEY, of Rochester, son of Joshua[4] and Rosamond[4] (Colman), *q.v.*
viii. SAMUEL, of Dover, b. 15 Aug. 1757, d. 1798, m. HANNAH HODSDON.

Children:
- 1) Joseph[7], of Dover, b. 1794, d. 1876, m. Mehitable Burroughs.
- 2) Mehitable, b. 1792, d. unm. 1870.
- 3) Hannah
- 4) Mary

8. ISSACHAR[5] DAM (John[4-1]), of Newington, bapt. 12 May 1722, d. 22 Nov. 1811, m. 12 May 1747, SARAH HODGKINS.

Children, baptized at Newington:
  i. HANNAH[6], bapt. 2 June 1754, m. ----- BICKFORD.
  ii. SARAH, bapt. 2 June 1754.
  iii. ELIZABETH, bapt. 2 June 1754.
  iv. THOMAS, bapt. 14 Dec. 1755.

9. THEODORE[5] DAM (John[4-1]), of Newington, bapt. 7 Oct. 1733, m. MARY -----.

Children, baptized at Newington:
  i. VALENTINE[6], bapt. 18 July 1756.
  ii. REBECCA, bapt. 23 Apr. 1758.
  iii. BENJAMIN, bapt. 3 Aug. 1760.
  iv. MARK, bapt. 1 Oct. 1769.
  v. HENRY, bapt. 1 Oct. 1769.
  vi. HANNAH, bapt. 1 Oct. 1769.
  vii. MARY, bapt. 6 Dec. 1772.

DAM (unconnected)

JONATHAN[2] DAM (Jonathan[1]) (Stackpole's *Kittery*, p. 337), of Kittery, m. 29 Dec. 1740, ABIGAIL NUTTER.

JOSHUA DAM, son of John[3] and Sarah, baptized 14 June 1741.

JETHRO DAM, son of John and Elizabeth, baptized 23 Aug. 1752.

ABIGAIL DAM, m. 16 Dec. 1762, JACOB CRUMMEL, of Durham.

MARY DAM, covenant, 19 Aug. 1770.

JOHN DAM, d. 17 July 1829, *aet.* 79 (*Register*, vol. 73, p. 197).

ABIGAIL DAM, widow, d. 8 Sept. 1835, *aet.* 78 (*id.*, p. 198).

CHARITY DAM, b. 17 Mar. 1743, d. 15 May 1760 (*Reg.* 80 - 307).

DAVIS

JAMES DAVIS, m. 29 Apr. 1725, MARY PLACE.

MARY DAVIS, wife of John, communion, 8 June 1740.

JOHN DAVIS, m. Feb. 18, 1755, EUNICE SEAVEY, of Rye.

DEAN

JOHN DEAN, mariner, m. 16 Aug. 1751, MIRIAM TRICKEY.

DECKER

1. JOHN DECKER, of Newington, m. SARAH -----.
Children, baptized at Newington:
    i. JOHN, bapt. 30 Sept. 1716.
    ii. SARAH, bapt. 30 Sept. 1716, m. 13 Oct. 1726, CLEMENT[2] MESERVY (1), son of Clement[1] and Elizabeth, *q.v.*
    iii. MARY, bapt. 30 Sept. 1716, m. 30 Jan. 1729, JOHN HODGDON.
    iv. HANNAH, bapt. 30 Sept. 1716, m. 7 Feb. 1731, HATEVIL[4] NUTTER (15), son of John[3], *q.v.*
    v. ELIZABETH, bapt. 30 Sept. 1716, m. 19 Sept. 1734, JOSEPH MOODY, of Scarborough, Me., b. at Salisbury, Mass. (*Register*, vol. 25, p. 121).
    vi. JOSEPH, bapt. 30 Sept. 1716.
    vii. DAVID, bapt. 4 Oct. 1719, m. 9 Apr. 1741, EUNICE PLACE (*Register*, vol. 27, p. 13), dau. of John and Eunice (Rowe), *q.v.*

viii. ABIGAIL, bapt. 3 Feb. 1723, m. 24 Dec. 1740, JOHN LOUD (*Register*, vol. 27, p. 9), of Portsmouth.

DENBOW

SELATHIEL[2] DENBOW (Selathiel[1]) (Stackpole's *Durham*, vol 2, p. 129), m. 19 Dec. 1720, RACHEL PEVEY, senior, of Newington.

He, or his son, m. 10 Sept. 1740, MARY HILL, of Durham.

DENEFORD

ELIZABETH DENEFORD, of Kittery, Me., m. 1 Jan. 1716/7, THOMAS HAMMETT, of Shadwell, Middlesex, Eng. (*Register*, vol. 23, p. 393).

DENNETT

1. **DAVID DENNETT**, of Newington, m. 21 Apr. 1751, DOROTHY[5] DOWNING (7-iii), dau. of Joshua[4] and Susanna (Dennett), *q.v.*

Children, born at Newington:
  i. LYDIA, bapt. 10 May 1753.
  ii. SAMUEL (twin), bapt. 17 May 1756.
  iii. EBENEZER (twin), bapt. 17 May 1756.
  iv. ELIZABETH, bapt. 12 Feb. 1758.
  v. JOHN, bapt. 6 July 1760.

1. **CHARLES DENNETT**, of Newington, m. 13 Sept. 1753, HANNAH[5] NUTTER, dau. of Hatevil[4] and Hannah (Decker) (15-ii), *q.v.*

Child:
  i. HANNAH, bapt. 13 July 1760.

DENNETT (unconnected)

WILLIAM DENNETT, m. 31 Oct. 1765, SARAH PAUL, both of Kittery.

HANNAH DENNETT, of Portsmouth, m. 12 Dec. 1765, CHARLES HODGDON.

MARK DENNETT, m. 17 July 1767, MARY DENNETT, both of Kittery.

MARY DENNETT, m. 17 July 1767, MARK DENNETT, both of Kittery.

MARY DENNETT, m. 13 May 1768, JOSEPH ADAMS, both of Kittery.

MARY DENNETT, m. 5 Jan. 1775, AARON HODGDON, both of Portsmouth.

HANNAH DENNETT, m. 17 Aug. 1775, JOHN CHASE, both of Kittery.

POLLY DENNETT, dau. of Moses, bapt. 30 June 1782.

HANNAH DENNETT, dau. of Moses and Mary, of Portsmouth, bapt. 12 Sept. 1784.

DITTEY

FRANCIS DITTEY, of Winbird Dorsetshire, m. 26 May 1715, ELIZABETH FURBER, of Portsmouth (*Register*, vol. 23, p. 272).

DIXON

THOMAS^4 DIXON (Thomas^3, Peter^2, William^1) (Stackpole's *Kittery*, p. 354), m. 19 Oct. 1768, SUSANNA REMICK, of Kittery.

LUCY^4 DIXON (Stephen^3, Peter^2, William^1) (Stackpole's *Kittery*, p. 354), m. 20 Dec. 1768, STEPHEN PETTIGREW, of Kittery.

DOCKUM

MARY DOCKUM, acknowledged the covenant, 26 May 1765.

DOE

SAMUEL^4 DOE (Samuel^3, Sampson^2, Nicholas^1) (Stackpole's *Durham*, vol. 2, p. 133), of Newmarket, m. 25 Apr. 1763, ELIZABETH PICKERING.

DONALD

THOMAS DONALD, m. 25 Jan. 1774, EUNICE HOYT, of Portsmouth.

DORE (*Libby's Dictionary*, p. 200)

1. RICHARD^1 DORE, of Portsmouth (Sagamore Creek), m. TAMSON -----.
In this will, dated 16 Feb. 1715/6, proved 17 Mar. 1715/6, he names his wife, Tamson, executrix, and "all my children," sureties, in the bond of the executrix,

William Cotton, Jr., and Richard Gerrish, Jr. (*N.H. State Papers*, vol. 31, p. 784).
Children, born at Portsmouth (*Libby's Dictionary*, p. 200):
  i. ? MARY, m. (1) 23 Dec. 1692, JAMES HOUSTON, m. (2) 3 Nov. 1715, JOHN GARDNER, of Co. Glouces., England.
  ii. JOANNA, m. (1) in 1692, DAVID[1] CANE, of Portsmouth, m. (2) JOHN BOURNE, m. (3) 25 Feb. 1716/7, STEPHEN NOLE, from Nahant, Cornwall, fisherman.
  iii. BRYAN, m. MARTHA (JACKSON) BOULTER, wid. of John Boulter.
  iv. PHILIP, of Portsmouth, Newington, 1717, Dover, 1735, m. 20 May 1708, SARAH CHILD, dau. of Henry[1] and Sarah (Nason) Child.
  Children:
   1) ? William[3], of Rochester, 1737, m. ? 24 Apr. 1740, Mary Wallingford, b. 1707, d. 23 Apr. 1785.
   2) ? Sarah, m. Richard Child.
   3) Philip, of Rochester, bapt. 5 July 1730, m. Lydia Mason.
     Children baptized 3 Mar. 1745/6 (*N.H. Gen. Rec.*, vol. 6, p. 69):
      a) Richard
      b) Elizabeth
      c) Mary
      d) Olive
      e) Lydia
      f) Philip
      5 more children
   4) Henry, of Rochester, bapt. 6 Aug. 1727, m. Mary Wallingford, dau. of John.
   5) Elizabeth, bapt. 6 Aug. 1727.
   6) Frances, bapt. 6 Aug. 1727, m. Abijah Stevens, d. 1804.
   7) John, of Rochester, bapt. 5 July 1730, m. 15 July 1753 (*N.H. Gen. Rec.*, vol. 4, p. 146), Hannah Edgerly.
  v. JOHN, of Portsmouth, bapt. 1784, m. Aug. 1714, MARY WIGGIN.
  vi. ? SOLOMON

PHILIP DORE, of Newington, m. SARAH[3] CHILD, dau. of William[2] and Elizabeth (Stackpole's *Kittery*, p. 320), bapt. in South Berwick, Me., 1 Sept. 1713.
Children, baptized at Newington:
  i. HENRY, bapt. 6 Aug. 1727.
  ii. ELIZABETH, bapt. 6 Aug. 1727, m. ? 10 June 1753, at Rochester, PAUL FARNUM (4 *N.H. Gen. Rec.*, 146).
  iii. FRANCES, bapt. 6 Aug. 1727.
  iv. PHILIP, of Rochester, bapt. 11 Mar. 1728 (See further *N.H. Gen. Rec.*, vol. 6, p. 69).

v. JOHN, bapt. 5 July 1730, m. at Rochester, 15 Aug. 1753, HANNAH EDGERLY, (N.H. Gen. Rec., vol. 4, p. 146)

DORE (unconnected)

WILLIAM DORE, of Cocheco, m. 24 Apr. 1740, MARY WALLINGFORD.

DOW

MOSES DOW, m. 19 Mar. 1736, SARAH PHILLIPS, of Portsmouth.

JOHN DOW, 5 Sept. 1736, communion.

SARAH DOW, wife of John, 17 Oct. 1736, communion.

JEREMIAH DOW, m. 25 Sept. 1746, ABIAH BROWN, both of Hampton.

DOWNING

Wills and administrations, 1750-1775.

Will of **JOHN DOWNING**, of Newington, N.H., dated 5 Sept. 1755, proved 12 Mar. 1766, mentions sons Harrison and Richard; John Samuel, Jonathan, Elizabeth, Sarah (children of late son, John); Samuel, Josiah, Abigail, Elizabeth (children of William and late daughter, Susanna Shackford); daughter, Temperance, and her husband, Lemuel Bickford, and son, John Bickford; Nicholas, John, James, Temperance (children of daughter, Mary Pickering) (N.H. Prov. Prob. Rec., vol. 24, p. 157).

25 Nov. 1760. Administration on the estate of Jonathan Downing, of Kingston, granted to his widow, Sarah Downing. (N.H. Prov. Prob. Rec., vol. 21, p. 534).

1. Capt. **JOHN**[1] **DOWNING**[+], of Newington, elder, 1724, b. about 1659, d. 16 Sept. 1744 (Thompson's *Landmarks*, p. 158), m. (1) about 1683, SUSANNA MILLER, dau. of John (Stackpole's *Kittery*, p. 361), d. 31 May 1733 (from family

------

[+]Dennis Downing was at Kittery, Me., as early as 1652. He had a son, John. A John Downing was in court in 1653 for disobedience to his father. These are, perhaps, the grandfather and father of Capt. John[1] Downing (Stackpole's *Kittery*, p. 361). It has been suggested, also, that Capt. John Downing descended from Richard, of the Trelawney Papers. The frequent occurrence of that name among his descendants lends color to this suggestion.

Bible at N.H.H.S), m. (2) 1734, ELIZABETH (STOVER) (HUNNEWELL) WALFORD, wid. of ----- HUNNEWELL, first husband, and JEREMIAH³ WALFORD, second husband, d. 31 May 1753.

In 1734, he and his wife, Elizabeth, conveyed to Benjamin Downing, lands at New Castle, formerly of Jeremiah Walford, devised by him to his widow, then wife of John Downing (*N.H. Colonial Deeds*, vol 20, p. 466).

He deposed in 1734, *aet.* 74, that about 52 or 53 years before, he went to Cape Porpoise (Kennebunk) to live on a farm of Maj. Vaughn and remained there for 5 years until driven away by the Indians (*N.H. Deeds*, vol. 20, p. 242), and again in 1742, that he came to Portsmouth about 60 years before (N.H. Court Files, No. 21813).

In his will, dated 23 Feb. 1743, proved 21 Sept. 1744, he mentions his wife, Elizabeth, sister or sister-in-law, Sarah, and his children (*N.H. State Papers*, vol. 32, p. 196). He died 16 Sept. 1744 (from family Bible at N.H.H.S.).

Children, as mentioned in his will:

2   i. JOHN², b. 10 Apr. 1684 (from family Bible at N.H.H.S.).

ii. RICHARD, of Newington, yeoman, b. 1686, d. *s.p.*, m. 24 Apr. 1709, ALICE⁵ DOWNING (Stackpole's *Kittery*, p. 362), dau. of Joshua² (Dennis¹) and Patience (Hatch) Downing (*Libby's Dictionary*, p. 204), b. at Kittery, Me.

In his will, dated 2 Apr. 1747, proved 30 Oct. 1754, he mentions his cousin (*sic*), Richard³ Downing, and Alice, his wife, to whom he gives his lands in Barnstead and the remainder interest in his other estate (*N.H. State Pap.*, vol. 33, p. 447).

The will of Joshua Downing dated 25 Apr. 1717, proved 25 May 1718 mentions his daughter, Alice, wife of Richard Downing and provides for her death without issue (*Maine Wills*, p. 197).

iii. HANNAH, b. 1688, m. JETHRO³ BICKFORD (2), son of John² and Susanna (Furber), *q.v.*

3   iv. JONATHAN, b. 1690.
4   v. JOSEPH, b. 1692.
5   vi. BENJAMIN, b. 1695.
6   vii. JOSHUA, b. 1698.

viii. JOSIAH, he had, by his father's will, lands in Rochester.

2. Col. JOHN² DOWNING (John¹), of Newington, mariner, shipwright, member of the Council, first selectman of Newington, 1713 (*Register*, vol. 58, p. 250), the leading man of the town in his time., b. 10 Apr. 1684, d. 14 Feb. 1766 (*Brewster's Rambles*, vol. 1, p. 65), m. (1) 26 Nov. 1706 (from family Bible at N.H.H.S.), ELIZABETH HARRISON, dau. of Nicholas and Mary (Bickford), b. 4 Jan. 1679 (from family Bible at N.H.H.S.), d. 27 July 1740 (from family Bible at N.H.H.S.), m. (2) 10 Apr. 1742 (from family Bible at N.H.H.S.), SARAH (LIT-

TLE) (GILMAN) THING, wid. of NICHOLAS GILMAN, first husband, and Maj. BARTHOLOMEW THING, second husband, d. 11 Jan. 1754 (from family Bible at N.H.H.S.).

In his will, dated 5 Sept. 1755, proved 12 Mar. 1766, he mentions his children and grandchildren (*N.H. Probate*, vol. 24, p. 157). His inventory was £ 30,000 and 20,000 acres of land in some 30 towns.

The will of Nicholas Harrison, dated Mar. 5, 1757, proved 1 June 1708, mentions his daughter, Elizabeth Downing (*N.H. State Paps.*, vol. 31, p. 620).

Children, born at Newington (family Bible in possession, 1920, Jackson Hoyt's record):

 i. MARY³, b. 31 Aug. 1707 (from family Bible at N.H.H.S.), m. 7 Feb. 1726/7, THOMAS³ PICKERING (5), son of Thomas² and Mary, *q.v.*

 ii. SUSANNA, b. 2? Feb. 1709 (from family Bible at N.H.H.S.), d. 3 Mar. 1752 (from family Bible at N.H.H.S.), m. 5 Oct. 1727, Capt. WILLIAM³ SHACKFORD (7), son of Samuel² and Abigail (Richards), *q.v.*

 iii. HARRISON, of Newington and Kennebunkport, b. 4 July 1710, d. 26 July 1761 (from family Bible at N.H.H.S.), m. 11 July 1750, SARAH WALKER.

 iv. JOHN, of Newington, b. 24 Sept. 1711, d. about 1750, m. PATIENCE³ HAM, dau. of John² and Elizabeth, who m. (2) 7 May 1752, WILLIAM³ SHACKFORD (8), son of Samuel² and Abigail (Richards), *q.v.*. Administration on his estate 24 Nov. 1750 to his widow, Patience.

 Children, baptized at Newington (as mentioned in the will of Col. John² Downing):

  1) John⁴ (See unconnected).

  2) Samuel

  3) Jonathan, bapt. 16 Oct. 1746, m. 10 Feb. 1774, Alice Nutter, *q.v.*

  4) Elizabeth, m. ? 9 Feb. 1769, Jotham⁵ Nutter (7-v), son of Anthony⁴ and Mary³ (Downing), *q.v.*

  5) Sarah

 v. TEMPERENCE, b. 12 Apr. 1713 (from family Bible at N.H.H.S.), d. 18 Jan. 1770, m. (1) LEMUEL³ BICKFORD (1-viii), son of John² and Susanna (Furber), *q.v.*, m. (2) JONATHAN TRICKEY.

7 vi. RICHARD, b. 24 June 1718 (from family Bible at N.H.H.S.).

3. JONATHAN² DOWNING (John¹), of Newington, b. 1690, m. 15 Mar. 1716, ELIZABETH³ NELSON, dau. of John² and Elizabeth (Haley) (Stackpole's *Kittery*, p. 341), b. at Kittery, Me.

Children, baptized at Newington:

 i. MARY³, bapt. 5 May 1717, m. 18 May 1740, ANTHONY⁴ NUTTER (7), son of Hatevil³ and Sarah, *q.v.*

 ii. RICHARD, bapt. 27 July 1718.

iii. HANNAH, bapt. 28 Feb. 1721.
iv. ALICE, bapt. 15 Apr. 1722, m. ? her cousin, RICHARD^3, DOWNING (7), son of John^2 and Elizabeth (Harrison), *q.v.*
v. NELSON, bapt. 1 Nov. 1724.
vi. JONATHAN?, bapt. 2 July 1727, d. in infancy.
vii. ELIZABETH, bapt. 1 Mar. 1730.
viii. JONATHAN, bapt. 19 Sept. 1738.

4. JOSEPH^2 DOWNING (John^1), of Newington, husbandman, b. 1692, m. 21 June 1716 (*Register*, vol. 23, p. 392), SARAH^3 SPINNEY, dau. of James^2 and Grace (Stackpole's *Kittery*, p. 740), b. at Portsmouth.

Children, born at Newington:
i. JOSHUA^3, bapt. 10 Feb. 1723.
ii. JOSEPH. In 1749, James Spinney made a conveyance to his grandson, Joseph Downing (*N.H. Deeds*, vol. 85, p. 480).

5. Deac. BENJAMIN^2 DOWNING (John^1), of Newington and Arundel, Me., (Kennebunk), 1728, town clerk, 1750-53, b. 1695, d. 1753, m. 3 Dec. 1724, ELIZABETH^3 FABIAN (2-iv), dau. of Lieut. John^2 and Mary (Pickering), *q.v.*

Children, the first three and the eleventh baptized at Newington, the others born, doubtless, at Arundel, Me.:
i. ALICE^3, b. 11 Oct. 1725 (town rec.), bapt. 10 Apr. 1726, d. 15 Jan. 1790 (town rec.), m. ? 5 Jan. 1744, her cousin, RICHARD^3 DOWNING (7), son of Jonathan^2 and Elizabeth (Nelson), *q.v.*
ii. SAMUEL, of Newington, bapt. 8 Jan. 1727, m. PATIENCE -----.
   Child, baptized at Newington:
   1) Samuel^6, bapt. 4 Jan. 1740/1.
iii. ELIZABETH, b. 20 July 1728, m. (1) 28 Jan. 1748, RICHARD^5 FURBER (10), son of Richard^4 and Mary^3 (Shackford), *q.v.*
iv. BENJAMIN, of Kennebunk, Me., town clerk, b. 12 Mar. 1732, d. 27 Jan. 1797, m. 26 Mar. 1756, MARY FAIRFIELD.
v. JONATHAN, m. SARAH CLEAVES.
vi. RICHARD, of Frenchman's Bay.
vii. SUSANNA, m. THOMAS GOODWIN.
viii. SARAH, m. ADAM CLARK.
ix. HANNAH, bapt. 27 Dec. 1749, d. 18 Mar. 1818, m. THOMAS BOOTHBY, b. 1735, d. 2 Jan. 1807.
x. PHEBE, m. JONATHAN STONE.
xi. MARY, d. in infancy.
xii. TEMPERENCE, m. EPHRAIM WILDES.

6. JOSHUA^2 DOWNING (John^1), of Newington, b. 1698, d. 1747, m. 18 Nov.

1724, SUSANNA³ DENNETT, dau. of Alexander² and Mehitable (Tetherly) (Stackpole's *Kittery*, p. 351), b. at Eliot, Me.

In his will dated 8 June 1747, proved 28 Oct. 1747, he mentions his wife, Susanna, and his children as listed below (*N.H. State Pap.*, vol. 31, p. 478).

Children, baptized at Newington:

8   i. JOSIAH³, bapt. 2 Jan. 1726.

    ii. SUSANNA, bapt. 3 Mar. 1728, *non compos* 1794 (*Rockingham Deeds*, vol. 141, p. 381), d. 5 Feb. 1804, m. 15 May 1747, WILLIAM³ HUNTRESS (4), son of Samuel² and Abigail (Ham), *q.v.*

    iii. DOROTHY, bapt. 22 Mar. 1730, m. 21 Apr. 1751, DAVID DENNETT, of Newington, *q.v.*

    iv. TEMPERENCE, bapt. as Deborah, 30 Apr. 1732.

9   v. JOSHUA, bapt. 6 Oct. 1734.

    vi. IZETTE, bapt. 4 Dec. 1737.

    vii. ELIZABETH, bapt. 18 May 1740.

    viii. HANNAH, bapt. 7 Nov. 1740.

    ix. MARY

7. Maj. RICHARD³ DOWNING (John$^{2\text{-}1}$), of Newington, bapt. 27 July 1708, d. 25 Sept. 1796 (town rec.), m. 5 Jan. 1743/4, his cousin ALICE³ DOWNING (3-vi), dau. of Jonathan² and Elizabeth (Nelson), *q.v.*

Children, baptized at Newington:

    i. ALICE⁴, bapt. 18 Nov. 1744, m. 26 Oct. 1765, HENRY HART, of Portsmouth.

    ii. SUSANNA, b. 7 Nov. 1746 (town rec.), bapt. 9 Oct. 1746, m. 15 Sept. 1763, MARK MILLER (1), *q.v.*

    iii. RICHARD, b. 4 Apr. 1748 (town rec.), d. 20 July 1804 (town rec.).

    iv. MARY, b. 18 Dec. 1749 (town rec.) d. unm. 2 Sept. 1791.

    v. BARTHOLOMEW, of Newington, b. 29 Nov. 1752 (town rec.), bapt. 17 Dec. 1752, d. 22 June 1828 (town rec.), m. DEBORAH -----, b. 1751, d. 5 Mar. 1829, *aet.* 78 yrs. (*Register*, vol. 73, p. 197).

Child, baptized at Newington:

    1) John Harrison⁷, b. 23 July 1780, m. 1 July 1804, Olive Bickford, b. 1772, d. 26 June 1849 (*Register*, vol. 73, p. 201).

    vi. THEODOSIA, bapt. 22 June 1755, b. 7 June 1755 (town rec.), d. unm. Nov. 1799 (town rec.).

    vii. JOHN HARRISON, b. 28 Oct. 1757 (town rec.), bapt. 3 Nov. 1757, d. in infancy.

    viii. ELIZABETH HARRISON, b. 1 May 1759 (town rec.) bapt. 6 May 1759, d. 27 Nov. 1847 (*Register*, vol. 73, p. 200), m. 28 Aug. 1777, her second cousin, JOSHUA⁴ DOWNING (8-1), son of Josiah³ and Elizabeth (Rollins), *q.v.*

8. JOSIAH³ DOWNING (Joshua², John¹), of Newington, bapt. 2 Jan. 1726, d. 17 Dec. 1811 (town rec.), ELIZABETH³ ROLLINS (2-vii), dau. of Joseph² and Sarah, *q.v.*

Children, baptized at Newington:
- i. JOSHUA⁴, bapt. 29 Feb. 1756, d. 8 Oct. 1846 (? 7 June 1804), m. 28 Aug. 1777, his second cousin, ELIZABETH H.⁴ DOWNING (7-viii), dau. of Richard³ and Alice³ (Downing), *q.v.*
- ii. DAVID DENNETT, bapt. 10 Apr. 1757.
- iii. HANNAH, bapt. 29 Oct. 1758.
- iv. SAMUEL, bapt. 25 May 1760, d. 28 Dec. 1837 (*Register*, vol. 73, p. 198), m. ELIZABETH⁴ ROLLINS (7-i), dau. of Noah³ and Elizabeth, *q.v.*
- v. EBENEZER, of Newington, bapt. 12 Sept. 1762, m. ? ABIGAIL ALLEN (Parson's *Rye*, p. 336).
- vi. ELIZABETH, bapt. 19 Feb. 1764.

DOROTHY WIGGIN DOWNING, ? wife of JOSIAH DOWNING, d. 17 May 1851, *aet.* 65.

Mrs. ELIZABETH DOWNING, d. 14 Aug. 1811, at Newington (town rec.).

JOSHUA DOWNING, d. 7 June 1804, at Newington.

BETSEY DOWNING, widow, d. 24 July 1836, *aet.* 87 (*Register*, vol. 73, p. 198).

9. JOSHUA³ DOWNING (Joshua², John¹), of Newington, bapt. 6 Oct. 1734, m. 30 Sept. 1756 (*N.E.H. Gen. Register*, vol. 82, p. 286), MARY RICHARDS, dau. of Capt. George.

Children, baptized at Newington (See *N.E.H. Gen. Register*, vol. 82, p. 35, bapt. of George Richard Downing, son of Joshua, So. Ch. Recs. - Portsmouth, 5 June 1757):
- i.
- ii. SUSANNA⁴, 14 May 1769.
- iii. SARAH, 14 May 1769.
- iv. LYDIA, 14 May 1769.
- v. JOHN, 14 May 1769.
- vi. DENNIS, 14 May 1769, d. 10 July 1804 (town rec.).

JOSHUA DOWNING and **MARY**, *ux.*, 22 Apr. 1769, convey lands at Rochester (*N.H. Deeds*, vol. 95, p. 456).

JOSHUA DOWNING and MARY, *ux.*, 20 Apr. 1769, convey lands willed to Mary (then Mary Richardson) by Capt. George Richardson (*id.*, vol. 96, p. 62).

NOTE:
Family record owned by Marie Downing Singles, of Charleston, West Virginia, 1 Nov. 1940, contained the following:

   vii. JOSHUA, b. Jan. 1769.
   viii. BENJAMIN, b. 28 May 1772.
   ix. SAMUEL, b. 1 Dec. 1775.

Baptized at Rochester, N.H., 23 July 1789 (See *N.H. Gen. Rec.*, vol. 6, p. 175).

DOWNING (unconnected)

JOHN[4] DOWNING (? John[3-1]), of Newington, m. 1 Aug. 1765, MARY DOWNING.
Children, baptized at Newington:
   i. JOHN, bapt. 11 Jan. 1767.
   ii. ALICE, bapt. 22 May 1768.
   iii. ELIZABETH, bapt. 15 July 1770.
   iv. RICHARD, bapt. 17 Jan. 1773.

SARAH DOWNING, m. 4 Dec. 1775, SAMUEL THOMPSON.

LOIS DOWNING, m. 13 Jan. 1757, EBENEZER[5] ADAMS (3), son of Rev. Joseph[4] and Elizabeth (Knight) (Janvrin), *q.v.*

SARAH DOWNING, m. 16 Dec. 1766, BENJAMIN HOYT, of Scarborough.

ELIZABETH DOWNING, m. 9 Feb. 1769, JOTHAM[5] NUTTER (7-v), son of Anthony[4] and Mary (Downing).

ELSIE DOWNING, b. 8 Sept. 1788, at Newington, m. 10 Sept. 1810, JAMES SPEED, of Newmarket (*N.H. Gen. Rec.*, vol. 6, p. 157).

LYDIA DOWNING, d. 17 Mar. 1832, *aet.* 42 (*Register*, vol. 73, p. 197).

BARTHOLOMEW DOWNING, d. 14 Jan. 1844, *aet.* 59 (*Register*, vol. 73, p. 199).

JOSIAH DOWNING, d. 8 Oct. 1846, *aet.* 80 (*i.d.*, p. 200).

THOMAS DOWNING, m. 14 Aug. 1796, MARTHA NORRIS, of Greenland (Parson's *Rye*, p. 575).

DREW

LYDIA DREW, m. 28 Nov. 1720, FRANCIS MATTHEWS, both of Oyster River.

DURGIN

ELIZABETH DURGIN (perhaps wid. of John^3) (Stackpole's *Durham*, vol. 2, p. 160), m. 15 Dec. 1756, JOHN LEONARD, of Durham.

DWYER

JAMES DWYER, of Portsmouth, m. 3 Apr. 1766, ELIZABETH SMITH, of Durham.

EDGERLY

SAMUEL EDGERLY, m. 12 July 1759, OLIVE DAM (6-ix).

JAMES EDGERLY, m. 4 May 1773, RACHEL KENT, both of Durham.

EMMONS

JANE EMMONS, 8 July 1756, covenant.

FABYAN

1. JOHN^1 FABYAN, of Portsmouth, 1660, constable, m. SARAH HALL, dau. of John (*Libby's Dictionary*, p. 227).

Children, born at Portsmouth, baptisms in North Church (*N.H. Gen. Rec.*, vol. 2, p. 53):

2   i. JOHN^2, b. about 1681, bapt. 26 Mar. 1693.
3   ii. JOSEPH, bapt. 26 Mar. 1693.
4   iii. SAMUEL, bapt. 26 Mar. 1693.
     iv. SARAH, bapt. 26 Mar. 1693. She was living in 1748 when her brother, John, made his will.

2. Lieut. JOHN² FABYAN (John¹), of Dover (Newington) 1709, tailor, deacon, J.P., ensign, 1715, lieutenant, 1720, first selectman of Newington (*Register*, vol. 58, p. 250), representative, 1745, b. about 1681, bapt. 26 Jan. 1693, d. 30 Mar. 1756, m. 25 Dec. 1702 (*N.H. Gen. Rec.*, vol. 4, p. 12), MARY³ PICKERING (2-iv), *q.v.*, dau. of Thomas² and Mary Pickering.

In his will, dated 6 Aug. 1748, proved 28 Apr. 1756, he names his wife, Mary; sister, Sarah; and children Samuel, John, Joseph, Elizabeth Downing, Mary Woodman, Phebe Furber, and Mehitable Walker (*N.H. State Pap.*, vol. 33 p. 587).

Children (baptisms, except the last, in the North Church, Portsmouth):

    i. Capt. JOHN³, of Scarborough, Me., 1733, b. about 1704, bapt. Oct. 1710 (*N.H. Gen. Rec.*, vol. 4, p. 56), d. unm. 3 June 1782, *aet.* 77-6 (tombstone).

5   ii. JOSEPH, b. 1 Apr. 1707, bapt. (*N.H. Gen. Rec.*, vol. 4, p. 56).

    iii. ELIZABETH, bapt. Oct. 1710 (*ibid.*), m. 3 Dec. 1724, BENJAMIN² DOWNING (5), *q.v.*, son of Capt. John¹ and Susanna (Miller) Downing.

    iv. MARY, bapt. Oct. 1710 (*ibid.*), m. 11 Sept. 1732, JOHN⁴ WOODMAN, of Durham, merchant, town officer, b. at Durham, 6 Mar. 1701, d. 15 July 1777, son of Lieut. Jonathan³ and Elizabeth (Downing) Woodman (Stackpole's *Durham*, vol. 2 p. 393).

6   v. SAMUEL, b. Dec. 1710.

    vi. PHEBE, bapt. 6 Sept. 1713 (*N.H. Gen Rec.*, vol. 4, p. 39), m. 17 Sept. 1733, JETHRO⁴ FURBER (7), *q.v.*, son of William³ and Sarah Furber.

    vii. MEHITABLE, bapt. 29 Apr. 1716, m. ----- WALKER.

3. JOSEPH² FABYAN (John¹), of Scarborough, Me., 1730, b. 1 Apr. 1707, d. 15 Mar. 1789, *aet.* 81-11 (tombstone), m. Oct. 1739, MARY BRACKETT, dau. of Joshua and Mary (Haines) (*Anthony Brackett Family*, p. 4), b. at Greenland, 1716, d. 1 May 1800.

Children, born at Scarborough, Me. (*Maine Gen. and Fam. Hist.*, p. 2267):

7   i. JOSHUA³, b. Mar. 1743, bapt. 27 Mar. 1743.

    ii. MARY, bapt. 2 Feb. 1746, m. (1) 20 Dec. 1768, JOHN BRACKETT, m. (2) PELETIAH MARCH.

4. SAMUEL³ FABYAN (John²⁻¹), of Newington, yeoman, b. 3 Dec. 1749, d. 30 Mar. 1756, m. (1) 29 Nov. 1733, ROSAMOND⁴ NUTTER (5-vi), dau. of John³, *q.v.*, m. (2) 12 Dec. 1745, ELIZABETH³ HUNTRESS (i-vi), dau. of Samuel² and Abigail (Ham), *q.v.*, m. (3) at Greenland, 11 Mar. 1777 (town rec.), MARY BERRY.

He had his father's farm at Newington. His will dated 21 Sept. 1782, proved 17 Mar. 1790, mentions his wife, Mary, and children as below, except the first, John, and the first, Rosamond (*Rockingham Probate*).

Children by first wife, baptized at Newington:
  i. JOHN[4], bapt. 4 May 1735, d. in infancy.
8 ii. JOHN, b. 6 Mar. 1737.
  iii. MARY, bapt. 11 Mar. 1739, m. 13 Dec. 1764, JAMES[4] PICKERING (15), son of Thomas[3] and Mary (Downing), *q.v.*
  iv. ROSAMOND, bapt. 14 June 1741, d. in infancy.
Children by second wife, baptized at Newington:
  v. ELIZABETH, bapt. 12 Oct. 1746, d. 27 Apr. 1838 (*Register*, vol. 73, p. 198), m. 1 Apr. 1768, DENNIS[5] HOYT (4), son of John[4] and Lydia (Miller), *q.v.*
9 vi. SAMUEL, bapt. 7 Aug. 1748.
  vii. ABIGAIL, b. 1750, d. 3 July 1829, m. 26 Jan. 1776, WILLIAM[5] PICKERING (15), son of Thomas[4] and Mary[2] (Janvrin), *q.v.*
  viii. ROSAMOND, bapt. 21 June 1752, b. 14 June 1752 (town rec.), d. 13 Feb. 1802 (town rec.), m. 4 Oct. 1770, LEVI[5] FURBER (11-viii), son of Nehemiah[4] and Abigail (Leighton), *q.v.*

----- FABIAN, of Newington, m. about 1736, MARY[4] BRACKETT, b. 1716 (*Piscataqua Pioneer*, p. 49)

5. JOSHUA[3] FABYAN (Joseph[2], John[1]), of Scarborough, Me., farmer, town officer, receiver of taxes, member of General Court, 1776, J.P., overseer of Bowdoin College, 1794-8, b. Mar. 1742, bapt. 27 Mar. 1743, d. 30 June 1779, m. 9 Jan. 1766, SARAH BRACKETT, b. at Yarmouth, Me., 9 Apr. 1740.
Children, born at Scarborough, Me. (*Maine Gen. and Fam. Hist.*, p. 2267):
  i. JOHN[4], of Leeds, Me., b. 1 Nov. 1766, m. at Portland Me., 1 Jan. 1789 (Cumberland Co. Commissioners' rec.), SARAH BRACKETT.
  ii. JOSEPH, b. 23 Apr. 1768, d. unm.
  iii. SAMUEL, b. 6 July 1770, d. unm.
  iv. GEORGE, of Scarborough, Me., mariner, b. 20 Mar. 1773, d. unm.?
  v. SARAH, b. 8 Apr. 1775, d. 1845, m. 10 Oct. 1797, EZRA CARTER.
  vi. MARY, d. 12 Sept. 1778.
  vii. JOSHUA, of Scarborough, Me., b. 28 Mar. 1782, bapt. 17 June 1782, d. 23 Jan. 1824, m. 26 Nov. 1803, MARY CLARK DOWNING, dau. of John, b. at Kennebunk, Me.
  Their son, George[5] was an overseer of Harvard College and his son, George[6], of Bliss Fabyan & Co. gave $250,000 to Harvard University to establish a chair of Comparative Pathology in memory of his father.

6. JOHN[4] FABYAN (Samuel[3], John[2-1]), of Newington, bapt. 6 Mar. 1737, d. 1805, m. at Greenland, 25 Feb. 1768 (town rec.), MEHITABLE BERRY.
In 1790, he had two males under 16 and five females in his family (Census).

His will dated 4 May 1805, proved 18 July 1805 mentions his children as follows.

Children, baptized at Newington:
- i. WILLIAM BERRY[5], of Newington, bapt. 19 Feb. 1769, d. *s.p.* 17 May 1826 (*Register*, vol. 73, p. 196). Administration 15 June 1826 on his estate, insolvent, to Samuel[5] Fabian (*Rockingham Probate*).
- ii. ROSAMOND, bapt. 4 Nov. 1770, d. 17 July 1814 (*Register*, vol. 73, p. 198), m. as his first wife, THOMAS[5] PICKERING (14-iv), son of John Gee[4] and Deborah (Furber) (Mills) Fabyan, *q.v.*
- iii. ELIZABETH, m. JOSHUA[5] PICKERING (11-v), son of Ephraim[4] and Lydia (Colman), *q.v.*
10   iv. SAMUEL, bapt. 24 May 1778.
- v. MARY, bapt. 16 Aug. 1780, b. 23 Mar. 1780 (town rec.), m. JOHN GEE[5] PICKERING (14-iii), son of John Gee[4] and Deborah (Furber) (Mills), *q.v.*

7. **SAMUEL[4] FABYAN** (Samuel[3], John[2-1]), of Newington, bapt. 7 Aug. 1748, d. 14 Apr. 1811 (town rec.), m. 18 Aug. 1778, ANNA[5] PICKERING (11-i), dau. of Maj. Ephraim[4] and Lydia (Colman), *q.v.*

His will dated 9 Apr. 1811, proved 20 May 1811, mentions his wife, Nancy; and children Mary Pickering, Lydia Dow, Elizabeth Dow, Olive Dennett, Joseph and John, executor and residuary legatee (*Rockingham Probate*). Her will dated 18 Sept. 1818, proved 14 Jan. 1834, supplies the names of the sons-in-law (*Rockingham Probate*).

In 1790, he had one male under 16 and five females in his family (Census).

Children, baptized at Newington:
- i. MARY[5], bapt. 17 Oct. 1779, m. JOSEPH PICKERING.
- ii. LYDIA, bapt. 15 Nov. 1780, m. AMOS DOW.
- iii. ELIZABETH, bapt. 12 Sept. 1784, m. HENRY DOW.
  Child:
  1) Elizabeth
- iv. OLIVE, m. 1. Mar. 1810, MARK[5] DENNETT, son of Jeremiah[4] and Susanna[5] (Peverly) (statement, 1923, of Alexander Dennett, of Kittery, Me.), of Portsmouth, b. 30 Mar. 1783, d. 19 Aug. 1858 at Portsmouth.
  Child, born at Portsmouth (*i.d.*):
  1) Ann Sherburn[6], b. 26 Mar. (or 11 Feb.) 1811, m. 9 May 1838 (town rec.), John S. Huntress, of Portsmouth, baker.
11   v. JOHN, of Newington, b. 2 Sept. 1787 (town rec.).
12   vi. JOSEPH, of Portsmouth, d. 1835.

8. **SAMUEL[5] FABYAN** (John[4], Samuel[3], John[2-1]), of Newington, farmer, bapt.

24 May 1778, d. 21 Oct. 1858 (*Register*, vol. 73, p. 204), m. ELIZABETH -----, b. 1773.
   Children, born at Newington (Census of 1850):
   i. JAMES P.[6], b. 1814.
      On 14 Oct. 1728, he was appointed guardian to his son, James P., to receive a bequest from the son's aunt, Rosamond[5] (Fabian) Pickering (*Rockingham Probate*).
   ii. FRANCIS A., b. 1824.
   iii. JOSHUA P., b. 1826.

9. **JOHN[5] FABYAN** (Samuel[4-3], John[2-1]), of Newington, farmer, b. 2 Sept. 1787 (town rec.), m. 8 Dec. 1811 (town rec.), CATHERINE[5] DENNETT, dau. of Jeremiah[4] and Susanna[5] (Peverly), b. at Portsmouth, 1788.
   Children, born at Newington (town rec.):
   i. SUSAN D.[6], b. 20 Mar. 1813.
   ii. HARRIET W., b. 30 Mar. 1815.
   iii. ELIZABETH H., b. 5 Dec. 1817, d. 6 Oct. 1818.
   iv. SAMUEL, b. 4 Mar. 1820.
   v. WILLIAM D., b. 13 July 1824, d. 11 Jan. 1839, in infancy.

JOHN S. FABIAN, farmer, d. at Newington, Sept. 1849, *aet.* 32 (Census of 1850).

10. **JOSEPH[5] FABYAN** (Samuel[4-3], John[2-1]), of Portsmouth, d. 1825.
   Children:
   i. JOSEPH[6]
   ii. RHODA ANN
   iii. SARAH MARIA
   On 13 Jan. 1835, James Edney, of Greenland, was appointed guardian of these children all under 14 years of age; Mark Dennett and John Fabian, sureties (*Rockingham Probate*).

SAMUEL FABIAN, of Hollis, Me., farmer, b. 1806, m. OLIVE -----.
   Children (Census of 1850):
   i. JOSHUA, b. 1831.
   ii. MARY, b. 1835.
   iii. GEORGIANNA, b. 1841.
   iv. CHARLES
   v. OLIVE ANN

FELNIG (See FIELDING)

FERNALD

TOBIAS[4] FERNALD (Nathaniel[3], Samuel[2], Renald[1]) (Stackpole's *Kittery*, p. 384), of Kittery, Me., m. 1729, ABIGAIL SMITH, of Kittery, Me.

ABRAHAM[4] FERNALD (Thomas[3], John[2], Renald[1]) (Stackpole's *Kittery*, p. 384), m. 16 May 1742, MARY TRICKEY (7-vi).

MARY FERNALD, of Portsmouth, m. 9 Nov. 1752, WILLIAM JENKINS, of Greenland.

MARY[5] FERNALD (Thomas[4-3], John[2], Renald[1]), (Stackpole's *Kittery*, p. 383), of Kittery, Me., m. 30 Aug. 1770, GEORGE ROGERS, of Kittery, Me.

WILLIAM FERNALD, son of John, bapt. 24 Sept. 1775.

ABIGAIL FERNALD, m. 26 Dec. 1776, WILLIAM PICKERING, of Greenland.

FICKETT (See PHICKETT)

FIELD

HANNAH FIELD, wid. of Zachariah[3] (Stackpole's *Durham*, vol. 2, p. 191), of Dover, m. 16 May 1716, RICHARD HUSSEY, of Dover.

JOSEPH[2] FIELD (Stephen[2]) (Stackpole's *Kittery*, p. 401), of Kittery, Me., m. 29 Oct. 1745, ABIGAIL PILLSBURY, of Kittery, Me.

ABIGAIL FIELD, m. 8 Aug. 1773, JOSEPH MEADER, both of Durham.

FIELDING

JOHN FIELDING, of Portsmouth, m. 20 Dec. 1748, ELIZABETH LARY, of Kittery, Me.

FITZGERALD

RICHARD FITZGERALD, m. 13 Oct. 1748, SARAH MEAD, both of Portsmouth.

FOGG

EUNICE[4] FOGG (James[3], Daniel[2], Samuel[1]) (Stackpole's *Kittery*, p. 404), m. 6 Oct. 1767, JOSEPH STAPLES, both of Kittery, Me.

ENOCH FOGG, of Scarborough, m. 4 June 1772, LOIS NUTTER.

FOLLETT

1. **NICHOLAS[1] FOLLETT**, of Dover, mariner, b. about 1626, m. ABIGAIL -----, b. about 1626, who m. (2) RICHARD[1] NASON, of Kittery, Me. (Stackpole's *Kittery*, p. 625). She was living in 1700 *aet.* about 80 yrs. (*N.H. State Papers*, vol. 31, p. 340).

   Children, born at Dover (*Register*, vol. 39, p. 827):
   i. NICHOLAS
   ii. MARY, m. WILLIAM WILLAM, of Dover.
   iii. SARAH, b. about 1654, m. JOHN[2] MEADER, son of John[1] and Abigail (Tuttle) (Stackpole's *Durham*, vol. 2, p. 275), of Durham, weaver. She was living 1706, about 52 yrs. old (*N.H. State Papers*, vol. 31, p. 340).

2. **NICHOLAS[2] FOLLETT** (Nicholas[1]), of Portsmouth, mariner, m. HANNAH -----.

   In his will dated 29 Apr. 1700, proved 19 Aug. 1700, he names his wife, Hannah; and children Nicholas, Philip, and Caleb (*N.H. State Papers*, vol. 31, p. 461). It appears from the papers that he had also a son, Benjamin "about 8 years old" 2 Oct. 1705.

   Children, born at Portsmouth:
   i. NICHOLAS[3], "eldest son" (*N.H. State Papers*, vol. 31, p. 340), of Portsmouth, tailor, b. 5 Nov. 1667, d. 29 Aug. 1722, m. 12 Sept. 1700, MARY HULL, dau. of Capt. Reuben and Hannah (Alcock) (Farniside) (Stackpole's *Durham*, vol. 2, p. 225).
      Children, baptized in North Church:
      1) Samuel, 1707/8 (*N.H. Gen. Rec.*, vol. 4, p. 52).
      2) Nicholas, 1707/8 (*ibid.*)
   ii. PHILIP
   iii. CALEB
   iv. BENJAMIN, of Stratham, cordwainer, b. about 1697, m. DEBORAH LYFORD, dau. of Francis and Rebecca Lyford, b. at Exeter. In the will of Francis Lyford, dated 17 Dec. 1723, he names his daughter, Deborah Follett (*N.H. State Papers*, vol. 32, p. 190)
      Administration on the estate of Benjamin was granted to Deborah, his wife, 24 Sept. 1746 (*N.H. State Papers*, vol. 33, p. 397).

v. ELIZABETH, bapt. in North Church, 21 July 1695 (*N.H. Gen. Rec.*, vol. 3, p. 54).

FOLLETT (unconnected)

Administration, 17 Nov. 1690, on **WILLIAM FOLLETT**, of Durham, cooper, to his widow, ELIZABETH (*N.H. State Papers*, vol. 31, p. 339). She was wid. of WILLIAM DREW and m. Follett, 20 July 1661. It appears from the administration proceedings that he was "second cousin" to Nicholas[1] Follett and died *s.p.*

There was an **ICHABOD FOLLETT**, at Dover, who m. as early as 1720, TEMPERANCE ----- (*Register*, vol. 39, p. 82).

THOMAS FOLLETT, b. in the Island of Jersey, m. 1 Oct. 1730, SUSANNA COOLBRUTH (*Register*, vol. 25, p. 117).

SUSANNA FOLLETT, 19 Nov. 1732, covenant.

THOMAS FOLLETT, son of Susanna, bapt. 19 Nov. 1732.

SUSANNA FOLLETT, 17 Oct. 1736, communion.

SUSANNA FOLLETT, m. May 10, 1739, JOSEPH ROLLINS (3), *q.v.*

FOLSOM

MARY FOLSOM, of Newmarket, m. 27 Aug. 1766, JONATHAN PHILBROOK, of Rye.

FOSS

WALTER FOSS, and wife, 15 June 1728, covenant.

WALTER FOSS, son of Walter, bapt. 15 June 1728.

ZACHARIAH FOSS, of Newcastle, m. 22 Aug. 1734, SARAH WATERHOUSE, of Portsmouth.

BENJAMIN FOSS, m. 2 Feb. 1735, ANN HODGDON, both of Rochester.

FOX

SARAH FOX, of Newmarket, m. 17 July 1755, JOHN WILLEY, of Durham.

FRY

CATHERINE FRY, m. 5 Nov. 1766, JONATHAN WOODMAN, both of Kittery, Me.

FURBER

1. Capt. WILLIAM[1] FURBER, of Dover Neck, 1639, and Bloody Point, 1657 (*Register*, vol. 6, p. 258; vol. 4, p. 248), constable, 1645, freeman, 1653, sergeant, 1657, b. in England about 1614 (*id.*, vol. 23, p. 153), came in the *Angel Gabriel* with John Cogswell from London in 1635 and was wrecked at Pemaquid (*ibid.*). He was dead in 1699, when John Dam and John and Thomas Bickford who had married his daughters prayed for distribution of his estate in the hands of his son, William[2] (*N.H. State Pap.*, vol. 31, p. 451). He m. (1) ELIZABETH ----- (*N.H. Gen. and Fam. Hist.*, vol. --, p. --), and had a wife, SUSANNA, in 1664 (*Register*, vol. 7, p. 119).

Children, born at Dover:
- i. HANNAH[2], m. ROGER[2] PLAISTED, son of Roger[1] and Olive (Colman) (Stackpole's *Kittery*, p. 666), of Kittery, Me., b. at Kittery, d. 16, Oct. 1675, killed by Indians.
- ii. ELIZABETH, b. about 1644, m. 9 Nov. 1664 (*Register*, vol. 7, p. 118) as his second wife, Serg't. JOHN[2] DAM, son of John[1] and Elizabeth (Pomfret) (*id.*, vol. 65, p. 213), of Bloody Point.
- iii. WILLIAM, b. about 1646.
- iv. BRIDGET, b. about 1660, m. THOMAS[2] BICKFORD, son of John[1] (Stackpole's *Durham*, vol. 2, p. 17), of Durham, b. about 1660.
- v. JETHRO, b. about 1662.
- vi. SUSANNA, b. 5 May 1664 (*Register*, vol. 7, p. 119; *Dover Historical Collections*, p. 112), d. 1731, m. about 1684, JOHN[2] BICKFORD (1), son of John[1], q.v.
- vii. ?MOSES
- viii. ?BERTHA
- ix. ?ESTHER

2. Lieut. WILLIAM[2] FURBER (William[1]), of Welch Cove, Bloody Point, ensign, 1694 (*Register*, vol. 6, p. 258), ferryman (*id.*, vol. 60, p. 96); *Dover Landmarks*, p. 80), member of the Colonial Assembly, 1698 (*Register*, vol. 17, p. 315), b. about 1648, deposed 1674 about 26 years of age (*N.H. Court Pap.*, 1674-7, pp. 37, 269), d. 14 Sept. 1707 (*N.H. Gen. Rec.*, vol. 3, p. 150), m. (1)? ELIZABETH -----, m. (2) 13 Aug. 1694 (*Register*, vol. 33, p. 395; *Dover Historical Collection*, p. 129) ELIZABETH (HURD) NUTE, dau. of Capt. John and Elizabeth[2] (Hull) Hurd (Stackpole's *Durham*, vol. 2, p. 234), and wid. of JAMES NUTE (*ibid.*), b. at Dover, 16 Feb. 1653, d. 9 Nov. 1705 (*N.H. Gen. Rec.*, vol. 3, p. 145), m. (3) in 1706, ELIZABETH (MARTYN) KENNARD, dau. of Richard, and wid. of EDWARD KENNARD, b. at Portsmouth, who m. (3) 27 Dec. 1708, BENJAMIN NASON, of Kittery, Me.

Administration on his estate in Oct. 1707, on the prayer of William, "eldest son," to his mother-in-law (stepmother), Elizabeth (*N.H. State Pap.*, vol. 31, p. 604). The intestate had made an antenuptial agreement 3 Apr. 1706, to settle his estate on Elizabeth Kennard, widow, of Kittery, Me., excepting lands at Welchman's Cove, Bloody Point, conveyed that day to his sons, William and Jethro. The widow, Elizabeth, was Elizabeth Nason, 7 Sept. 1710. Administration 6 Mar. 1712/3 to William[3]; sureties, Jethro[3] and Hatevil Nutter.

Children, born at Newington (*Piscataqua Pioneers*, p. 847):

4   i. WILLIAM[3], b. 1672.
5   ii. JETHRO
     iii. ?DANIEL, a Daniel Furber is mentioned 1686/7 in the account book of Capt. John Gerrish, of Dover (*Register*, vol. 36, p. 74).
     iv. ?ELIZABETH, m. 18 Dec. 1719, FRANCIS WEBBER, of Kittery, Me.
     v. ?JOSHUA

3. JETHRO[2] FURBER (William[1]), of Newington, master mariner, b. about 1662, m. AMY[2] COWELL, dau. of Edward[1] and Agnes, b. at Portsmouth, she m. (2) NATHANIEL[2] AYRES (7), *q.v.*, of Portsmouth and Boston, son of Capt. John[1] and Anna (Symonds), *q.v.*

Administration on his estate was granted 6 Oct. 1686, to Nathaniel Ayres and his wife, Amy, "formerly widow of the deceased" (*N.H. State Pap.*, vol. 31, p. 304).

Administration *de bonis non* on Edward Cowell's estate was granted 2 May 1682, his widow, Agnes, having died, to Jethro Furber who married Annie (*sic*) their daughter (*id.*, p. 204)

Child:

6   i. JETHRO[3], b. 1682.

4. WILLIAM[3] FURBER (William[2-1]), of Newington, b. 1672, d. 20 Mar. 1757 (town rec.), m. SARAH NUTE, dau. of James, b. 1675, d. 28 Apr. 1762.

His will dated 12 Nov. 1741, proved 25 May 1757, names his wife, Sarah; sons Moses and Nehemiah; grandson, Richard, under age; and daughters Jerusha Pierce, and Bethiah (*N.H. State Pap.*, vol. 33, p. 81).

Children, born at Newington:
7 i. JOSHUA⁴, b. about 1690.
8 ii. MOSES, b. about 1698.
9 iii. RICHARD, bapt. in North Church, Portsmouth, 3 Feb. 1714 (*N.H. Gen. Rec.*, vol. 4, p. 99), b. about 1700.
10 iv. JETHRO, bapt. in North Church, Portsmouth, 17 Oct. 1708 (*N.H. Gen. Rec.*, vol. 4, p. 53) as son of Sarah.
11 v. NEHEMIAH, b. 21 Jan. 1710.
 vi. BETHIAH, bapt. at Newington, 1 June 1718 (dau. of Thomas?).
 vii. JERUSHA, bapt. at Newington, 7 Aug. 1720, b. 8 Mar. 1719 (town rec.) m. 25 Mar. 1738 (*Register*, vol. 25, p. 378), GEORGE⁴ PEIRCE, son of George³, of Portsmouth, b. at Portsmouth.

5. JETHRO³ FURBER (William²⁻¹), of Newington, master mariner, m. LEAH NUTE, dau. of James, who m. (2) 16 May 1716, as his second wife, HATEVIL³ NUTTER (3), son of Anthony² and Sarah (Langstaff), *q.v.*

Administration on his estate 2 Mar. 1715/6 to Leah, his widow; Hatevil Nutter and Moses Dam, sureties (*N.H. State Pap.*, vol. 31, p. 785).

Children, born at Newington (*N.H. Deeds*, vol. 23, p. 548):
12 i. JETHRO⁴, b. 1682.
 ii. MARY, d. 29 Mar. 1777, m. at Greenland, 31 Mar. 1734 (*Register*, vol. 65, p. 353), JAMES⁴ LIBBEY, son of Capt. John³ and Eleanor (Kirke) (*Libby Family*, p. 54), of Scarborough, Me., b. at Portsmouth, 1700, d. 18 Feb. 1776.
 iii. ESTHER, d. 1 Oct. 1756, m. Lieut. ANDREW³ LIBBY, son of Matthew² and Elizabeth (Brown) (*Libby Family*, p. 52), of Scarborough, Me., sawmiller, b. at Kittery, Me., 1 Dec. 1700, d. 5 Jan. 1773.
 iv. ABIGAIL, m. 1 Jan. 1724, JAMES NUTTER (15), son of John, *q.v.*
 v. HANNAH, m. MATTIAS NUTTER (14), son of John, *q.v.*
 vi. ELIZABETH, m. at Newington, 4 Oct. 1727, THOMAS BICKFORD, of Portsmouth.

6. JETHRO³ FURBER (Jethro², William¹), of Portsmouth, b. 1682, d. 9 Apr. 1738 *aet.* 56 (Locke's Tombstones), m. ELIZABETH -----.

Children, baptized at Portsmouth (*Register*, vol. 81, p. 425):
13 i. NATHANIEL⁴, bapt. 3 Mar. 1716.
14 ii. JAMES, bapt. 28 Mar. 1718/9.

JETHRO FURBER, was living in Boston, 1739/40, where Nathaniel Ayres had settled (*N.H. Deeds*, vol. 24, p. 534; *id.*, vol. 25, p. 24).

7. JOSHUA[4] FURBER (William[3-1]), of Portsmouth, mariner, b. about 1690, m. ELIZABETH KENNARD. She m. (2) 26 May 1715 (*Register*, vol. 23, p. 272), FRANCIS DITTY, of Winbird, Dorset, m. (3) Capt. RICHARD WATERHOUSE, m. (4) MOSES DAM, of Newington (*Libby's Dictionary*, p. 196).

In 1746, Elizabeth Dam, wife of Moses of Newington, and formerly wife of Joshua[4] Furber of Portsmouth, quitclaims her interest in lands formerly of William[3] Furber to Jethro[4], Moses[4], and Nehemiah[4] Furber, his brothers (*N.H. Deeds*, vol. --, p. --).

His will dated 19 May 1708, proved 6 Dec. 1712, names his wife, Elizabeth; his father, William, who gave him lands at Welchman's Cove in 1707; and son, Joshua (*N.H. State Pap.*, vol. 31, p. 623). It appears from the administration papers that he had also a son, Edward, and a child who died during the administration, and that his widow married Ditty and had an allowance for bringing up her son, Joshua, from the age of 5 1/2 to 7 yrs. and son, Edward, from the age of 1 to 7.

Children, born at Portsmouth:

15   i. JOSHUA[5], b. 1709.
    ii. EDWARD, bapt. in the North Church, 5 Aug. 1711 (*N.H. Gen. Rec.*, vol. 4, p. 56).
16   iii. ? WALLIS, bapt. in the North Church, 22 June 1712 (*id.*, p. 57).

8. Deac. MOSES[4] FURBER (William[3-1]), of Newington, b. about 1698, m. 31 July 1727 (*Register*, vol. 24, p. 359), ANNA (BICKFORD) WALKER (1-vi), dau. of John and Susanna[2] (Furber) and wid. of Samuel, *q.v.*, b. at Newington, 18 Sept. 1698.

His will dated 23 Aug. 1764, mentions his wife, Anna; and children William, Joshua, Moses, Thomas, Keturah, Elizabeth, Anna and Sarah (Hoyt) (*N.H. Probate*, vol. 24, p. 124).

Children, baptized at Newington:

    i. WILLIAM[5], b. about 1728, bapt. 12 Aug. 1733, not mentioned in the will.
    ii. SARAH, b. about 1730, bapt. 12 Aug. 1733, not mentioned in the will.
    iii. JOSHUA, b. about 1732, bapt. 25 Nov. 1733, not mentioned in the will.
    iv. KETURAH, bapt. 13 June 1736.
    v. SARAH, bapt. 5 Nov. 1738, m. (1) 26 Sept. 1757, JOHN HOYT[5] (3-iv), son of John[4] and Lydia (Miller), *q.v.*, m. (2) JONATHAN[4] TRICKEY (10), son of Thomas[3] and Mary, *q.v.*
17   vi. WILLIAM, bapt. 3 May 1741.
18   vii. JOSHUA, bapt. 3 June 1744.
    viii. ELIZABETH, bapt. 7 Sept. 1746, m. ?19 Nov. 1767, JOHN[5] DAM (5-viii), son of Richard[4] and Elizabeth (Leighton), *q.v.*
    ix. HANNAH, bapt. 4 Oct. 1748, d. in infancy.
19   x. MOSES
20   xi. THOMAS, bapt. 28 Apr. 1751.

xii. ANNA, bapt. 17 Apr. 1757 (as dau. of Anna).

THOMAS FURBER, m. SARAH FROST BLUNT, dau. of Rev. John and Sarah (Frost) (Brewster's *Rambles*, vol. 1, pp. 892-91).

9. RICHARD⁴ FURBER (William$^{3-1}$), of Newington, cordwainer, m. 22 Nov. 1722 (*N.H. Gen. Rec.*, vol. 5, p. 44), MARY³ SHACKFORD (2-vii), dau. of Samuel² and Abigail (Richards), *q.v.*, who m. (2) ALEXANDER HODGDON (37), son of Alexander³ and ? Jane Shackford, *q.v.*

Administration of his estate 20 Aug. 1728, to his widow, Mary, then wife of Alexander Hodgdon (*N.H. State Pap.*, vol. 32, p. 336).

Children, bapt. at Newington:
  i. FRANCIS⁵, bapt. 8 Dec. 1723.
21 ii. RICHARD, bapt. 12 Sept. 1725.

10. JETHRO⁴ FURBER (William$^{3-1}$), of Newington, bapt. 17 Oct. 1708, m. 17 Sept. 1733, PHEBE³ FABYAN (2-vi), dau. of Lieut. John² and Mary³ (Pickering), *q.v.*

Administration on his estate, 1761, to his son, Jethro (*N.H. Probate*, vol. 22, p. 43).

Children, baptized at Newington:
  i. JETHRO⁵, bapt. 2 June 1734, d. in infancy.
  ii. A CHILD, bapt. 7 Dec. 1735.
22 iii. JETHRO, bapt. 4 June 1738.
  iv. LEAH, bapt. 31 Aug. 1740.
23 v. JOHN, bapt. 7 Nov. 1742.
24 vi. JOSEPH, bapt. 28 Oct. 1744.
25 vii. ELI, bapt. 29 Mar. 1747.
  viii. PHEBE, bapt. 4 June 1749.

11. NEHEMIAH⁴ FURBER (William$^{3-1}$), of Newington, husbandman, b. 21 Jan. 1710, m. (1) 5 Dec. 1732, ABIGAIL⁵ LEIGHTON, (1-vi), dau. of Thomas⁴ and Deborah, *q.v.*, m. (2) 12 Nov. 1780, MARY HART.

In his will dated 5 Nov. 1785, proved 18 July 1787, he names his wife, Mary; and children Elizabeth Pickering, Jerusha Pickering, Abigail Hill, Deborah Pickering, Sarah Roberts and Levi, executor (*Rockingham Probate*).

Children, baptized at Newington (births in *Register*, vol. 9, p. 366):
  i. ELIZABETH⁵, bapt. 30 May 1736, b. 26 Apr. 1733, m. ----- PICKERING, *q.v.*
  ii. MARY, b. 5 May 1735, d. 18 Apr. 1736.
  iii. JERUSHA, bapt. 7 Jan. 1738, b. 6 Jan. 1738, m. 10 July 1759, THOMAS⁴ PICKERING (8), son of James³ and Mary (Nutter), *q.v.*

    iv. ABIGAIL, bapt. 22 June 1740, b. 12 June 1740, m. ----- HILL.
    v. DEBORAH, bapt. 19 Apr. 1742, m. (1) 11 Oct. 1764, LUKE[2] MILLS, son of Luke[1] and Hannah[2] (Lang) (*John Lang Family*, 1-x), of Portsmouth, master mariner, bapt. at Portsmouth, 17 Jan. 1741/2, m. (2) 10 June 1773, JOHN GEE[4] PICKERING (12), son of Thomas[3] and Mary[5] (Downing), *q.v.*
    vi. SARAH, bapt. 10 Mar. 1744/5, b. 1 Mar 1744/5, m. 16 July 1761, TIMOTHY[5] ROBERTS, son of Timothy[4] and Anna (Waldron) Roberts, of Rochester, yeoman, bapt. at Rochester, 11 May 1740 (McDuffee's *Rochester*, p. 587).
    vii. NEHEMIAH, bapt. 24 Apr. 1748, b. 24 Apr. 1748, d. 23 Feb. 1754.
26   viii. LEVI, bapt. 26 May 1751, b. 16 May 1751.
27   ix. FABIAN, b. 14 June 1752, d. 13 Feb. 1802, m. ? DOROTHY[5] NUTTER (80iv), dau. of Maj John[4] and Anna (Symmes), *q.v.*

12. JETHRO[4] FURBER (Jethro[3], William[2-1]), of Portsmouth, shipjoiner, born 1682, m. about 1716, ? ELIZABETH MORRILL, dau. of Nicholas.

    Children, born at Portsmouth (*N.H. Deeds*, vol. 67, p. 79):
28   i. JETHRO[5], of Boston.
    ii. MARY, m. JONATHAN BOURNE, of Boston.
    iii. MARGARET, bapt. 14 Mar. 1735/6 (*Register*, vol. 81, p. 442).
    iv. ELIZABETH, d. unm. before 30 Apr. 1763.
29   ?v. THOMAS, of Portsmouth, m. (1) SARAH -----, m. (2) ? BETHIA -----, who m. (2)JOHN COTTON.
    In 1767, Thomas Furber and Sarah, his wife, convey lands formerly of Jethro (*N.H. Deeds*, vol. --, p. --)

12. WALLIS[5] FURBER (Joseph[4], William[3-1]), of Portsmouth, cooper, bapt. 22 June 1712, m. JERUSHA -----.

    Children, baptized at Portsmouth (*Register*, vol. 81, p. 442):
    i. A CHILD[6], bapt. 10 Apr. 1743 (*Register*, vol. 81, p. 442).
30   ii. JAMES, bapt. 24 Mar. 1744/5 (*ibid.*).
    iii. ANDREW, bapt. 5 Aug. 1750 (*id.*, vol. 82, p. 26).
    iv. MORRILL, bapt. 7 June 1751 (*ibid.*).
    v. ? THOMAS, of Portsmouth, ? 1755, m. 14 June 1776 (South Church rec.), ELIZABETH BURNHAM.
    Children, born at Portsmouth:
      1) Wallis, bapt. 12 Sept. 1766 (*Register*, vol. 82, p. 36).
      2) William, bapt. 29 Nov. 1767 (*ibid.*).
      3) Abigail, bapt. 13 Oct. 1769.

13. WILLIAM⁵ FURBER (Moses⁴, William³⁻¹), of Newington, farmer, bapt. 3 May 1741, m. (1) MARY⁵ COLMAN, dau. of Phineas⁴ and Abigail³ (Huntress), b. at Newington, 1 June 1741, m. (2) ----- PEAVY. He had the ferry (road?), owned 1925 by Arthur Schurman. Administration on his estate was granted 14 Jan. 1834, to Jeremiah H. Neal (*Rockingham Probate*).

Children by first wife, born at Newington:
    i. LYDIA⁶, m. ?----- LANG.
    ii. -----

Children by second wife, born at Newington:
    iii. LUCY, b. 1791, m. 21 Nov. 1711, JEREMIAH H. NEAL, of Newington, d. 7 Aug. 1834 (*Register*, vol. 73, p. 198).
    iv. AUGUSTUS, m. SARAH FURBER, dau. of Levi, b. 1797, d. 19 June 1831 (*Register*, vol. 73, p. 197), of Newington.
    v. -----

14. Capt. JOSHUA⁵ FURBER (Moses⁴, William³⁻¹), of Northwood, 1767, potash manufacturer, officer in the Revolution, b. 24 May 1744, bapt. 3 June 1744, d. 27 Apr. 1827, m. ELIZABETH PAGE.

His will dated 29 Mar. 1826, proved 10 May 1827, names his wife, Elizabeth; and children David, executor, Moses, Catherine Marsh, Nancy Hill, Polly Crawford, Thomas, Joshua, William, Samuel and John, deceased, and his heirs (*Rockingham Probate*).

Children, born at Northwood (Cogswell's *Nottingham*, pp. 687-8):
    i. MOSES⁶, of Northwood, b. 6 Jan. 1768, d. 3 Aug. 1826, m. DOROTHY ROLLINS.
    Children, born at Northwood:
      1) Moses⁷, b. 1790.
      2) Benjamin, b. 1792.
    Moses, m. at Northwood, 26 Jan. 1803, Tamsen Evans (t. 2).
    Adm. on Moses, of Northwood, 12 Dec. 1827, to wid. Tamsen, est. insolvent; Edward Evans of Nottingham, and Wi. Evans of Barrington, husbandman, sureties (*Rockingham Probate*).
    ii. CATHERINE, b. 22 Dec. 1769, d. 25 Aug. 1840, m. as his second wife, SAMUEL MARSH, of Northwood, b. 23 Apr. 1762, d. 27 Aug. 1827.
    Children, born at Northwood:
      1) James⁷, b. 15 Oct. 1797.
      2) David, b. 19 Feb. 1801, m. 4 July 1827, Elizabeth Burnham, dau. of Jacob and Lydia, b. 19 Apr. 1801, d. 25 Sept. 1876.
      3) Nancy, b. 22 Aug. 1803.
      4) Samuel, b. 30 Apr. 1808.
    iii. JOHN, of Northwood, b. 8 May 1772, d. 17 Feb. 1824, m. 22 Mar. 1789 (town rec.), OLIVE⁷ BATCHELDER, dau. of John⁶ and Sarah (Mur-

ray) (*Batchelder Genealogy*, p. 156), b. at Northwood.

Administration on his estate, insolvent, 9 Mar. 1824, to his widow, Olive (*Rockingham Probate*); Nathaniel Batchelder, of Northwood and William Batchelder, of Nottingham, sureties. The widow, Olive, was guardian of her children Sarah, Olive, Hazen Kimball, Mary Ann and Theodore.

Children, born at Northwood (town rec.):

1) McLaurin[7], b. 21 July 1798, d. unm.
2) Elizabeth, b. 28 Apr. 1801, m. John A. Ring.
3) Nancy, b. 9 Aug. 1803, d. unm.?
4) John Langdon, b. 14 July 1805.
5) Mary Ann, b. 20 July 1807.
6) Theodore, b. 1 Apr. 1810.
7) Sarah, b. 4 Apr. 1813, d. 29 July 1872, m. 7 Apr. 1836, Oliver[6] Cotton, son of John[5] and Hannah (Lane), of Boston, Portsmouth and Northwood, machinist, postmaster, b. at Gilmanton, 11 Oct. 1811, d. 3 Oct. 1887.
8) Olive, b. 11 Apr. 1815, m. Lewis Bradford.
9) Hazen Kimball, b. 8 Mar. 1822.

iv. NANCY, b. 31 Aug. 1774, d. 1842, m. NOAH HILL.

Children:

1) Elizabeth[7]
2) Joshua
3) Bradbury, of Woonsocket, R.I.
4) Jonathan, d. unm. ?
5) Pearl, d. unm. ?

v. ELIZABETH, b. 8 Mar. 1777, d. 20 Sept. 1795.

vi. THOMAS (twin), of Northwood, b. 10 Apr. 1779, d. 31 Dec. 1831, m. (1) 16 Mar. 1802 (town rec.), SARAH NEALLEY, dau. of John and Dorothy (Burleigh) (Cogswell's *Nottingham*, p. 761), b. at Nottingham, m. (2) ELIZABETH DEMERITT, dau. of Moses[4] and Lydia (Odell) Demeritt (Stackpole's *Durham*, vol. 2, p. 122). She m. (2) SAMUEL BEAN, of Deerfield (*ibid.*).

Children by first wife, born at Northwood (town rec.):

1) Joseph[7], b. 25 Sept. 1802.
2) Lavinia, b. 15 Oct. 1805, d. unm.?
3) Dorothy, b. 29 Sept. 1808, d. unm.?

Children by second wife:

4) Sarah, b. 1812, d. unm.
5) William H. H., of Boston, butcher, b. 1814.
6) Page, of Boston, butcher, b. 1816.
7) Lydia O., b. 1 June 1818, m. 31 Aug. 1836, James Bean, son of

Samuel and Deborah (Avery), of Deerfield, b. at Deerfield, 18 Apr. 1815.

8) Eliza, b. 1820, d. unm.?

9) Thomas J.

vii. JOSHUA (twin), of Northwood, farmer, deputy sheriff, b. 10 Apr. 1779, d. 6 Feb. 1828, m. ALCEY NEALLEY, dau. of John and Dorothy (Burleigh) (Cogswell's *Nottingham*, p. 261), b. at Nottingham.

Administration on his estate, insolvent, 19 Mar. 1828, to his widow, Alcey (*Rockingham Probate*); Joseph Nealley, Esq., and John Nealley, innholder, both of Northwood, sureties; Joseph Nealley was appointed guardian of Joshua's children: Lyman, John N., Mary Jane, Charles, and Alcey N.

Children, born at Northwood:

1) Lyman[7], of Lawrence, Mass., foreman machinist, b. 1810, d. 1855.

2) John Nealley, of Corrington, Ky., 1865, lawyer, b. 28 Feb. 1813, d. 21 July 1878, m. (1) Margaret A. Linn, b. in Ohio, m. (2) 1857, Martha M. Smith, dau. of John, b. at Salem.

3) Mary Jane, m. (1) James T. Adams, of Dover, clergyman, m. (2) ----------.

4) Charles, of Andover, Mass., machinist, member of the General Court, 1857.

5) Alcey Nealley, m. Vachel Weldon, of Augusta, Ky., merchant.

viii. MARY, b. 26 June 1781, d. 26 May 1857, m. JOHN CRAWFORD.

Children:

1) Benjamin[7]

2) William

3) Mary, m. Joseph Dunn.

ix. WILLIAM, of Nottingham, b. 9 Feb. 1783, d. 18 Mar. 1853, m. 12 Feb. 1812 (town rec.), DORCAS BUTLER, (Not in Jas. Butler fam.).

Children:

1) Elizabeth[7], b. 1814, d. unm.?

2) Isabel, b. 1816, d. unm.?

3) Sarah, b. 1818, d. unm.?

4) Henry, b. 1820.

5) Abigail, b. 1822, d. unm.?

6) Ward, b. 1825.

x. DAVID, of Northwood, farmer, saw miller, b. 12 Sept. 1787, d. 31 Dec. 1858, m. SARAH HALEY, b. at ? Epping.

Children, born at Northwood (*N.H. Gen. and Fam. Hist.*, vol. --, p. --):

1) Samuel H.[7] (twin), of Northwood, b. 1810, m. Mary F. Leavitt.

2) William (twin), b. 1810.

3) Franklin, of Holliston, Mass., Methodist preacher, b. 1812.

4) Martha, b. 1814, m. Samuel F. Leavitt, of Northwood.

xi. SAMUEL, of Northwood, b. 4 Jan. 1791, d. 27 May 1829, m. 9 July 1801 (town rec.), LUCY[7] BATCHELDER, dau. of John[6] and Sarah (Murray) (*Batchelder Genealogy*, p. 156), b. at Northwood.

Administration on his estate 1 Sept. 1829, to his widow, Lucy (*Rockingham Probate*); Samuel Batchelder, Gent., and Nathaniel Tasker, joiner, both of Northwood, sureties; William Batchelder, of Nottingham, was appointed guardian 11 Nov. 1829, of Samuel's children: John B., George W., Lucy Maria, Caroline, Samuel Greenleaf, Susan G., and Olive Sanborn (*id.*).

Children, born at Northwood:
1) John Batchelder[7], of Northwood, b. 1803.
2) George W., of New Bedford, Mass., b. 1805.
3) Lucy Maria, b. 1807, d. *s.p.*, m. 26 Aug. 1865, as his second wife, Thomas[8] Garland, son of Benjamin[7] and Sarah (Philbrick) (*Garland Genealogy*, p. 121), of Newmarket, b. 15 Sept. 1819.
4) Caroline, b. 1810, d. unm.?
5) Samuel Greenleaf, b. 1812.
6) Susan G., b. 1815, d. unm.?
7) Olive Sanborn, b. 1820, m. William B. Small, of Newmarket.

15. MOSES[5] FURBER (Moses[4], William[3-1]), m. 28 June 1770, HANNAH HOYT.

17. RICHARD[5] FURBER (Richard[4], William[3-1]), of Newington and Lee, 1769, soldier at Louisburg in 1747 (*Register*, vol. 25, p. 267), bapt. 12 Sept. 1725, m. (1) ABIGAIL WADLEIGH (*N.H. Deeds*, vol. 38, p. 552), dau. of John, m. (2) 28 Jan. 1748, ELIZABETH[3] DOWNING (5-iii), dau. of Benjamin[2] and Elizabeth[3] (Fabyan), *q.v.*

Children, baptized at Newington:
i. SAMUEL[6], of Rochester, bapt. 7 May 1749, m. 12 Sept. 1776, MARY[5] EMERSON (*Register*, vol. 25, p. 56; *Dover Historical Collections*, p. 175), dau. of Samuel[4] and Dorothy (Chamberlain) Emerson (Stackpole's *Durham*, vol. 2, p. 178) (*Dover Historical Collections*, p. 56), b. at Dover, 14 Feb. 1756.

ii. BENJAMIN, of Rochester, bapt. 8 Mar. 1752, m.? 18 Dec. 1777, DEBORAH TIBBETTS (*N.H. Gen. Rec.*, vol. 4, p. 148).

iii. Gen. RICHARD, of Rochester, officer in the Revolution, bapt. 30 Sept. 1753, m. (1) 18 June 1780, ALICE[5] COLMAN (5-i), dau. of John[4] and Mary (Woodman), *q.v.*, m. (2) 12 Oct. 1786, MARY POWERS.

Child by first wife, baptized at Newington:
1) Alice Colman[7], bapt. 1 July 1781.

iv. ELIZABETH DOWNING, bapt. 31 Aug. 1755, m. JAMES[5] CHESLEY, son of Thomas[4] and Mary (Hill) (Stackpole's *Durham*, vol. 2 p. 64), of Durham, b. at Durham, 25 Jan. 1750, d. at Rochester, 13 Jan. 1851 (*Register*, vol. 5, p. 267).

Children, born at Durham (Stackpole, *loc. cit.*):
1) Mary[7], m. 12 Nov. 1791, James Horn.
2) Elizabeth, m. 25 Dec. 1800, Stephen Place.
3) Thomas, m. 15 Oct. 1801, Elizabeth Brewster.
4) Richard Furber, b. 24 Oct. 1781, m. 30 Jan. 1806, Nancy Twombly.
5) Abigail, b. 26 June 1785, m. 25 Sept. 1806, Daniel Hayes.
6) Sarah, b. 28 Oct. 1787, m. 9 July 1809, Joseph Patterson[6] Huntress, son of Mark[5].
7) Isaac Buzzell (twin), b. 14 June 1789.
8) Jacob (twin), b. 14 June 1789.
9) James, b. 2 Oct. 1791.
10) Deborah, b. 14 Sept. 1794, m. 8 June 1823, John[6] Huntress, son of Mark[5].

v. FRANCES, bapt. 9 Apr. 1758.
vi. MARY, bapt. 1 July 1759, m. ? 21 Dec. 1786, DEARBORN JEWETT (*N.H. Gen. Rec.*, vol. 5, p. 2), of Rochester.
vii. ALICE, bapt. 25 Apr. 1762.

18. JETHRO[5] FURBER (Jethro[4], William[3-1]), of Newington, bapt. 4 June 1738, m. MARY[4] SHERBURN, dau. of Deac. Samuel[3] and Mercy (Wiggin) (*Register*, vol. 59, p. 56), b. at Portsmouth, 16 Jan. 1740, d. 1792.

Children, baptized at Newington:
43 i. JETHRO[6], bapt. 11 Dec. 1763, had one leg only.
    ii. PHEBE, bapt. 15 Mar. 1767.
    iii. MARY, bapt. 25 June 1769.
    iv. ABIGAIL, bapt. 8 Dec. 1771, m. ? JAMES C.[5] PICKERING (10-vii), son of Maj. Ephraim[4] and Lydia (Colman), *q.v.*

22. LEVI[5] FURBER (Jeremiah[4], William[3-1]), of Newington, bapt. 26 May 1751, b. 16 May 1751 (town rec.), d. 19 Jan. 1829 (*Register*, vol. 73, p. 198), m. 4 Oct. 1770, ROSAMOND[4] FABYAN (3-viii), dau. of Samuel[3] and Elizabeth[3] (Huntress), *q.v.*

Administration on his estate 11 Feb. 1829, to his eldest son, William, of Rochester; Richard Furber and James C. Pickering, both of Newington, sureties; Simon Davis, of Newington and Thomas Brackett, of Portsmouth, sons-in-law, estate insolvent (*Rockingham Probate*).

Children, born at Newington (town rec.):
i. DEBORAH[6], b. 2 May 1771.

  ii. NEHEMIAH, b. 27 June 1773, d. unm. 14 Aug. 1825 (*Register*, vol. 73, p. 196). Administration on his estate 16 Oct. 1826 (*Rockingham Probate*).

45 iii. SAMUEL, b. 1 July 1775, d. before 1843, m. SARAH -----, d. 11 Nov. 1843 (*Register*, vol. 73, p. 199).

46 iv. WILLIAM, of Rochester, b. 30 Apr. 1778.
  v. ELIZABETH, b. 17 May 1780.
  vi. ABIGAIL, b. 12 June 1782.
  vii. DOROTHY, b. 24 Mar. 1784, d. 31 Mar. 1784.
  viii. NATHANIEL, b. 26 Apr. 1785, d. 3 May 1785.
  ix. MARY, b. 13 Apr. 1786.
  x. MEHITABLE, b. 16 Aug. 1788.
  xi. ROSAMOND DAME, b. 13 Feb. 1791.
  xii. LEVI, b. 10 June 1793, d. unm. 1825, administration on his estate 30 Aug. 1825 (*Rockingham Probate*).
  xiii. SARAH, b. 6 Jan. 1796.

23. JOHN[5] FURBER (if this is the man) (Jethro[4], William[3-1]), of Barnstead, clockmaker, b. 7 Nov. 1742, m. (1) ----- -----, m. (2) Mar. 1782, ABIGAIL LORD.

Children by first wife:
  i. MARTHA[6]
  ii. ELIZABETH
  iii. JOHN

In 1781, John Furber, of Barnstead, clockmaker, was appointed guardian of his children: Martha, Elizabeth, and John, all under 14; Joseph Cotton, boat-builder, and Samuel Bowles, merchant, both of Portsmouth, sureties (*Strafford Probate*).

45. SAMUEL[6] FURBER (Levi[5], Jeremiah[4], William[3-1]), of Newington, husbandman, b. 1 July 1775, d. 1 Aug. 1824 (*Register*, vol. 73, p. 186), m. (1) ----- -----, m. (2) SARAH -----.

His will dated 17 May 1823, proved 14 Sept. 1824, mentions his father, Levi, "his now wife, Sarah," and his children as below; widow, Sarah, administratrix *c.t.*; John Fabyan and Charles Hodgdon, sureties (*Rockingham Probate*).

Children, born at Newington:
  i. ANN MARIA[7], m. 10 Mar. 1845, THOMAS M. FOYE (*Register*, vol. 73, p. 193), of Newcastle.
  ii. ZERVIAH PARKER, b. 1806, d. 9 May 1836.
  iii. JOHN M., of Newington, husbandman, b. 1804, d. 3 Sept. 1861 (*Register*, vol. 73, p. 205), m. 26 June 1836, LYDIA DOW (*Register*, vol. 73, p. 192).
   Administration on his estate was granted 5 Nov. 1861, to his son, Samuel; the widow, Lydia, renouncing (*Rockingham Probate*).

iv. THOMAS GERRISH, of Newington, husbandman, m. 7 May 1837, ELIZABETH DOW (*ibid.*).

THEODORE FURBER, of Portsmouth, master mariner, merchant, b. 1741, d. 14 Jan. 1809 (*Locke's Tombstones*), m. LYDIA -----, b. 1764, d. 3 Jan. 1842 (*Locke's Tombstones*).

Administration on his estate 30 Feb. 1809, to Lydia, his widow; James C. Pickering, yeoman, and Joshua Pickering, Gent., sureties (*Rockingham Probate*). The citation was addressed to Stephen Pickering of Greenland and to the "heirs and representatives of Dorothy Rollins, dec'd., who was wife of James Rollins, of Somersworth," and the proceedings mention his sons, Theodore P., mariner, dec'd., and McLaurin, dec'd. Service was admitted by James Rollins and Lydia A. Rollins, of Somersworth, and Mary B. Rollins, of Greenland.

Her will dated 3 Jan. 1838, mentions her daughter, Lydia Pickering (and her children: Maturin F., Stephen Hale, and Theodore F.); and the following grandchildren: Lydia Amanda Woodman, Mary Buxsell Clark, Olive Pickering Rollins, Dorothy Ann Gault (dau. of McLaurin Furber and wife of Samuel), Mary Elizabeth Drew, Theodore Furber Rollins of East Boston, and Charles Rollins of East Boston (children of Dorothy Rollins), Lydia Furber Pickering, Abby Frances Pickering, Eliza Perkins Pickering, and Hosea Clark of Cambridge, Mass., executor; John Fabyan and Jacob S. Pickering, sureties (*Rockingham Probate*).

Children:
    i. THEODORE P., of Portsmouth, mariner, b. 1799, d. unm. 12 May 1818 *aet.* 19 (*Locke's Tombstones*).
    ii. MCLAURIN
        Child:
        1) Dorothy Ann, m. Samuel Gault.
    iii. LYDIA, m. STEPHEN PICKERING, of Greenland.
        Children:
        1) Maturin F.
        2) Stephen Hale
        3) Theodore F.
    iv. DOROTHY, m. JAMES ROLLINS, of Somersworth.
        Children:
        1) Mary Elizabeth, m. ----- Drew.
        2) Theodore Furber, of East Boston.
        3) Charles, of East Boston.

JOHN M.[7] FURBER (Samuel[6], Levi[5], Jeremiah[4], William[3-1]), of Newington, farmer, b. 1804, d. 3 Sept. 1861, m. 26 June 1836, LYDIA DOW, b. 1812.

Administration on his estate 5 Nov. 1861 to Samuel Furber, his eldest son, the widow, Lydia, renouncing Isaac Furber of Newington and William G. Nutter, of

Portsmouth, sureties (*Rockingham Probate*).

Children, born at Newington (Census):

    i. SAMUEL[8], b. 1837, of Newington.

    Child:

       1) Carl S., of Centralia, Wash.

    ii. ISAAC, b. 1839, d. 29 May 1919, m. CAROLINE L. who administered his estate.

    Children, born at Newington:

       1) John M., of N.Y. City (care Lord & Taylor).

       2) Fred, of Smutty Ridge, Ports.

       3) Maryan (?), of Portsmouth.

       4) Ella F., m. George S. French.

       5) Annie M.

    iii. SARAH F., b. 1841, m. ----- MILLER, of Portsmouth.

    Children:

       1) Prof. Edward F., of Newton Center, Mass.

    iv. JOHN, b. 1843.

    v. LYDIA, b. 1846, d. unm. 29 May 1919. Her will dated 27 June 1895, proved July 1, 1919, names her brothers, Samuel and Isaac, and her sister, Sarah Miller.

THOMAS GERRISH[7] FURBER (Samuel[6], Levi[5], Jeremiah[4], William[3-1]), of Newington, farmer, b. 1812, m. ELIZABETH -----.

Children, born at Newington (Census):

    i. SOPHIA[8], b. 1839.

GAINES

JOHN GAINES, b. at Ipswich, Mass., m. 18 Jan. 1727/8, RUTH WATERHOUSE, of Portsmouth (*Register*, vol. 24, p. 360).

Maj. GEORGE GAINES, only son of John (*Brewster's Rambles*, pp. 133-5, 334), m. (1) MARY DAME, dau. of Col. Theophilus, of Portsmouth, b. 1747, d. 16 Apr. 1780 (*N.H. Gazette* of 22 Apr. 1780), m. (2) 28 May 1782, SARAH PICKERING.

GAMMON

WILLIAM GAMMON, of Kittery, Me., m. 31 Oct. 1717, MARY HEPWORTH, of Portsmouth (*Register*, vol. 23, p. 394).

GERRISH

ABIGAIL GERRISH, m. 8 Oct. 1773, BENJAMIN BROWN, both of Madbury.

GLEER

THOMAS GLEER, m. 2 Apr. 1736, ELIZABETH CRAWFORD.

GODSO

Lieut. JOHN³ GODSO (William²⁻¹), (Stackpole's *Kittery*, p. 450), m. 13 Sept. 1741, MARY ROGERS, both of Kittery, Me.

GOSS

SARAH GOSS, m. 1 July 1754, REUBEN LIBBY, both of Rye.

GOTHAM

EDWARD GOTHAM, soldier, m. 27 Mar. 1777, MERCY PEVEY.

EDWARD and SAMUEL GOTHAM, children of Mercy, bapt. 12 Aug. 1781.

JAMES GOTHAM, son of Mercy, bapt. 5 Nov. 1782.

GOVE

ENOCH GOVE, of Hampton, m. 9 Feb. 1749, HANNAH LUCY, of Portsmouth.

GOWEN

MERCY GOWEN, m. 16 Nov. 1773, JAMES PICKERING.

GRAY

JAMES GRAY, at Newington, 1713, (*Register*, vol. 58, p. 249).

----- GRAY, dau. of James and Tamsen, bapt. 25 May 1717.

GEORGE GRAY, son of James and Tamsen, bapt. 22 Nov. 1719.

JAMES GRAY, son of James and Tamsen, bapt. 7 Sept. 1723.

MARY GRAY, m. 3 Jan. 1725, GEORGE MARRINER.

GREEN

BETHIAH GREEN, m. 25 Apr. 1758, JOHN CROCKER, both of Kittery, Me.

GREENOUGH

SAMUEL GREENOUGH, m. 27 Oct. 1761, LUCY TRIPE.

PELATIAH GREENOUGH, m. 4 Oct. 1769, EUNICE WITHAM, both of Kittery, Me.

GROVE (GROVER)

HANNAH GROVE(R), of Ipswich, Mass., m. 9 Nov. 1727, WILLIAM MURRAY, of Charleston, S.C. (*Register*, vol. 24, p. 35).

NATHANIEL GROVE(R), m. 5 Feb. 1736, ELIZABETH (DELIVERANCE) WALKER, dau. of Edward[2] and Deliverance (Gaskin), *q.v.*

SAMUEL GROVE(R), son of Nathaniel, bapt. 13 Mar. 1737.

SARAH GROVE(R), dau. of Nathaniel, gr. dau. of Edward Walker, bapt. 6 Nov. 1748.

SARAH GROVE(R), dau. of John, bapt. 27 Apr. 1737.

SARAH GROVE(R), dau. of John, bapt. Dec. 1738.

ELIZABETH GROVE(R), dau. of John, bapt. 6 Feb. 1742/3.

MARTHA GROVE(R), wife of John, communion, 8 June 1755.

MARY GROVE(R), m. 3 Feb. 1756, ROBERT SINNOTT, both of Newmarket.

HALL

MEHITABLE HALL, covenant, 3 Mar. 1734.

HAM

(See *Register*, vol. 26)

DORCAS HAM, m. 1 Dec. 1723, JOHN RICHARDS.

JUDAH HAM, covenant, 15 June 1728.

JOHN LEIGHTON HAM, of Newington, m. 7 Nov. 1728, ABIGAIL HAM, of Portsmouth (*Register*, vol. 24, p. 360).

BENJAMIN, TOBIAS, REUBEN, NATHANIEL, and SAMUEL HAM, children of John and Judah, bapt. 18 Aug. 1728.

JUDAH HAM, communion, 1 July 1739.

PATIENCE[3] HAM, dau. of John[2] and Elizabeth, m. ----- SHACKFORD (*Register*, vol. 26, p. 389).

SAMUEL HAM, m. 10 Apr. 1755, ELIZABETH BICKFORD.

WILLIAM HAM, m. 12 Jan. 1779, ANNA WALKER, both of Portsmouth.

HAMMET

THOMAS HAMMET, of Shadwell, Middlesex, Eng., m. 1 Jan. 1716/7, ELIZABETH DENEFORD, of Kittery, Me. (*Register*, vol. 23, p. 393).

THOMAS HAMMET, and wife, covenant, 8 Apr. 1753.

THOMAS HAMMET, son of Thomas, bapt. 8 Apr. 1753.

HAMMOND

ELISHA[5] HAMMOND (Jonathan[4], Joseph[3-2], William[1]) (Stackpole's *Kittery*, p. 492), m. 11 June 1780, SARAH LIBBY, both of Kittery.

HARRIS

----- HARRIS, dau. of Sarah, bapt. 14 Apr. 1728.

HART

SAMUEL HART, of Portsmouth, m. 23 Dec. 1725, BRIDGET CUTT, of Kittery, Me. (*Register*, vol. 24, p. 358).

HENRY HART, of Portsmouth, m. 26 Oct. 1765, ALICE DOWNING.

MARY HART, m. 12 Nov. 1780, NEHEMIAH FURBER.

RICHARD D. HART, d. 29 May 1843, *aet.* 77 (*Register*, vol. 73, p. 199).

HASTY

LETTICE HASTY, m. 13 Nov. 1732, JOHN HOYT, of Portsmouth.

HAYNES

SAMUEL HAYNES, m. 14 Mar. 1721, PATIENCE PRYOR, of Greenland.

DORCAS HAYNES, m. 7 Dec. 1732, WILLIAM BABB, of Portsmouth.

ELIZABETH HAYNES, m. 27 Apr. 1740, SIMON LEVERITT, of parish of Santua, Isle of Jersey (*Register*, vol. 27, p. 8).

HEARD

JOSEPH HEARD, of Dover, m. 9 Aug. 1722, REBECCA RICHARDS.

HEPWORTH

MARY HEPWORTH, of Portsmouth, m. Sept. 1716, JOSHUA REMICK, of Kittery, Me. (*Register*, vol. 23, p. 393).

MARY HEPWORTH, of Portsmouth, m. 31 Oct. 1717, WILLIAM GAMMON, of Kittery, Me. (*Register*, vol. 23, p. 394).

MARY HEPWORTH, formerly of Ireland, m. 20 July 1718, JOHN ABBOTT, of Portsmouth (*Register*, vol. 23, p. 395).

MARY HEPWORTH, m. May 1723, JOHN WOODMAN, of Kittery (Stackpole's *Kittery*, p. 805)

HILL

SAMUEL HILL, of Kittery, Me., m. 22 Nov. 1716, MARY NELSON.

ELIZABETH HILL, dau. of Samuel and Mary, bapt. 3 Sept. 1721.

SAMUEL HILL, son of Samuel and Mary, bapt. 3 Sept. 1721.

SUSANNA HILL, wid. of Joseph^2 (John^1) (Stackpole's *Kittery*, p. 516), m. 2 Jan. 1724, JOHN LYSSEN, both of Kittery.

MARY HILL, m. 10 Sept. 1740, SELATHIEL DENMORE, both of Durham.

JONATHAN^4 HILL (Samuel^3, Nathaniel^2, Valentine^1) (Stackpole's *Durham*, vol. 2, p. 210), of Durham, m. 24 Mar. 1757, MARY KNIGHT.

JOHN HILL, m. 17 June 1766, LUCY CHICK, both of Kittery, Me.

HILLARD

NICHOLAS HILLARD, of Portsmouth, m. 16 Dec. 1718, ELIZABETH HOYT, wid. of William, of Newington (*Register*, vol. 23, p. 395).

CHARLES HOYT HILLARD, son of Elizabeth, bapt. 18 Aug. 1728.

ELIZABETH HILLARD, m. 2 Nov. 1732, JOHN^1 DAM (1), *q.v.*

HODGDON

1. ALEXANDER^3 HODGDON (Jeremiah^2, Nicholas^1) (*Hodsdon-Hodgdon Families*, p. 22), of Newington, m. JANE^2 SHACKFORD (1-vi), dau. of William^1, and Deborah^2 (Trickey), *q.v.*
    Children, born at Newington (*Hodsdon-Hodgdon Families, loc. cit.*):
3   i. ALEXANDER^4
4   ii. JOSEPH
    iii. JEREMIAH, of Newington and Falmouth, Me., 1732, m. 16 Apr. 1721, SARAH DRAKE.
        Children, the first one baptized at Newington, the others at Falmouth, Me.

(*Hodsdon-Hodgdon Families*, p. 37):
1) Sarah[5], bapt. 3 Oct. 1731.
2) James, bapt. 20 Aug. 1732.
3) Benjamin, bapt. 20 Aug. 1732.
4) Elizabeth, bapt. 20 Aug. 1732.
5) Seth, bapt. 17 Sept. 1732.
6) Ann, bapt. 1734.
7) Jeremiah, bapt. 1737.
8) Mary, bapt. 1740.

iv. JOHN

v. BENJAMIN, of Boston, m. there 30 Oct. 1738, REBECCA MARSHALL.

vi. ANN, m. ? ZACHARIAH[4] EMERY, son of Daniel[3] and Margaret (Gowen) (Stackpole's *Kittery*, p. 368), of Kittery, Me., b. 12 Mar. 1704/5.

vii. ELIZABETH, bapt. at Newington, 17 Oct. 1716.

2. JOHN[3] HODGDON (Jeremiah[2], Nicholas[1]), of Newington, m. MARY BABB, dau. of Sampson, b. at Portsmouth.

The will of Sampson Babb, of Portsmouth, dated 5 Feb. 1736, proved 30 May 1739, mentions "my daughter, Mary Hodgdon" (*N.H. State Pap.*, vol. 32, p. 564).

Children (*Hodsdon-Hodgdon Families*, p. 23):

    i. JEREMIAH[4]

6   ii. JOHN

3. ALEXANDER[4] HODGDON (Alexander[3], Jeremiah[2], Nicholas[1]), of Newington and Rochester, 1753, m. at Greenland, 9 July 1727, MARY[3] (SHACKFORD) FURBER (1-vii), dau. of Samuel[2] and Abigail (Richards), and wid. of Richard[4] (6), *q.v.*

The will of Samuel Shackford, proved 4 Mar. 1730/1 mentions his daughter, Mary Hodgdon (*N.H. State Pap.*, vol. 32, p. 405).

Children, baptized at Newington:

    i. ELEAZER[5], bapt. 19 Sept. 1731, of Dover.

    ii. SAMUEL, bapt. 19 Sept. 1731.

    iii. ANN, bapt. 25 June 1732.

    iv. ABIGAIL, bapt. 14 Apr. 1734, m. 19 Aug. 1770, as his second wife, CHRISTOPHER[4] HUNTRESS (3-i), son of Christopher[3] and Mary (Chick), *q.v.*

    v. REBECCA, bapt. 30 Nov. 1735.

    vi. Capt. ALEXANDER, bapt. 19 Oct. 1740 d. 26 Apr. 1732 (*Register*, vol. 80, p. 307), m. his cousin, LYDIA[4] SHACKFORD (6-ii), dau. of Joshua[3] and Lydia (Lovejoy), *q.v.*

Children, baptized at Rochester:

1) A son (Joshua?), bapt. 26 July 1767.
2) Theodore, bapt. 13 Mar. 1774.
3) Joseph, of Rochester, bapt. 3 Nov. 1776, d. 24 Nov. 1846 (*Register*, vol. 80, p. 307), m. (1) Mary L. -----, b. 1768, d. 10 Aug. 1800 (*ibid.*), m. (2) Abigail -----, b. 1779, d. 20 Jan. 1845 (*ibid.*).
4) John, bapt. 11 July 1779.
5) Nathaniel, bapt. 20 May 1781.

4. JOSEPH[4] HODGDON (Alexander[3], Jeremiah[2], Nicholas[1]), of Newington, m. PATIENCE -----.

Children, baptized at Newington:
  i. A CHILD[5], bapt. 26 June 1720.
  ii. PATIENCE, bapt. 26 June 1720, d. in infancy.
  iii. A CHILD, bapt. 1722.
  iv. ALEXANDER, bapt. 30 Oct. 1723.
  v. JOHN, bapt. 10 July 1727.
  vi. PATIENCE, bapt. 10 July 1727.
  vii. LYDIA, bapt. 19 Dec. 1736.
  viii. ABIGAIL, bapt. 19 Dec. 1736, m. ? WILLIAM[4] HARN, son of Eleazer[3] and Elizabeth (Carr) (*Register*, vol. 26, p. 391), of Vt., b. at Rochester.

5. JOHN[4] HODGDON (Alexander[3], Jeremiah[2], Nicholas[1]), of Newington, m. MARY -----.

Children, baptized at Newington:
  i. MARY[5], bapt. 19 June 1727.
  ii. MEHITABLE, bapt. 19 June 1727.
  iii. ELIZABETH, bapt. 19 June 1727, m. 7 Aug. 1755, DANIEL BICKFORD, of Portsmouth.
  iv. JOHN, bapt. 3 Mar. 1728.

6. JOHN[4] HODGDON (John[3], Jeremiah[2], Nicholas[1]), of Newington, m. 30 Jan. 1729, MARY DECKER, dau. of John and Sarah, *q.v.*

Children, baptized at Newington:
  i. JANE[5], bapt. 22 Feb. 1730, m. PITMAN[2] COOLBROTH (3), son of George[1] and Mary, *q.v.*
  ii. JOHN, bapt. 16 Sept. 1733, d. in infancy.
  iii. A CHILD, bapt. 7 Dec. 1735.
  iv. TEMPERENCE, bapt. 3 Nov. 1739.
7 v. CHARLES, bapt. 18 Oct. 1741.
  vi. HANNAH, bapt. 12 Feb. 1743/4.
8 vii. JOHN, bapt. 5 Jan. 1745/6.
9 viii. BENJAMIN, bapt. 20 May 1750.

  ix. SARAH, bapt. 22 Dec. 1751, m. 2 Sept. 1773, STEPHEN⁴ AYRES (14-x), son of Thomas³, *q.v.*
10 x. JOSEPH, bapt. 19 June 1755.

  7. Deac. CHARLES⁵ HODGDON (John⁴⁻³, Jeremiah², Nicholas¹), of Newington and Barnstead, 1768, member of the legislature, bapt. 18 Oct. 1741, d. 1815, m. 12 Dec. 1764, HANNAH DENNETT.
  Children, baptized at Newington:
   i. ELIZABETH⁶, bapt. 10 Aug. 1766.
   ii. BENJAMIN, of Newington, m. 25 Nov. 1771, NANCY SAYWARD, b. at Dover *q.v.* 1775, d. 24 Oct. 1838, *aet.* 63 (*Register*, vol. 73, p. 198).
   iii. OLIVE⁺, bapt. 10 Mar. 1771, m. NATHANIEL⁶ ADAMS (2-x), son of Dr. Joseph⁵ and Johanna (Gilman), *q.v.*
   iv. CHARLES, bapt. 22 Aug. 1773, of Barnstead, lawyer, town clerk 1800-5, member of the Legislature, m. ELIZABETH⁷ ADAMS (5-v), dau. of Ezekiel Gilman⁶ and Mary (Hoyt), *q.v.*
   v. NANCY, bapt. 10 Mar. 1776.

  8. JOHN⁵ HODGDON (John⁴⁻³, Jeremiah², Nicholas¹), of Newington, bapt. 5 Jan. 1745/6, m. 25 Feb. 1773, TEMPERENCE⁵ PICKERING (11-i), dau. of Nicholas⁴ and Hannah (Bickford), *q.v.*
  Children, baptized at Newington:
   i. ELIZABETH⁶, bapt. 16 Jan. 1774.
   ii. MARY, 24 Sept. 1775, m. ? at Greenland, 18 Nov. 1798, WILLIAM⁴ LANG, son of Lieut. Thomas³ and Mary (Weeks) (*John Lang Family*, no. 36), of Acton, farmer, b. at Greenland, 2 Feb. 1776 (town rec.), d. 13 June 1855.
   Only child, born at Acton:
    1) John⁷, of Acton, farmer, b. 20 Feb. 1800, d. 27 Nov. 1852, m. 17 May 1825, Mary J. Webb, dau. of Henry and Mary (Colbath), b. at Portsmouth, 22 Nov. 1804, d. 25 June 1884.
   iii. JEREMIAH, bapt. 9 Nov. 1777.
   iv. JOHN, bapt. 8 Aug. 1779.
   v. SARAH, bapt. 15 Apr. 1781.
   vi. LOIS, bapt. 9 June 1782.

  9. BENJAMIN⁵ HODGDON (John⁴⁻³, Jeremiah², Nicholas¹), of Newington and Barnstead, bapt. 20 May 1750, town clerk, 1787-89, m. 8 Apr. 1776,

---

+Lang Ms. - says she married Thomas⁴ Lang, Dec. 1786.

ROSAMOND⁵ COLMAN (2-iv), dau. of Phineas⁴ and Abigail (Huntress), *q.v.*
Children, baptized at Newington:
  i. LYDIA⁶, bapt. 23 Mar. 1772.
  ii. EPHRAIM, bapt. 21 Mar. 1779.
  iii. BENJAMIN, 17 June 1781.
  iv. SARAH AYRES (*Henry Adams Family*, p. 415), m. (1) 29 Apr. 1806, JOHN⁷ ADAMS (5-vi), son of Ezekiel Gilman⁶ and Mary (Hoyt), *q.v.* m. (2) N. D. STOODLEY.

10. JOSEPH⁵ HODGDON (John⁴⁻³, Jeremiah², Nicholas¹), of Newington, bapt. 29 June 1755, m. at Greenland, 13 Nov. 1775 (town rec.), SARAH⁵ PEVERLY, dau. of George⁴ and Ann, b. at Portsmouth, 21 July 1754.
Children, born at Newington (town rec.):
  i. ROBERT PEVERLY, b. 26 Nov. 1780.
  ii. JOHN, b. 20 Feb. 1782.
  iii. MARY, b. 3 May 1787.
  iv. JOSEPH, b. 27 Feb. 1790.
  v. SARAH, b. 31 Aug. 1792.

HODGDON (unconnected)

SARAH HODGDON, m. 25 Feb. 1725, JOHN BICKFORD.

ANN HODGDON, m. 2 Feb. 1735, BENJAMIN FOSS, both of Rochester.

SAMUEL HODGDON, son of Mary, bapt. 25 July 1736.

ANN HODGDON, dau. of Elizabeth, bapt. 21 June 1747.

ELIZABETH HODGDON, m. 14 Aug. 1754, GEORGE WARREN, of Portsmouth.

ELIZABETH HODGDON, m. 7 Aug. 1755, DANIEL BICKFORD, both of Portsmouth.

AARON HODGDON, gr. son of John and Mary, bapt. 3 July 1757.

TEMPERENCE HODGDON, m. 17 Oct. 1764, JOHN BOYNTON, of Wiscasset.

ABIGAIL HODGDON, of Berwick, m. 9 Aug. 1770, CHRISTOPHER BENSON.

BENJAMIN HODGDON, m. 25 Feb. 1771, HANNAH SAYWARD, both of Dover.

HANNAH HODGDON, dau. of Hannah, bapt. 30 May 1773.

AARON HODGDON, m. 5 Jan. 1775, MARY DENNETT, both of Portsmouth.

SALLY HODGDON, wife of C. HODGDON, d. 15 July 1824 (*Register*, vol. 73, p. 196).

ZERVIAH P. HODGDON, wife of CHARLES, d. 6 Apr. 1846, *aet.* 64 (*id.*, p. 200).

HODGKINS

SARAH HODGKINS, m. 12 May 1747, ISSACHAR DAM.

HOLDEN

WILLIAM HOLDEN, m. 20 Dec. 1725, ELIZABETH WALKER.

ELIZABETH HOLDEN, dau. of William, bapt. 26 Nov. 1727.

WILLIAM HOLDEN, bapt. 25 Feb. 1728.

HONEYWELL

JEMIMA HONEYWELL, covenant, 7 Apr. 1745.

HORN

MOSES HORN, of Dover, m. 11 Oct. 1764, HANNAH ROLLINS, of Rochester.

HOYT

1. **WILLIAM³ HOYT** (Thomas², John¹) (*Hoyt-Haight-Hight Families*, pp. 28, 113), of Kittery, Me., b. at Amesbury, Mass., 8 Apr. 1676, m. 10 Mar. 1701/2 (*Pike's Journal*), ELIZABETH (HALEY) NELSON, dau. of Andrew and Deborah (Wilson) (Stackpole's *Kittery*, p. 483) and wid. of John, b. at York, Me., 1666, who

m. (3) 16 Dec. 1718, NICHOLAS HILLIARD, of Portsmouth and (4) 2 Nov. 1732, Deac. JOHN³ DAM (1), *q.v.*, and d. in Feb. 1765, *aet.* 99 yrs. (*N.H. Gazette*, of 8 Mar. 1765).

    Children, born at Kittery, Me. (Hoyt's *Salisbury*, p. 757):

      i. SARAH⁴, , m. 18 May 1725, SAMUEL⁴ NUTTER (10), son of Henry³ and Mary² (Shackford), *q.v.*

      ii. ABIGAIL, m. 31 Aug. 1730, GEORGE BOYD, of Boston.

3   iii. JOHN

      iv. ELIZABETH, m. 28 Nov. 1734, GEORGE² COOLBROTH (1-i), son of George¹ and Mary, *q.v.*

      v. WILLIAM⁺, of Berwick, Me., m. 24 Oct. 1734, ELIZABETH WALTON.

      vi. CHARLES⁺, of Portsmouth.

2. ISRAEL³ HOYT (Thomas², John¹), (*Hoyt-Haight-Hight Families*, pp. 29, 118), of Portsmouth, b. 16 July 1678, m. GRACE TAPRILL, dau. of Robert.

    Children, baptized at Newington:

      i. DOROTHY⁴, bapt. 14, June 1719, m. at Greenland, 29 Apr. 1725 (*Register*, vol. 24, p. 357), SAMPSON BABB, of Portsmouth.

      ii. ISRAEL, bapt. 14 June 1719.

        Child, baptized at Newington:

          1) Esther⁵, bapt. 30 Mar. 1740.

      iii. JOHN, bapt. 14 June 1719, m. 13 Nov. 1732, LETTICE HASTY.

        Child, baptized at Newington:

          1) Elizabeth⁵, bapt. 9 May 1736.

      iv. ABISHA, bapt. 14 Nov. 1719, m. 15 June 1739, JOEL WHITMORE, of Portsmouth.

      v. FRANCES, bapt. 14 June 1719.

3. JOHN⁴ HOYT (William³, Thomas², John¹), of Newington, m. 10 Dec. 1728 (*Register*, vol. 24, p. 360), LYDIA MILLER, dau. of Benjamin.

The will of Benjamin Miller, proved 30 May 1750, mentions his daughter, Lydia Hoyt (*N.H. State Pap.*, vol. 33, p. 423).

    Children, born at Newington:

      i. SARAH⁵, bapt. 26 Oct. 1729.

      ii. ELIZABETH, bapt. 7 Oct. 1733, d. in infancy.

      iii. MARY, bapt. 2 Dec. 1733, d. in infancy.

4   iv. JOHN, bapt. 14 Sept. 1735.

      v. ELIZABETH, bapt. 1 Jan. 1738.

+Statement, 1923, of Jackson M. Hoyt, of Newington.

                vi. WILLIAM, bapt. 10 Feb. 1739/40, d. in infancy.
5   vii. WILLIAM, bapt. 3 Aug. 1740.
6   viii. BENJAMIN, bapt. 2 Apr. 1742.
7   ix. DENNIS, bapt. 13 May 1744.
                 x. MARY, bapt. 8 May 1748, d. May 1798, m. 24 Dec. 1771, EZEKIEL GILMAN⁶ ADAMS (5), son of Dr. Joseph⁴ and Johanna (Gilman), *q.v.*.
8   xi. ENOCH, bapt. 10 June 1750.
9   xii. JOSEPH, bapt. 30 Dec. 1753.

4. JOHN⁵ HOYT (John⁴, William³, Thomas², John¹), of Newington, bapt. 14 Sept. 1837, m. 26 Sept. 1757, SARAH⁵ FURBER (5-v), dau. of Moses⁴ and Anna (Bickford) (Walker), *q.v.*, who m. (2) JONATHAN⁴ TRICKEY (10) (*Register*, vol. 73, p. 206).

Children, born at Newington (*ibid.*):
   i. LYDIA⁶, b. 12 Feb. 1758, d. 18 Dec. 1836 (*id.*, p. 198), m. 20 Apr. 1779, EBENEZER⁶ ADAMS (7), son of Joseph⁵ and Johanna (Gilman), *q.v.*
   ii. HANSON, m. MARY LORD.
   iii. WILLIAM, of Newington, b. 1762, d. 2 Aug. 1832, *aet.* 72 (*Register*, vol. 73, p. 197), m. CHARLOTTE PICKERING.
   iv. ANNA (NANCY), b. 1765, d. 16 Nov. 1843 (*Register*, vol. 73, p. 199), m. 16 Apr. 1798, JAMES⁵ PICKERING (9-ii), son of Winthrop⁴ and Phebe (Nutter), *q.v.*

6. BENJAMIN⁵ HOYT (John⁴, William³, Thomas², John¹, of Rochester, bapt. 2 Apr. 1742, m. 16 Dec. 1766, SARAH⁴ DOWNING, dau.? of John³ and Patience (Ham).

7. Capt. DENNIS⁵ HOYT (John⁴, William³, Thomas², John¹), of Newington, bapt. 13 May 1744, d. 22 Apr. 1818, m. 1 Apr. 1768, ELIZABETH⁴ FABIAN (4-v), dau. of Samuel³ and Elizabeth⁴ (Huntress), *q.v.*

Children, born at Newington:
   i. JOHN⁶, of Vt., bapt. 19 Feb. 1769, m. ----- NUTTER.
   ii. MARY PICKERING, bapt. 1 July 1770.
   iii. SAMUEL FABIAN, of Newington, b. 5 Aug. 1772, bapt. 22 Aug. 1772, d. 23 Feb. 1843, m. 24 May 1801, NANCY⁷ ADAMS (5-iii), dau. of Ezekiel Gilman⁶ and Mary (Hoyt), *q.v.*
   iv. GEORGE, bapt. 6 Nov. 1774.
   v. ELIZABETH, bapt. 18 Aug. 1776, m. 22 May 1794, THOMAS HENDERSON, of Dover.
   vi. LYDIA, bapt. 17 May 1778, d. 10 Sept. 1839, m. JOHN⁴ WINKLEY, son of John³ (Stackpole's *Kittery*, p. 803), of Kittery, Me, b. at Kittery, 1757, d. 18 May 1813.

8. ENOCH⁵ HOYT (John⁴, William³, Thomas², John¹), of Rochester, bapt. 10 June 1750, m. 17 July 1771, ELIZABETH⁵ COLMAN (4-iii), dau. of Phineas⁴ and Abigail (Huntress), *q.v.*

9. JOSEPH⁵ HOYT (John⁴, William³, Thomas², John¹), of Newington, Rochester, and Athens, Me., 1800, bapt. 30 Dec. 1753, m. 13 Sept. 1776, MARY⁵ AYRES, dau.? of Nathaniel⁴ and Ruth (Shapleigh), *q.v.*

Children, born at Newington:
  i. WILLIAM⁶, bapt. 6 Sept. 1778.
  ii. FRANCES, bapt. 31 Jan. 1779.
  iii. POLLY AYRES, bapt. 9 Sept. 1781.
  iv. LYDIA MILLER, bapt. 12 Sept. 1784.
  v. JOSEPH, bapt. 11 July 1787.

HOYT (unconnected)

MARY HOYT, of Portsmouth, m. 1 Sept. 1768, THEODORE CARLETON, of Exeter.

DANIEL HOYT, m. 27 Jan. 1770, ELIZABETH BROWN, of Hampton.

HANNAH HOYT, m. 28 June 1770, MOSES FURBER.

EUNICE HOYT, of Portsmouth, m. 25 Jan. 1774, THOMAS DONALD.

JOHN HOYT, m. 1 Nov. 1826, ELIZABETH DAME (*Register*, vol. 77, p. 191).

HUNTRESS

1. SAMUEL² HUNTRESS (George¹) (*N.H. Gen. Rec.*, vol. 6, p. 177), of Newington, b. 1687, d. 28 Apr. 1758 (*Thompson's Landmarks*, p. 37), m. (1) ABIGAIL HAM, b. at Portsmouth, m. (2) MARY -----.

Children, baptized at Newington:
4 i. WILLIAM³, bapt. 15 Sept. 1717.
  ii. SAMUEL, of Newington, joiner, bapt. 15 Sept. 1717, m. 31 Jan. 1742, MARY⁴ COLMAN (1-iii), dau. of Eleazer³ and Anna (Nutter), *q.v.* Administration on his estate 5 Aug. 1773, to Solomon Huntress, of Newmarket (*Rockingham Probate*). The will of Samuel² Huntress, of 1758, mentions two sons then living of Samuel³ Huntress, then dead.
  Children, born at Newington:

1) Solomon[4], of Canterbury and Strafford, Vt., b. 16 Jan. 1749, m. at Newmarket, 17 Mar. 1771 (town rec.), Lucy[5] Burleigh, dau. of Jacob[4] and Abigail (*Burleigh Family*, p. 21), b. at Newmarket, 29 July 1754, d. 23 Apr. 1825.

iii. ABIGAIL, bapt. 15 Sept. 1717, m. 22 Apr. 1739, PHINEAS[4] COLMAN (2), son of Eleazer[3] and Anna (Nutter), *q.v.*

iv. GEORGE, of Portsmouth, bapt. 2 Nov. 1718, m. 26 May 1743, MARY[4] RING, dau. of Deac. Seth and Elizabeth (Libby), *q.v.*

Children, baptized in South Church, Portsmouth:
1) Mary[4], bapt. 10 June 1744.
2) Hannah, bapt. 27 July 1746.

v. SOLOMON, bapt. 11 Dec. 1720.

vi. ELIZABETH, bapt. 7 Apr. 1723, m. as his second wife, 12 Dec. 1745, SAMUEL[3] FABIAN (2), son of John[2] and Mary[3] (Pickering), *q.v.*

vii. PAUL, bapt. 4 June 1727.

viii. JOSEPH, bapt. 28 Apr. 1734.

Samuel's grave stone on the Upper Huntress (cemetery)? owned 1892 by Miss Mary Huntress.

2. JOHN[2] HUNTRESS (George[1]), of Newington, yeoman, b. about 1690, m. MARY -----.

His will dated 11 July 1746, proved 29 May 1751 (*N.H. State Pap.*, vol. 33, p. 387) mentions his wife, Mary, and all his children.

Children, baptized at Newington:
i. HANNAH[3], bapt. 9 Dec. 1716.

ii. JOHN, bapt. 2 Nov. 1718.

iii. TAMSEN, bapt. 11 Dec. 1720, m. 1 Feb. 1741, JOHN PARSHLEY, of Portsmouth.

iv. MARY, bapt. 21 Apr. 1723, m. 7 June 1741, MICHAEL MARTIN, of Portsmouth.

Child, baptized at Newington:
1) William[4], bapt. 20 Dec. 1741.

v. HEPWORTH, bapt. 13 Dec. 1724.

5 vi. JONATHAN, bapt. 19 Mar. 1727.

vii. DEBORAH, bapt. 17 Dec. 1732.

3. CHRISTOPHER[3] HUNTRESS (George[2-1]), of Newington, mason, b. about 1703, d. 6 Aug. 1782, m. 1724, MARY[3] CHICK, dau. of Richard[2] and Martha (Lord) (Stackpole's *Kittery*, p. 319), b. at Kittery, Me., about 1703.

His will dated 1 Oct. 1763, proved 31 Oct. 1782, mentions all the following children but Martha, David, and Mark; and his granddaughter, Martha Lord (*Rockingham Probate*).

Children, baptized at Newington:

    i. CHRISTOPHER[4], bapt. 13 Oct. 1728, m. (1) 22 Sept. 1752, ELIZABETH PEARSON, b. at ?Hampton, m. (2) 19 Aug. 1770, ABIGAIL[5] HODGDON (3-iv), dau. of Alexander[4] and Mary (Shackford) (Furber), *q.v.*

    ii. MARTHA, bapt. 13 Oct. 1728, m. 28 Sept. 1750, JOSEPH LORD, of Berwick, Me.

    iii. DARLING, of Berwick, Me., bapt. 19 Apr. 1730, m. 6 Dec. 1751 (*Register*, vol. 55, p. 313), LOVE[3] EARL, dau. of Etherington[2] and Hannah (Goodwin) (Stackpole's *Kittery*, p. 513).

    Children, baptized at Newington:

      1) Mary[5], bapt. 12 Nov. 1752.

      2) Hannah, bapt. 26 May 1754.

    iv. MARY, bapt. 7 May 1732, m. 12 Apr. 1753, SAMUEL[4] ROLLINS (11), son of Samuel[3] and Alice (Davie), *q.v.*

    v. GEORGE, bapt. 3 Feb. 1734.

    vi. DAVID, bapt. 13 Mar. 1737, not mentioned in the will.

6   vii. NATHAN, b. about 1739.

    viii. NOAH, bapt. 20 Feb. 1742/3, m. ABIGAIL[5] PICKERING (6-ix), dau. of John and ? Mary (Nutter), *q.v.*

    ix. ELIZABETH, bapt. 18 Mar. 1743/4, m. ----- STEVENS.

    x. MARK, bapt. 20 Feb. 1743/4 (*Register*, vol. 25, p. 286).

4. WILLIAM[3] HUNTRESS (Samuel[2], George[1]), of Newington, d. 1786, m. 15 Mar. 1747, SUSANNA[5] DOWNING (9-ii), dau. of Joshua[4] and Susanna (Dennett), *q.v.*

Children, baptized at Newington:

    i. LYDIA[4], bapt. 8 May 1748, m. 9 Nov. 1774, JONATHAN[5] SWETT, son of Jonathan[4] and Jane (Rowe), of Windsor, b. at Hampton Falls, 27 Aug. 1748.

    ii. SAMUEL, bapt. 10 June 1750.

    iii. JOSHUA, bapt. 21 June 1752.

    iv. ELIZABETH (twin), bapt. 21 Aug. 1757, m. 21 Oct. 1779, JOEL[6] LEIGHTON (4-vi), son of Thomas[5] and Mary (Smithson), *q.v.*

    v. LOIS DOWNING (twin), bapt. 21 Aug. 1757, *non compos* 1786 (*Rockingham Probate*).

5. JONATHAN[3] HUNTRESS (John[2], George[1]), of Newington, m. 5 Feb. 1747, MARY[3] WALKER (1-iii), dau. of Edward[2] and Deliverance (Gaskin), *q.v.*

Children, baptized at Newington:

i. ENOCH⁴, bapt. 3 Nov. 1747, m. DEBORAH⁵ NUTTER (7-vi), dau. of Samuel⁴ and Mary (Downing), *q.v.*
   Child, baptized at Newington:
   1) George⁵, bapt. 23 Dec. 1770.
ii. OLIVE, bapt. 18 June 1749.
iii. JONATHAN, bapt. 18 Aug. 1751.
iv. GIDEON, bapt. 17 Feb. 1754.
v. DEBORAH, bapt. 16 May 1756.
vi. SETH, of Portsmouth, bapt. 27 May 1759, m. ? at Portsmouth, 2 Sept. 1784, SARAH⁵ DAME (6-v), dau. of Eliphalet and Abigail⁴ (Nutter), *q.v.*
vii. NOAH, bapt. 4 Oct. 1761.
viii. DANIEL, bapt. 21 Aug. 1768 (bapt. as son of John and Mary).
ix. BENJAMIN, bapt. 16 Aug. 1772.

6. NATHAN⁴ HUNTRESS (Christopher³, George²⁻¹), of Newington and Parsonsfield, Me., 1799, b. about 1739, m. (1) before 24 Dec. 1769, when she renewed her covenant, SUSANNA -----, m. ? (2) SUSANNA -----, who as his "present wife" renewed her covenant, 16 June 1771.
   Children, baptized at Newington:
   i. MARY⁵, bapt. 16 June 1771.
   ii. JOSEPH CHICK, bapt. 16 June 1771.
   iii. SARAH, bapt. 6 June 1773.
   iv. JOHN FABIAN, bapt. 16 Nov. 1779.
   v. HANNAH, bapt. 16 Nov. 1779.
   vi. A CHILD, bapt. 20 Nov. 1785.

HUSSEY

RICHARD HUSSEY, m. 16 May 1716, HANNAH FIELD.

JACKSON

THOMAS JACKSON, of Casco Bay, m. 12 Apr. 1734, MARY RICHARDS.

BENJAMIN JACKSON, son of Thomas, bapt. 16 Mar. 1735.

BETHIAH JACKSON, dau. of Thomas and Mary, bapt. 22 May 1737.

JACOBS

DOROTHY JACOBS, m. 23 May 1773, JOHN TUTTLE, both of Durham.

JANVRIN

1. **JOHN¹ JANVRIN**, of Portsmouth, mariner, son of Jean and Elizabeth (Le Couteur) (Hurd's *Rockingham*, p. 346), b. at St. Hellier, Island of Jersey, d. 1717, m. 12 Sept. 1706 (*N.H. Gen. Rec.*, vol. 4, p. 12), ELIZABETH² KNIGHT (i-iv), dau. of John and Bridget (Sloper) (Stackpole's *Durham*, vol. 2, p. 244), *q.v.*

Administration on his estate 13 Oct. 1720 to his widow, Elizabeth (*N.H. State Pap.*, vol. 32, p. 125).

Children, baptized at Portsmouth:

2   i. JOHN², b. 8 July 1707, bapt. 2 Oct. 1709 (*N.H. Gen. Rec.*, vol. 4, p. 55).

    ii. GEORGE, of Portsmouth, bapt. 19 July 1713 (*N.H. Gen. Rec.*, vol. 4, p. 97), d. *s.v.p.* m. 10 Nov. 1738 (*Register*, vol. 26, p. 379), ELIZABETH⁴ MENDUM, dau. of Nathaniel³ and Frances (Stackpole's *Kittery*, p. 606). (ABIGAIL PICKERING???)

    Child, baptized at Portsmouth:

    1) Ebenezer³, bapt. 7 Apr. 1754 (*N.H. Gen. Rec.*, vol. 5, p. 129), d. unm.

    iii. MARY, mentioned in the will of John¹ Knight, communion, 5 Nov. 1738, m. 19 May 1743 as his second wife, THOMAS³ PICKERING (5), son of Thomas² and Mary, *q.v.*

    iv. ELIZABETH, d. unm.

Widow JANVRIN, d. 16 Feb. 1830, *aet.* 100 yrs. (*Register*, vol. 73, p. 197).

2. **JOHN² JANVRIN** (John¹), of Newington, Hampton Falls, 1756, and Seabrook, teacher, farmer, b. 8 July 1707, d. 7 Oct. 1780, m. 9 Oct. 1751, ELIZABETH STICKNEY (*Piscataqua Pioneers*, p. 118), dau. of Moses, b. at Newburyport ?, 12 Jan. 1722, d. 12 Apr. 1809.

His will dated 5 Nov. 1777, proved 25 Oct. 1780, names his wife, Elizabeth, and children as below. The inventory was $61,000 including silver plate $650 (*Rockingham Probate* files).

Children, the first two baptized at Newington:

3   i. JOHN³, bapt. 3 Feb. 1754.
4   ii. WILLIAM, bapt. 21 Aug. 1755.
5   iii. JAMES
6   iv. GEORGE, b. 26 Mar. 1762.
    v. ELIZABETH

3. **JOHN³ JANVRIN** (John², John¹), of Portsmouth and Seabrook, bapt. 3 Feb. 1754, m. (1) 5 May 1772, CATHERINE⁵ LANG, dau. of Daniel⁴ and Martha⁴ (Moses) (*Robert Lang Family*, 23-ii), *q.v.*, m. (2) 1784, ELIZABETH⁶ ADAMS (2-vii), dau. of Dr. Joseph⁵ and Joanna (Gilman), *q.v.* (Jewett's *Barnstead*, p. 151)

His will dated 23 Oct. 1837, proved 15 Nov. 1837, names his children as below and grandchildren: John Janvrin, Matilda Locke, Sarah Chase, Mary Jane Evans, Belinda Peeling, Dennis Janvrin, Olive Blackburn, Elizabeth A. Walton, John William Walton, and Joshua Janvrin (*Rockingham Probate* files).

Children:
    i. WILLIAM^4, (residuary legatee)
    ii. OLIVE, m. ----- EATON.
    iii. JOSEPH ADAMS, of Seabrook, master mariner, and Lowell, Mass., merchant.

4. WILLIAM^3 JANVRIN (John$^{2\text{-}1}$), of Seabrook, bapt. 21 Aug. 1755, m. at Gilmanton, 24 Nov. 1796 (town rec.), ABIGAIL^6 ADAMS (2-viii), dau. of Dr. Joseph and Joanna (Gilman), *q.v.* (Jewett's *Barnstead*, p. 151).

JOS. ADAMS JANVRIN, m. 14 Nov. 1822, LYDIA ANN COLMAN, both of Exeter, viz.

5. JAMES^3 JANVRIN (John$^{2\text{-}1}$), of Seabrook, m. at Hampton Falls, 15 Mar. 1786, POLLY CHASE.

6. GEORGE^3 JANVRIN (John$^{2\text{-}1}$), of Seabrook, b. 6 Mar. 1762, m. 4 June 1789, DOROTHY LOVERING.

Children, born at Seabrook (town rec.):
    i. SARAH^4, b. 27 Apr. 1790.
    ii. DOROTHY, b. 30 Apr. 1792.
    iii. GEORGE, b. 9 Nov. 1794.
    iv. LORANA, b. 23 Jan. 1797.
    v. RUTH LAMPREY, b. 8 Dec. 1798.
    vi. FRANCES, b. 26 Sept. 1801.
    vii. JEFFERSON, b. 5 May 1803.
    viii. MARINDA, b. 19 Mar. 1805.
    ix. ELIZA, b. 25 July 1808.

JAQUES

DEBORAH JAQUES, m. 24 Sept. 1724, PAUL WENTWORTH, of Kittery, Me.

JENKINS

WILLIAM JENKINS, of Greenland, m. 9 Nov. 1752, MARY FERNALD, of Portsmouth.

JOSEPH² JENKINS (Roland¹) (Stackpole's *Kittery*, p. 553), m. 15 Dec. 1771, KATHARINE WOODMAN, of Kittery.

JOHNSON

SARAH JOHNSON, dau. of Capt. James, of Greenland, m. 15 Feb. 1749, THOMAS⁴ SHERMAN, son of Deac. James³ and Margaret (Rowe), of Greenland (*Register*, vol. 59, p. 60).

JONES

MARTHA⁴ JONES (Stephen³) (Stackpole's *Durham*, vol. 2, p. 233), of Durham, m. 29 June 1769, NATHANIEL MESERVY.

ELIZABETH BARKER JONES, dau. of Sarah, bapt. 23 Nov. 1777.

STEPHEN JONES, m. 3 July 1782, ALICE BICKFORD.

KENNARD

RUTH³ KENNARD (Michael²) (Stackpole's *Kittery*, p. 565), m. 15 July 1749, JAMES TUCKER, both of Kittery.

ELIZABETH⁴ KENNARD (Edward³) (Stackpole's *Kittery*, p. 563), m. 4 Dec. 1764, ROBERT STAPLES.

WILLIAM⁴ KENNARD (Michael³) (Stackpole's *Kittery*, p. 566), m. 24 Apr. 1773, HANNAH SARGENT, both of Kittery.

DIAMOND⁴ KENNARD (Michael³) (Stackpole's *Kittery*, p. 562), m. 20 Jan. 1774, ELIZABETH CHANDLER, of Kittery.

KENT

RACHEL KENT, probably gr. dau. of John (Stackpole's *Durham*, vol. 2, p. 241), m. 4 May 1773, JAMES EDGERLY, both of Durham.

KNIGHT

1. JOHN¹ KNIGHT (*alias* Chevalier), of Portsmouth, merchant, b. 30 Aug. 1659, d. 11 May 1721, m. 29 Mar. 1684, BRIDGET SLOPER, dau. of Richard and

Mary (Sherburn) (Stackpole's *Durham*, vol. 2, p. 244), b. at Portsmouth.

His will dated 29 Nov. 1720, proved 7 June 1721, mentions his wife, Bridget; sons John, William, and Temple; daughters Elizabeth Adams and Mary Knight; and grandchildren John, Nicholas and Mary Knight (children of his son, John) and John and Mary Janvrin (children of his daughter, Mary (Knight) Janvrin) (*N.H. State Pap.*, vol. 3, p. 125).

Administration on the estate of Bridget Knight was granted 30 July 1740 to her son, Capt. John (*id.*, p. 790).

Children, born at Portsmouth:

    i. ELIZABETH[2], b. 8 July 1685 (*Piscataqua Pioneers*, p. 117), d. 10 Feb. 1757, m. (1) 12 Sept. 1706, JOHN[1] JANVRIN, *q.v.*, m. (2) 10 Oct. 1720 (*Register*, vol. 24, p. 14), Rev. JOSEPH[4] ADAMS, *q.v.*

2   ii. JOHN

    iii. WILLIAM, b. about 1700, m. 29 Nov. 1722, DEBORAH PENHALLOW, dau. of Samuel[1].

        Administration on his estate was granted 11 Jan. 1732/3 to his widow, Deborah (*N.H. State Pap.*, vol. 32, p. 463).

    iv. TEMPLE, d. unm. ?

        Administration on his estate was granted 27 Apr. 1741 to John Knight (*id.*, vol. 33, p. 52).

    v. MARY

2. Capt. JOHN[2] KNIGHT (John[1]), of Newington, representative, m. ELIZABETH HEARD, dau. of Tristram.

His will dated 8 Nov. 1765, proved 24 Jan. 1766, mentions his children as below.

Children, baptized at Newington:

    i. Ensign JOHN[3], of Durham, d. at Newington, 22 Feb. 1770 (*Register*, vol. 74, p. 127, *N.H. Gazette* of 2 Mar. 1770), m. (1) 14 Apr. 1743, PATIENCE[3] SMITH, dau. of Col. Samuel[2] and Hannah (Burnham) (Stackpole's *Durham*, vol. 2, p. 334), b. at Durham, 6 Apr. 1722, m. (2) 15 Mar. 1759, TEMPERENCE[4] PICKERING (5-vi), dau. of Thomas[3] and Mary (Downing), *q.v.*

3   ii. NICHOLAS

    iii. MARY, bapt. 5 May 1717, d. in infancy.

    iv. DANIEL, bapt. 24 Jan. 1720.

    v. BRIDGET, bapt. 1 Oct. 1721, m. 6 July 1740, JAMES[5] CHADBOURN, son of James[4] and Sarah (Hatch) (Downing) (Stackpole's *Kittery*, p. 313), of Kittery, Me., b. at Kittery, 23 May 1714.

    vi. ALICE, bapt. 20 Mar. 1723, m. THOMAS HATCH.

    vii. SUSANNA, bapt. 18 Feb. 1728.

    viii. MARY, bapt. 3 Aug. 1729, m. 24 Mar. 1757, JONATHAN[5] HILL, son of

Samuel[4] and Sarah (Thompson) (Stackpole's *Durham*, vol. 2, p. 210), of Durham, bapt. 28 Aug. 1726.
- ix. GEORGE, of Newington, bapt. 16 July 1732, m. (1) MARY -----, m. (2) SUSANNA[6] CHESLEY, dau. of George[5] and Sarah (Sampson) (Stackpole's *Durham*, vol. 2, p. 62), bapt. at Durham, 21 Mar. 1741.
- x. A DAUGHTER, bapt. 16 Oct. 1734.
- xi. DEBORAH, bapt. 16 Mar. 1735, m. 1752, NATHANIEL[3] ADAMS, son of Matthew[2] and Muriel (Cotton). Their son, Nathaniel, was the author of the *Annals of Portsmouth*.

3. NICHOLAS[3] KNIGHT (John[2-1]), of Newington, b. about 1715, m. 28 Nov. 1744, SARAH THOMPSON.

Children, baptized at Newington:
- i. WILLIAM[4], of Newington, bapt. 18 May 1746, m. ROSE -----.
  Children, baptized at Newington:
  1) Sarah[5], bapt. 18 June 1778.
  2) Mary, bapt. 18 June 1778.
- ii. CHARLES, bapt. 18 Dec. 1748.
- iii. SUSANNA, bapt. 14 Apr. 1751, m. 4 Mar. 1776, HUNKING[3] COOLBROTH (5), son of James[2] and Olive (Leighton), *q.v.*
- iv. NICHOLAS, bapt. 29 June 1755.

KNIGHT (unconnected)

NATHAN KNIGHT, was at Newington, 1713 (*Register*, vol. 58, p. 249).

Capt. WILLIAM KNIGHT, of Portsmouth, m. 27 Apr. 1774, in Boston, ANNA BORLAND, wid. of John (*N.H. Gazette* of 2 Mar. 1770).

JAMES KNIGHT, d. 18 Mar. 1848, at Rochester, *aet.* 61-10-0 (*Register*, vol. 80, p. 308).

JOHN KNIGHT, d. 30 Jan. 1850, *aet.* 87 yrs. (*Register*, vol. 73, p. 201).

LAMB

ELIZABETH LAMB, m. 12 Nov. 1758, ISAAC MEZEET, both of Portsmouth.

LANG

BENJAMIN[3] LANG (William[2], John[1]), of Rye, m. 10 July 1758, ELEANOR BURLEIGH.

CATHERINE[4] LANG (John[3], William[2], John[1]), of Portsmouth, m. 5 May 1772, JOHN JANVRIN.

LANGDON

WILLIAM[3] LANGDON (Tobias[2]) (Parson's *Rye*, p. 410), of Portsmouth, m. 15 Oct. 1778, MARY PICKERING.

LANGLEY

THOMAS[2] LANGLEY, (James[1]) (Stackpole's *Durham*, vol. 2, p. 246), m. 7 Sept. 1743, SARAH TRICKEY.

ESTHER LANGLEY, wid. of Thomas[2], *supra* m. 16 May 1780, WINTHROP BICKFORD.

LARY

ELIZABETH LARY, of Kittery, m. 20 Dec. 1748, JOHN FELING, of Portsmouth.

LEACH

MEHITABLE LEACH, m. 18 Oct. 1716, JAMES BERRY, of Dublin, Ireland. (*Register*, vol. 23, p. 393).

JOSEPH[2] LEACH (Nathaniel[1]) (Stackpole's *Kittery*, p. 573), m. 9 Feb. 1749, ABIGAIL MILLER, both of Portsmouth.

LEAVERS (? Seward)

WILLIAM LEAVERS, son of Henry, bapt. 15 Nov. 1719.

LEATHERS

JONATHAN[4] LEATHERS (Edward[5]) (Stackpole's *Durham*, vol. 2, p. 256), m. 25 Dec. 1740, KETURAH TRICKEY, (1-viii).

LE GOSSE

GEORGE LE GOSSE, communion, 24 Jan. 1742.

LEIGHTON

1. THOMAS⁴ LEIGHTON (John³ ?, Thomas²⁻¹) (Stackpole's *Durham*, vol. 2, p. 260), of Newington, m. DEBORAH -----.

Administration on his estate 29 Aug. 1744 to Deborah, his widow (*N.H. State Pap.*, vol. 33, p. 209)

Children, born at Newington (Stackpole, *loc. cit*):

 i. OLIVE⁵, m. JAMES² COOLBROTH (2), son of George¹ and Mary, *q.v.*

 ii. JOHN

 iii. ELIZABETH, m. 24 Jan. 1724, RICHARD⁴ DAM (5), son of John³ and June (Rowe), *q.v.*

3 iv. HATEVIL

 v. DEBORAH, m. 9 Oct. 1735, Capt. WILLIAM COLLINS, of Portsmouth.

 vi. ABIGAIL, m. 5 Dec. 1732, NEHEMIAH⁴ FURBER (8), son of William³ and Sarah, *q.v.*

 vii. KEZIAH, m. 30 Sept. 1739, ELEAZER⁴ COLMAN, son of Eleazer³ and Ann (Nutter), *q.v.*

4 viii. THOMAS

2. JOHN⁴ LEIGHTON (John³, Thomas²⁻¹), of Dover, b. about 1706, d. 1756, m. 7 Nov. 1728, ABIGAIL HAM, dau. of Samuel (*Register*, vol. --, p. --), b. at Portsmouth, 15 Mar. 1710.

The will of Samuel Ham, of Portsmouth, yeoman, proved 9 Dec. 1731, mentions his daughter, Abigail Leighton (*N.H. State Pap.*, vol. 32, p. 420).

Children, baptized at Newington:

 i. WILLIAM⁵, bapt. 30 Sept. 1736, b. 20 Aug. 1729 (*Register*, vol. 7, p. 256).

 ii. HATEVIL, bapt. 30 Sept. 1736, b. 13 May 1731 (*ibid.*).

 iii. MOSES, bapt. 30 Sept. 1736.

 iv. PAUL, bapt. 30 Sept. 1736, d. in infancy.

 v. TOBIAS, bapt. 30 Sept. 1736, b. 9 May 1736 (*ibid.*), m. ANN TUTTLE.

 vi. PAUL, bapt. 7 Oct. 1739, b. 3 Apr. 1739 (*ibid.*).

 vii. ABIGAIL, bapt. 4 Sept. 1740, b. 2 May 1740, m. JOHN KELLEY.

 viii. JONATHAN, b. 20 Jan. 1742 (*ibid.*), m. 3 Dec. 1777, MARY BAMPTON.

 ix. OLIVE, b. 29 Oct. 1743 (*ibid.*).

 x. MARY, b. 19 Feb. 1746 (*ibid.*).

 xi. DEBORAH, b. 23 Oct. 1747 (*ibid.*), m. 30 Nov. 1768, EBENEZER TUTTLE.

 xii. JAMES, b. 12 Oct. 1749 (*ibid.*), m. SARAH⁴ THOMPSON (3-iv), dau. of William² and Anna (Barker), *q.v.*

3. HATEVIL⁵ LEIGHTON (Thomas⁴, John³, Thomas²⁻¹), of Newington, m. 7 Dec. 1732, SARAH TRICKEY (7-iii), dau. of Capt. Thomas³ and Mary.

Children, baptized at Newington:
- i. ISAAC⁶, bapt. 30 Sept. 1736.
- ii. DEBORAH, bapt. 30 Sept. 1736.
- iii. MARK, bapt. 7 Oct. 1739.
- iv. JEMIMA, bapt. 7 Oct. 1739.
- v. THOMAS, bapt. 26 Oct. 1740.
- vi. SAMUEL, bapt. 18 Oct. 1756.
- vii. DAVID, bapt. 18 Oct. 1756.

4. THOMAS⁵ LEIGHTON (Thomas⁴, John³, Thomas²⁻¹), of Newington, m. 28 Oct. 1742, MARY SMITHSON.

Children, baptized at Newington:
- i. DEBORAH⁶, bapt. 12 Nov. 1743, m. 3 Dec. 1761, LEIGHTON³ COOLBROTH (4), son of James² and Olive, *q.v.*
- ii. MARY, bapt. 3 Mar. 1744/5, m. 21 Mar. 1771, CHRISTOPHER⁵ NUTTER (10-vi), son of Samuel⁴ and Sarah (Hoyt), *q.v.*
- iii. THOMAS, bapt. 25 May 1746.
- iv. JOHN SMITHSON, bapt. 20 Apr. 1748.
- v. SMITHSON, bapt. 1749.
- vi. JOEL, bapt. 3 Nov. 1751, m. 21 Oct. 1779, ELIZABETH⁴ HUNTRESS (4-iv), dau. of William³ and Susanna⁵ (Downing), *q.v.*

   Children, baptized at Newington:
   1) Temperance Pickering⁷, bapt. 8 Oct. 1780.
   2) Thomas, bapt. 20 Nov. 1785.
   3) William, bapt. 20 Nov. 1785.
- vii. LUKE, bapt. 14 Dec. 1753.
- viii. ELIZABETH, bapt. 15 Feb. 1756, m. 4 Jan. 1779, THOMAS⁴ PINDER, son of Joseph³ and Hepzibah (Davis) (Stackpole's *Durham*, vol. 2, p. 304), of Durham, bapt. 23 Dec. 1775.
- ix. GEORGE

   Child, baptized at Newington:
   1) Mary Smithson⁷, bapt. 26 Nov. 1780.

LEIGHTON (unconnected)

SARAH LEIGHTON, m. 12 May 1731, THOMAS TRIGGS, of Portsmouth (*Register*, vol. 25, p. 118).

CATHERINE[5] LEIGHTON (William[4]) (Stackpole's *Kittery*, p. 577), m. 17 Nov. 1768, DEPENDENCE SHAPLEIGH, both of Kittery, Me.

SARAH[5] LEIGHTON (William[4]) (Stackpole, *loc. cit.*), m. 16 Dec. 1773, Capt. WILLIAM RAITT, both of Kittery, Me.

LEONARD

JOHN LEONARD, of Durham, m. 15 Oct. 1756, ELIZABETH DURGIN.

LIBBY

JAMES LIBBY, m. 3 Dec. 1725, ELIZABETH MESERVY.

MARY LIBBY, m. 2 Dec. 1728, WILLIAM BERRY, of Scarborough, Me.

----- **LIBBY**, of Scarborough, Me., m. 1731, ESTHER FURBER.

ELIZABETH[3] LIBBY (Matthew[2]) (Stackpole's *Kittery*, p. 585), of Portsmouth, m. 26 Nov. 1734, JOHN SMITH, of Berwick, Me.

REUBEN[5] LIBBY (Isaac[4], Anthony[3-2], John[1]) (Parson's *Rye*, p. 416), m. 1 July 1754, SARAH GOSS, both of Rye.

MATTHEW[5] LIBBY (Matthew[4-3], David[2], John[1]), m. 1 Sept. 1754, LYDIA[5] LIBBY (Samuel[4], Matthew[3]), both of Kittery.

LYDIA[5] LIBBY (*supra*), m. 1 Sept. 1754, MATTHEW[5] LIBBY (*supra*).

JERUSHA[5] LIBBY (Matthew[4]) (Stackpole's *Kittery*, p. 585), m. 30 Nov. 1762, BENJAMIN STAPLES, both of Kittery.

AZARIAH[5] LIBBY (Matthew[4]), m. 16 Dec. 1762, ELIZABETH PAUL, both of Kittery.

STEPHEN LIBBY, of Scarborough, Me., m. 17 Oct. 1765, MARGARET MILLER, of Portsmouth.

SARAH[5] LIBBY (Samuel[4]), m. 11 June 1780, ELISHA HAMMOND, both of Kittery.

LITTLEFIELD

MABEL LITTLEFIELD, m. 15 May 1730, RICHARD BUSBEE, both of Wells, Me.

LORD

JOSEPH LORD, of Berwick, Me., m. 28 Sept. 1750, MARTHA HUNTRESS (3-ii).

LOUD

SOLOMON LOUD, son of William and Abigail (Abbott), b. 3 Sept. 1713, at Portsmouth (*Register*, vol. 24, p. 18).

SOLOMON LOUD, of Portsmouth, m. 7 Mar. 1735, ABIGAIL DAM (2-i).

JOHN LOUD, m. 24 Dec. 1740, ABIGAIL DECKER, both of Portsmouth (*Register*, vol. 27, p. 9).

LUCY

HANNAH LUCY, of Portsmouth, m. 9 Feb. 1749, ENOCH GOVE, of Hampton.

LYSSEN

JOHN[2] LYSSEN (Weymouth[1]) (Stackpole's *Kittery*, p. 602), m. 2 Jan. 1724, SUSANNAH HILL, both of Kittery.

MACDONALD

JAMES MACDONALD, of Barrington, m. 27 Nov. 1760, SARAH NUTTER.

MARRINER

GEORGE MARRINER, m. 3 Jan. 1725, MARY GRAY.

MARY MARRINER, of Kittery, m. 26 Sept. 1755, WILLIAM MULLALY, joiner.

MARSHALL

JOHN MARSHALL, of Portsmouth, m. 4 Oct. 1745, ELIZABETH WHITE.

MARSTON

MARY MARSTON, m. 12 Jan. 1744, JOHN MOULTON, both of Hampton.

MARTIN

MICHAEL MARTIN, of Portsmouth, m. 7 June 1741, MARY HUNTRESS (2-iv).

WILLIAM MARTIN, son of Michael and Mary, bapt. 20 Dec. 1741.

MASON

ROBERT^2 MASON (Joseph^1) (Stackpole's *Durham*, vol. 2, p. 263), of Newmarket, m. 3 May 1753, SUSANNA BICKFORD.

SUSANNA MASON wid of Robert^2 (*supra*), m. 19 Sept. 1762, JOHN CHAPMAN, of Newmarket.

MASSURE (See MUSHAWAY)

MATTHEWS (MATHES)

FRANCIS^4 MATTHEWS (MATHES), (Francis^3) (Stackpole's *Durham*, vol. 2, p. 264), m. 28 Nov. 1720, LYDIA DREW, both of Oyster River.

BENJAMIN^5 MATTHEWS (MATHES) (Francis^4), (*supra*), m. 20 June 1745, ANNA COLMAN (3-v).

MEDER

SARAH MEDER, m. 2 July 1767, JOHN WILLIAMS, both of Durham.

CHARITY MEDER, m. 2 July 1767, DANIEL RANDALL, both of Durham.

JOSEPH^5 MEDER (Joseph^4) (Stackpole's *Durham*, vol. 2, p. 280), m. 8 Aug. 1773, ABIGAIL FIELD, both of Durham.

MEED

SARAH MEED, m. 13 Oct. 1748, RICHARD FITZGERALD, both of Portsmouth.

MELOON

SAMUEL MELOON, covenant, 10 Nov. 1728.

SAMUEL and MARY MELOON, children of Samuel and Mary, bapt. 10 Nov. 1728.

JOHN MELOON, son of Samuel and Mary, bapt. 16 Nov. 1729.

MESERVEY

CLEMENT[2] MESERVEY (Clement[1]), of Newington, 1713, Scarboro, Me., 1727 (*Dover Landmarks*, p. 97), Gorham, Me., and Standish, Me., m. (1) 24 Sept. 1702, ELIZABETH JONES (Stackpole's *Durham*, vol. 2, p. 285), m. (2) 17 Oct. 1726, SARAH[2] DECKER, bapt. at Newington, 30 Sept. 1716, dau. of John[1] and Sarah Decker, *q.v.*, m. (3) at Scarboro, 14 Aug. 1738, SARAH (-----) STONE (McLellan's *Gorham*, p. 674).

Children by first wife, born at Newington:
  i. GEORGE[3], bapt. 19 Jan. 1724, m. 17 Feb. 1736/7 (*Register*, vol. 26, p. 377), ELIZABETH HAM, b. at Portsmouth.
  ii. PETER, bapt. 19 Jan. 1724, m. 31 Mar. 1737 (*ibid.*) SARAH LORD, b. at Portsmouth.
  iii. JOSEPH, bapt. 19 Jan. 1724.

Children by second wife, the first one born at Newington, the others at ----- (McLellan's *Gorham, loc. cit.*):
  iv. JOHN, of Standish and Bridgton, Me., bapt. 13 Oct. 1728, m. (1) Mar. 1757, MARY YEATON, b. at ? Standish, m. (2) SARAH STROUT, b. at ? Gorham.
  v. ELIZABETH, b. 2 Sept. 1730, m. EDMUND PHINNEY.
  vi. CLEMENT, of Bristol, Me., b. 2 Sept. 1733, m. MARY WORCESTER, b. at ? Standish.
  vii. MARGARET, m. WILLIAM WESCOTT, of Scarboro.
  viii. HANNAH, m. TIMOTHY CROCKER.
  ix. BENJAMIN, bapt. 4 July 1744.
  x. NATHANIEL, bapt. 26 July 1749, m. REBECCA MARTIN.

MESERVEY (unconnected)

ELIZABETH[3] MESERVEY (Daniel[2], Clement[1]), m. 23 Dec. 1725, JAMES LIBBY.

NATHANIEL MESERVEY, covenant, 23 Oct. 1726.

ANNA MESERVEY, m. 13 Sept. 1752, JOSEPH WELLS, both of Portsmouth.

NATHANIEL MESERVEY, m. 29 June 1769, MARTHA JONES, of Durham.

MEZEET

ISAAC MEZEET, m. 12 Nov. 1758, ELIZABETH LAMB, of Portsmouth.

MILLER

MARK MILLER, of Newington, m. 15 Sept. 1763, SUSANNA[4], DOWNING, bapt. at Newington, 9 Oct. 1746, dau. of Richard[3] and Alice[3] (Downing) Downing, *q.v.*

Children, born at Newington:
  i. ELIZABETH HARRISON, bapt. 1 June 1766.
  ii. BENJAMIN, of Portsmouth, bapt. 31 July 1768.
   Children, baptized at Portsmouth:
    1) Patty, bapt. 20 Jan. 1782 (*N.H. Gen. Rec.*, vol. 7, p. 13).
    2) Joseph, bapt. 19 Sept. 1784 (*id.*, p. 15).
  iii. NICHOLAS HARRISON, bapt. 17 Sept. 1769.
  iv. ALICE, bapt. 13 Oct. 1771.

MILLER (unconnected)

Mrs. MILLER, took communion, 28 June, 1716.

HANNAH MILLER, m. 23 Feb. 1725, PERCY BICKFORD (*N.H. Gen. Rec.*, vol. 2, p. 7).

BENJAMIN MILLER, JR., m. 23 Sept. 1731, ELIZABETH DENNETT, both of Portsmouth (*Register*, vol. 25, p. 118).

PETER MILLER, m. 28 July 1741, ELIZABETH TRICKEY, both of Portsmouth (*id.*, vol. 27, p. 9)

ABIGAIL MILLER, of Portsmouth, dau. of Benjamin, m. 9 Mar. 1742, as his first wife, JONATHAN^4 TRICKEY, of Newington, shipwright, b. about 1720, son of John^3 and Mary (Whittum) Trickey, *q.v.*

ABIGAIL MILLER, m. 7 Feb. 1749, JOSEPH LEACH, both of Portsmouth.

MARGARET MILLER, of Portsmouth, m. 17 Oct. 1765, STEPHEN LIBBY.

TEMPERENCE MILLER, of Scarboro, Me., d. 20 Jan. 1826, *aet.* 95 (*Register*, vol. 73, p. 196).

MILLS

Capt. **LUKE MILLS**, son of Luke and Hannah^2 (Lang) Mills, of Portsmouth, m. 11 Oct. 1764, DEBORAH^5 FURBER, bapt. at Newington, 19 Apr. 1742, dau. of Nehemiah^4 and Abigail (Leighton) Furber, *q.v.*

DEBORAH MILLS, communion, 28 May 1769.

DEBORAH (FURBER) MILLS, m. 10 June 1773, JOHN GEE^4 PICKERING, of Newington, bapt. at Newington, 24 Aug. 1735, d. 15 Aug. 1796, son of Thomas^3 and Mary (Downing) Pickering.

MOODY

JOSEPH MOODY, of Scarboro, Me., m. 19 Sept. 1734, ELIZABETH^2 DECKER, bapt. at Newington, 30 Sept. 1716, dau. of John^1, *q.v.*

JOSEPH MOODY, of Scarboro, Me., m. 30 Oct. 1760, MARY NUTTER.

MOORE

LAZARUS MOORE, of Portsmouth, m. 19 Feb. 1736, SARAH WHIDDEN, of Greenland.

MORRILL

ISAAC MORRILL, m. 2 June 1768, MARY SPINNEY, both of Kittery, Me.

MOULTON

PATIENCE MOULTON, covenanted, 3 July 1726.

JOHN MOULTON, m. 12 Jan. 1744, MARY MARSTON, both of Hampton.

MULLALY

WILLIAM MULLALY, joiner, m. 26 Sept. 1755, MARY MARRINER, of Kittery, Me.

MURDOCH

LETTICE MURDOCH, m. 23 Oct. 1724, JAMES CALDWELL, both of Londonderry.

MURRAY

WILLIAM MURRAY, of Charleston, S.C., m. 9 Nov. 1727, HANNAH GROVE, of Ipswich, Mass. (*Register*, vol. 24, p. 359).

SAMUEL MURRAY, son of William and Hannah, bapt. 2 Sept. 1734.

MUSHAWAY (MASSURE)

FRANCIS MUSHAWAY (MASSURE), of Portsmouth, m. 22 Oct. 1767, ALICE NUTTER.

NASON

RICHARD NASON, at Newington, 1713 (*Register*, vol. 58, p. 249).

NEAL

PHEBE NEAL, m. 7 Apr. 1748, SAMUEL AYRES, both of Portsmouth.

MARY NEAL, m. 6 Sept. 1770, JAMES AYRES, both of Greenland.

NELSON

ELIZABETH[3] NELSON (John[2], Charles[1]) (Stackpole's *Kittery*, p. 64), m. 15 Mar. 1716, JONATHAN[2] DOWNING, of Newington, b. about 1690, son of John[1] and Susanna (Miller) Downing, *q.v.*

MARY³ NELSON (Stackpole's *Kittery, ut supra*), m. 22 Nov. 1716, SAMUEL HILL, of Kittery.

LEADER NELSON, m. 2 Sept. 1750, ABIGAIL BREWSTER, of Portsmouth.

NORWOOD

SARAH NORWOOD, m. 30 Jan. 1758, SAMUEL BREWSTER, of Barrington.

NUTTER

1. HATEVIL¹ NUTTER, of Dover, 1635 (*Register*, vol. 7, p. 259), b. in England about 1604 (*N.H. State Pap.*, vol. 31, p. 157), d. 1675, m. (1) ----- -----, m. (2) ANN AYRES (*Tremain Family*, p. --).

In his will dated 28 Dec. 1674, proved 25 June 1675, he names his "present wife, Ann," and his children: Anthony, Mary Wingate, and Abigail Roberts (*N.H. State Pap.*, vol. 31, p. 157).

Children:

2   i. ANTHONY, b. 1630.

ii. MARY, m. JOHN WINGATE, of Dover, he m. (2) SARAH CANNEY, wid. of Thomas (*N.H. State Pap.*, vol. 31, p. 186).

In his will dated 12 Mar. 1673/4, and codicil thereto made after the birth of his daughter, Abigail, both proved 23 Mar. 1678/9, he names his wife, Sarah; children John, Moses, Ann, Joshua, Caleb, and Mary; father-in-law Nutter; brother, Anthony Nutter; and five unmarried children of Thomas Canney (*N.H. State Pap.*, vol. 31, p. 185).

Children, as mentioned in his will:

1) John³
2) Moses
3) Ann
4) Joshua
5) Caleb
6) Mary

iii. ABIGAIL, b. about 1630, m. ⁺(1) about 1656, JOHN² ROBERTS, of

---

⁺It is said in Stackpole's *Durham*, vol. 2, p. 231, that she married Stephen² Jones. This is probably an error. He married Abigail Bickford (*Ham's Marriages*, M.S.)

Dover, husbandman, marshall of the Province, delegate to the Convention of 1689, b. about 1629, d. 21 Jan. 1694/5, son of Thomas[1] and Rebecca (?Hilton) Roberts.

Children (surname *Roberts*), born at Dover:

1) John[3], of Dover, b. about 1657, m. Mary -----.
2) Thomas, of Dover, yeoman, b. about 1659, m. (1) ----- -----, m. (2) in 1711 or 1712, Elizabeth (Tucker) Hopley, b. at Portsmouth about 1670, dau. of John and Ursula Tucker, wid. of Robert Hopley.
3) Hatevil, of that part of Dover which became, 1729, the parish; and 1754, the town of Somersworth; and 1849, Rollinsford; b. about 1661 (depositions), d. 1724, m. his cousin, Lydia Roberts, b. at Dover about 1665, dau. of Thomas[2] and Mary[2] (Leighton) Roberts.
4) Joseph, of Dover, yeoman, b. about 1666, m. (1) Elizabeth Ham, b. at Dover, dau. of John Ham, m. (2) Abigail -----.
5) Abigail, b. about 1650, m. (1) 8 Nov. 1671, John[2] Hall, of Dover, representative, 1697, b. about 1649, d. 29 Apr. 1697, son of Deac. John[1] Hall, m. (2) 24 Oct. 1698, as his second wife, Thomas[2] Downs, of Cocheco, constable, b. in Boston, 17 Mar. 1653/4, d. (killed by Indians) 1711, son of Thomas[1] and Catherine Downs.
6) Mary, b. about 1670, m. Timothy Robinson.
7) Sarah, b. about 1665, m. Zacharias[2] Field, of Durham, b. there about 1648, son of Derby[1] and Agnes Field.

iv. ELIZABETH, m. THOMAS[2] LEIGHTON, of Durham, son of Thomas[1] Leighton.

2. Lieut. ANTHONY[2] NUTTER (Hatevil[1]), of Newington, member of the council, 1682, b. in England 1630, d. Feb. 19, 1686. (*Register*, vol. 7, p. 259), m. SARAH[2] LANGSTAFF, dau. of Henry[1].

Administration on his estate was granted June 1, 1720, to his sons, Hatevil and Henry, both of Newington; sureties Robert Pike and Tristram Heard.(*N.H. State Papers*, vol. 32, p. 105).

Children, born at Newington:

3 i. HATEVIL[3]
4 ii. HENRY
5 iii. JOHN, b. Dec. 27, 1663.
   iv. SARAH, b. about 1660, m. Capt. NATHANIEL[2] HILL (*Register*, vol. 7, p. 259), son of Valentine[1] and Mary (Eaton) (Stackpole's *Durham*, vol. 2, p. 209), of Durham, b. at Durham, 1 Mar. 1659, d. 1742.
   v. ? MARY, m. SHADRACK WALKER.

3. HATEVIL[3] NUTTER (Anthony[2], Hatevil[1]), of Newington, d. 1745, m. (1) SARAH -----, m. (2) 16 May 1716, LEAH (-----) FURBER, wid. of JETHRO[3] (2-

ii), son of William², *q.v.*

His will dated 22 Nov. 1745, proved 25 Dec. 1745, mentions his father, Anthony; wife, Leah, executrix; the following children except No. vi (Elizabeth); and his negro, Caesar; sureties John Downing and Jethro Furber. (*N.H. State Papers*, vol. 33, p. 310).

Children by first wife, born at Newington:

6   i. HATEVIL⁴, b. about 1705.
7   ii. ANTHONY, b. about 1710.
       iii. ELEANOR
       iv. SARAH, b. about 1712, m. at Greenland, 28 Dec. 1732, EDWARD³ WALKER (3), son of Edward² and Deliverance (Gaskin), *q.v.*

Children by second wife, baptized at Newington:

       v. ABIGAIL, b. 15 Sept. 1717, m. ELIPHALET⁴ DAM (6), son of Deac. Moses³ and Abigail (Huntress), *q.v.*
       vi. ELIZABETH, b. 29 Nov. 1719, d. in infancy.
8   vii. JOHN, b. 12 Mar. 1721.
       viii. ELIZABETH, b. 21 Sept. 1723, m. 21 Nov. 1742, EDWARD³ ROLLINS (4), son of James² and Deborah (Pevey), *q.v.*
       ix. OLIVE, m. 6 Jan. 1749, (*Register*, vol. 7, p. 260), ICHABOD³ ROLLINS (5), son of James² and Deborah (Pevey), *q.v.*
9   x. JOSHUA (*Register*, vol. 7, p. 260).

4. HENRY³ NUTTER (Anthony², Hatevil¹), of Newington, yeoman, d. 1739, m. 26 July 1703 (*N.H. Gen. Rec.*, vol. 4, p. 12), MARY² SHACKFORD (1-iii), dau. of William¹ and Deborah² (Trickey), *q.v.*

His will dated 4 Dec. 1739, proved 30 Jan. 1739/40, mentions his wife, Mary; and children Samuel (executor), Valentine, Joseph, Elizabeth Crockett, and Mary (*N.H. State Papers*, vol. 32, p. 771).

Children, as mentioned in the will:

10   i. SAMUEL⁴, covenant, 7 Apr. 1728.
11   ii. VALENTINE
12   iii. JOSEPH, of Durham, m. BRIDGET BARKER.
       iv. ELIZABETH, b. 1713, m. 25 Dec. 1733 (*Register*, vol. 65, p. 354), JOSHUA CROCKETT.
       v. MARY, b. 1715, d. 16 Jan. 1811, m. ? 28 Aug. 1740, JOHN⁴ PICKERING (6), son of James³ and Mary (Nutter).
13   vi. HENRY, bapt. 2 Sept. 1736.
       vii. ? GRAFTON

5. JOHN³ NUTTER (Anthony², Hatevil¹), of Newington, b. 27 Dec. 1663.

Children, born at Newington:

       i. JOHN⁴, of Newington, Gent., b. 1695?, d. *s.p* 1747, m. 8 Feb. 1718/9

(*Register*, vol. 24, p. 13), ABIGAIL WHIDDEN, dau. of Michael, b. at Portsmouth.

His will dated 20 Aug. 1746, proved 29 Apr. 1747, mentions his wife, Abigail; and brothers Matthias, James, and Hatevil (*N.H. State Papers*, vol. 33, p. 393).

The will of Michael Whidden proved 28 Mar. 1739, mentions his daughter, Abigail Nutter (*id.*, vol. 32, p. 729).

14   ii. MATTHIAS
15   iii. JAMES
16   iv. HATEVIL
      v. THOMAS, of Newington, m. DEBORAH -----.
      Child, baptized at Newington:
        1) Thomas^5, 13 May 1720.
     vi. ROSAMOND, m. 29 Nov. 1733, SAMUEL^3 FABIAN (3), son of John^2 and Mary (Pickering), *q.v.*

6. HATEVIL^4 NUTTER (Hatevil^3, Anthony^2, Hatevil^1), of Newington, b. 1705, m. 28 June 1727, REBECCA AYRES.

Children, baptized at Newington:
    i. HANNAH^5, bapt. 14 Apr. 1728.
    ii. ROSAMOND, bapt. 18 Jan. 1730.
    iii. MARY, bapt. 1 Oct. 1732, d. in infancy.
    iv. MARY, bapt. 6 Oct. 1734.
    v. MARK, bapt. 19 Dec. 1736.

7. ANTHONY^4 NUTTER (Hatevil^3, Anthony^2, Hatevil^1), of Newington and Barnstead, m. 18 May 1740, MARY^3 DOWNING (3-i), dau. of Jonathan^2 and Elizabeth (Nelson), *q.v.*

Children, baptized at Newington:
    i. ALICE^5, bapt. 15 Mar. 1740/1, m. 23 Nov. 1758, LEMUEL^4 TRICKEY (3), son of Capt. Thomas^3 and Mary, *q.v.*
    ii. ELEANOR, bapt. 5 June 1743.
    iii. LOIS, bapt. 3 Feb. 1744/5.
    iv. NELSON DOWNING, bapt. 12 Oct. 1746.
    v. JOTHAM, bapt. 22 May 1748, m. 9 Feb. 1769, ELIZABETH^4 DOWNING, dau. ? of John^3 and Patience (Ham).
    vi. DEBORAH, bapt. 26 Aug. 1750, m. ENOCH^4 HUNTRESS (5-i), son of Jonathan^3 and Mary^3 (Walker), *q.v.*
    vii. JONATHAN WARNER, bapt. 7 Apr. 1754.

ANTHONY NUTTER, of Portsmouth, d. (*N.H. Gazette*) 27 Aug. 1773.

8. **Deac. and Maj. JOHN⁴ NUTTER** (Hatevil³, Anthony², Hatevil¹), of Newington, deacon, 21 Mar. 1765, bapt. 12 Mar. 1721, d. 19 Sept. 1776, m. 17 Nov. 1747, ANNA SYMMES, dau. of John, b. at Portsmouth, 20 Oct. 1727, d. 11 Aug. 1793.

Children, baptized at Newington:

   i. HATEVIL⁵, bapt. 18 Dec. 1748, d. 25 Dec. 1831, m. 8 Mar. 1781, SUSANNA⁵ SHACKFORD (9-4), dau. of Capt. Samuel⁴ and Elizabeth (Ring), *q.v.*

     Child, baptized at Newington:

     1) John⁶, bapt. 12 Sept. 1784.

   ii. MARY, bapt. 26 Aug. 1750, m. 12 Feb. 1724, JAMES³ PEVEY (5), son of Hudson² and Madeline (Brown), *q.v.*

   iii. HANNAH, bapt. 14 June 1752, d. 12 June 1764, *q.v.*

   iv. DOROTHY, bapt. 11 Aug. 1754, m. ? FABIAN⁵ FURBER (8-ix), son of Nehemiah⁴ and Abigail⁵ (Leighton), *q.v.*

   v. Maj. JOHN⁺, bapt. 13 Mar. 1757, of Barnstead, officer in the Revolution, d. 1837, m. 24 June 1779, ELIZABETH⁵ DAM (6-vi), dau. of Eliphalet⁵ and Abigail (Nutter), *q.v.*

   vi. A CHILD, b. and d. 23 Apr. 1759.

   vii. ANN, bapt. 16 Mar. 1760, d. 17 Aug. 1813, m. 7 Nov. 1781, WILLIAM⁶ NUTTER (9-ii), son of Anthony⁵ and Sarah (Nutter), *q.v.*

   viii. JOSEPH SYMMES, of Newington, bapt. 21 Feb. 1762, d. 2 Jan. 1846 (*Register*, vol. 73, p. 200)

   ix. ANTHONY, bapt. 26 Feb. 1764, ? of Barnstead, m. ANNA -----.

   x. HANNAH, bapt. 12 July 1767, m. JOTHAM JOHNSON.

   xi. ABIGAIL, bapt. 30 Apr. 1769, d. 28 Aug. 1856, m. CYRUS FRINK.

HATEVIL NUTTER, covenant - his daughter, MARY DAM, bapt. 25 Nov. 1781.

9. **JOSHUA⁴ NUTTER** (Hatevil³, Anthony², Hatevil¹), of Newington, m. 22 Jan. 1749, SARAH RICHARDS, dau. of Benjamin and Elizabeth, *q.v.*

Children, baptized at Newington:

   i. ELIZABETH⁵, bapt. 29 Aug. 1756, m. ? 9 Jan. 1772, DEPENDENCE AYRES, son of Thomas, of Newington.

   ii. ESTHER, bapt. 26 Aug. 1759.

   iii. OLIVE, bapt. 31 Jan. 1762, m. ? 1796, SAMUEL TUCKER (*Oracle* - 20 Jan. 1796).

+John - Had Eliphalet, of Barnstead, who m. Love Locke, dau. of James (Jewett's *Barnstead*).

10. SAMUEL⁴ NUTTER (Henry³, Anthony², Hatevil¹), of Newington, m. 18 May 1725, SARAH HOYT.

Children, baptized at Newington:
- i. RICHARD⁵, of Rochester, bapt. 11 Sept. 1726, m. TEMPERENCE -----.
  Children:
  1) Anthony⁶
  2) Henry
  3) James, of Rochester, m. 5 Apr. 1786 (*N.H. Gen. Rec.*, vol. 5, p. 2), Elizabeth Heard.
  4) John
  5) Winthrop, of Rochester, m. 25 May, 1788, Charity Meader (*N.H. Gen. Rec.*, vol. 5, p. 3).
  6) Stephen
  7) Richard, of Rochester, m. 14 May 1789, Dorothy Place (*N.H. Gen. Rec.*, vol. 5, p. 4).
  8) Abigail
  9) Sarah, m. 19 Nov. 1788, John Bickford (*N.H. Gen. Rec.*, vol. 5, p. 4), son of John.
  10) Mary, m. 20 Sept. 1798, James Tibbetts (*N.H. Gen. Rec.*, vol. 5, p. 53 (*id.*, vol. 6, p. 130), of Rochester.
- ii. MIRIAM, bapt. 26 Jan. 1730, m. 15 Jan. 1755, JOHN NUTTER.
- iii. SAMUEL, bapt. 8 Apr. 1733.
- iv. LEMUEL, bapt. 21 Mar. 1739.
- v. CHRISTOPHER, of Newington, bapt. 18 Mar. 1755, m. 21 Mar. 1771, MARY⁶ LEIGHTON (4-ii), dau. of Thomas⁵ and Mary (Smithson), *q.v.*
- vi. ARABELLA, perhaps the "child" bapt. in the North Church, Apr. 1752 (*N.H. Gen. Rec.*, vol. 5, p. 90), covenanted at Newington, 27 Sept. 1761 (*N.H. Gen. Rec.*), m. 16 July 1764, JOSEPH³ PEAVEY (5), *q.v.*

11. VALENTINE⁴ NUTTER (Henry³, Anthony², Hatevil¹), of Portsmouth, m. MARY GOODE (*Shackford Family*, Ms.).

His will proved Jan. 1757, mentions his children as follows (*N.H. Probate*, vol. 20, p. 195):
- i. WILLIAM⁵
- ii. MARY, m. ----- WILLS.
- iii. ANTHONY
- iv. AGNES, m. ----- GREELEY.
- v. GRAFTON
- vi. HENRY
- vii. VALENTINE
- viii. ABIGAIL

Child, baptized at North Church, Portsmouth:
- ix. SARAH, bapt. 27 Nov. 1747, m. at Portsmouth, 29 Aug. 1770 (South Church rec.), BENJAMIN COLE, of Portsmouth.

12. JOSEPH[4] NUTTER (Henry[3], Anthony[2], Hatevil[1]), of Durham, m. BRIDGET BARKER (?), dau. of Enid (?) (*Shackford Family* Reg.).

13. HENRY[4] NUTTER (Henry[3], Anthony[2], Hatevil[1]), of Portsmouth, tanner, bapt. 2 Sept. 1736, m. MARGARET MARCH, dau. of Clement, d. 4 Mar. 1788. (North Church rec.)

Children, baptized in North Church, Portsmouth:
- i. MARY, bapt. 6 Oct. 1765, m. ? 2 May 1787, ELISHA ABBOTT, of Wolfeborough (See *Libby and Abbott Genealogies*).
- ii. REBECCA, bapt. 16 Aug. 1767, m. 8 Oct. 1784, BENJAMIN HOYT (*Hoyt Genealogy*, p. 120).
- iii. SARAH, bapt. 16 July 1769, d. in infancy.
- iv. SARAH, bapt. 24 Nov. 1771, m. ? 22 Dec. 1791, STEPHEN WENTWORTH (*Register*, vol. 63, p. 176).
- v. HENRY, bapt. 31 Oct. 1773.
- vi. JOHN, bapt. 10 Sept. 1775.
- vii. JACOB, bapt. 1 Jan. 1778, m. MARY SNELL (*N.H. Gazette* of 4 Nov. 1800).
- viii. CLEMENT MARCH, bapt. 25 June 1780.
- ix. CHARLES, bapt. 17 Aug. 1783, d. 1 May 1845, m. OLIVE DURGIN, dau. of Ebenezer and ----- (Taylor), b. 9 Jan. 1778, d. 24 Aug. 1846 (*History of Porter, Me.*, p. 23. Look also at *Runnells Family*, p. 139).

14. MATTHIAS[4] NUTTER (John[3], Anthony[2], Hatevil[1]), of Newington, m. (1) HANNAH[4] FURBER (2-ii-i), dau. of Jethro[3] and Leah (*Tremain*, p. 375), *q.v.*, m. (2) 25 Oct. 1749, SUSANNA[4] AYRES (13-iv), ? dau. of George and Abigail (Perkins), *q.v.*

Children by first wife, baptized at Newington:
17   i. MATTHIAS[5], bapt. 24 Oct. 1736.
- ii. THOMAS, bapt. 24 Oct. 1736.
- iii. ROSAMOND, bapt. 10 Sept. 1743, d. unm. ?
- iv. JOHN⁺, bapt. 5 June 1745/6.

Child by second wife, baptized at Newington:

⁺In 1755, he was John Nutter, Jr., and Maj. John (8) was John Nutter, Sr. There were no other Johns. John Nutter, Jr., married 15 Jan. 1755, Miriam[5] Nutter (10-ii).

v. JONATHAN, bapt. 4 Mar. 1754, d. unm. ?

15. JAMES⁴ NUTTER (John³, Anthony², Hatevil¹), of Newington, m. 1 Jan. 1724, ABIGAIL⁴ FURBER (2-ii-4), dau. of Jethro ? and Leah, *q.v.*
Children, baptized at Newington:
    i. ANN⁵, bapt. 30 Oct. 1726.
    ii. JOHN, bapt. 26 Oct. 1729.
    iii. TEMPERANCE, bapt. 26 Oct. 1729, d. unm. ?
    iv. MARY, bapt. 14 Sept. 1736, m. ? 30 Oct. 1760, JOSEPH MUNDY, of Scarborough, Me.
18   v. JAMES, bapt. 29 Sept. 1736.
19   vi. ANTHONY, bapt. 29 Sept. 1736.

16. HATEVIL⁴ NUTTER (John³, Anthony², Hatevil¹), of Newington, m. 17 Feb. 1731, HANNAH DECKER (1-ii), dau. of John and Sarah, *q.v.*
Children, baptized at Newington:
    i. SARAH⁵, bapt. 19 Nov. 1732.
    ii. HANNAH, bapt. 3 Feb. 1734, m. 13 Sept. 1753, CHARLES DENNETT.
    iii. JOSEPH, bapt. 17 Oct. 1736.
    iv. MARY, bapt. 18 Mar. 1739, m. ? 30 Oct. 1760, JOSEPH MOODY, of Scarborough, Me.
    v. JOHN, bapt. 23 May 1742.
    vi. BENJAMIN, bapt. 25 Nov. 1744, of Barnstead, d. 5 Dec. 1832 (Jewett's *Barnstead*, p. 235), m. ? 19 Dec. 1778, MARY⁵ TASKER, dau. of John⁴ and Mary (Young) (Stackpole's *Durham*, vol. 2, p. 355), d. 1830.
    vii. ELIZABETH, bapt. 21 June 1747, m. 27 Sept. 1764, DANIEL WALKER, of Portsmouth.
    viii. HATEVIL, bapt. 7 Apr. 1750, of Newington, covenant, 25 Nov. 1781, m. 11 Jan. 1781, ESTHER⁶ DAM (7-vi), dau. of Joseph⁵ and Mehitable (Hall), *q.v.*
    Child, baptized at Newington:
      1) Mary Dam⁶, bapt. 25 Nov. 1781.
    ix. LOIS, bapt. 24 Dec. 1752, m. 4 June 1772, ENOCH FOGG, son of Samuel and Rachel, of Scarborough, Me.
    x. ABIGAIL, bapt. 4 May 1755.

17. MATTHIAS⁵ NUTTER (Matthias⁴, John³, Anthony², Hatevil¹), of Newington, ship carpenter, bapt. 24 Oct. 1736, d. 3 Mar. 1818, m. (1) at Portsmouth, 8 Nov. 1764 (South Church Rec., *N.H. Gen. Rec.*, vol. 2, p. 94), MARTHA PERKINS, m. (2) ANNA (TRICKEY) VINCENT, m. (3) MARY FOLSOM (Hurd's *Rockingham*, p. 394), b. 1776, d. 1871, *aet.* 95 yrs.

His will dated 23 Dec. 1817, proved 18 Mar. 1818, mentions his wife, Mary, and the following children (*Rockingham Probate*).

Children by first wife, born at Newington:

i. JAMES⁶, of Portsmouth, gentleman, had all his father's real estate, paying legacies.

ii. MATTHIAS, m. (1) 21 June 1788, ELIZABETH COLBATH (Stackpole's *Durham*, vol. 1, p. 381), m. (2) SARAH WENTWORTH, dau. of John and Rebecca (Horne) (*Wentworth Genealogy*, vol. 2, p. 253).

iii. Capt. GEORGE, dead when his father made his will leaving children, b. 1767, d. 19 Sept. 1814, m. ABIGAIL⁶ ADAMS (4-viz), dau. of Benjamin³ and Abigail (Pickering), *q.v.*

iv. MARTHA, m. ----- COLMAN.

v. HANNAH, m. JOSEPH W.⁵ PICKERING (10-viii), son of Maj. Ephraim and Lydia (Colman), *q.v.*

vi. JOHN

vii. PHEBE, b. 27 June 1778, d. 22 Aug. 1849, m. 15 Apr. 1796, NATHANIEL COOPER⁵ SHACKFORD, son of Capt. Samuel⁴ and Elizabeth⁴ (Ring), *q.v.*

viii. MARY, m. ----- BURNHAM.

Children by second wife, born at Newington:

ix. JOSHUA, d. unm.

x. JOSEPH, of Newington, farmer, b. at Newington about 1795, d. in Wisconsin, 20 June 1863, m. 24 Aug. 1815 (town rec.), ELIZA D.⁶ PEVERLY, dau. of William⁵ and Joanna Peverly (*Peverly Family*, p. 18).

xi. ANNA, m. JAMES NUTTER.

xii. ABIGAIL, d. unm.?

xiii. MARK, of Newington, m. HANNAH -----, b. 1808, d. 1878.

xiv. HARRIET, b. 1802, d. 26 Aug. 1829, *aet*. 27 (*Register*, vol. 73, p. 197), m. KINSMAN⁶ PEVERLY, son of William⁵ and Johanna (Vicker), of Newington, farmer, b. about 1799, d. 21 Jan. 1846, *aet*. 46 (*Register*, vol. 73, p. 200).

Children by third wife, born at Newington (*Jackson Hoyt's Record*):

xv. ELIZABETH, b. 2 July 1807, d. unm. ?

xvi. WILLIAM WHITE, of Newington, member of the Legislature, 1808, b. 22 Sept. 1808, m. 1873, FRANCES I. (DOW) BRACKETT, dau. of Isaac, d. 15 July 1880.

xvii. LAVINA, b. 8 Apr. 1811, d. 6 May 1887, m. 19 Oct. 1844, JOSEPH R. PETTENGELL, son of Ansel and Augusta (Towne), of Augusta, Me.

xviii. SUSAN JANE, b. 21 Oct. 1814, d. unm. ?

xix. ALFRED, b. 6 June 1812, d. in infancy.

xx. ALFRED, d. unm. ?

xxi. OLIVE P., b. 5 Mar. 1817, d. unm. ?

18. JAMES[5] NUTTER (James[4], John[3], Anthony[2], Hatevil[1]), of Newington, bapt. 29 Sept. 1736, m. 18 Dec. 1755, ESTHER[5] DAM (4-xii), dau. of John[4] and Elizabeth (Hilliard), *q.v.*

Children, baptized at Newington:
- i. Deac. EBENEZER[6], bapt. 20 Nov. 1757, of Barnstead, 1783, soldier in the Revolution, b. 10 Oct. 1756, d. 18 Apr. 1840, m. 5 Feb. 1782, TEMPERENCE COOLBROTH, b. at Portsmouth, 1 Feb. 1759, d. 1829.

  Children:
  1) James[7], b. 30 Oct. 1784, m. Miriam Jenkins.
  2) George
  3) Elizabeth
  4) Dorothy
  5) John
  6) Nathaniel
  7) William
- ii. NATHAN, bapt. 2 May 1759, of Barnstead, soldier in the Revolution (Jewett's *Barnstead*, p. 119), d. at Halifax, N.S., a prisoner of war.
- iii. NATHANIEL, bapt. 25 Nov. 1770.
- iv. JETHRO, bapt. 25 Nov. 1770, of Barnstead, m. 1784, MARY ELLIOTT (Jewett's *Barnstead*, p. 136).
- v. ABIGAIL, bapt. 25 Nov. 1770.
- vi. DOROTHY, (*Genealogical Hist. of N.H.*, p. 1836).

19. ANTHONY[5] NUTTER (James[4], John[3], Anthony[2], Hatevil[1]), of Newington, bapt. 29 Jan. 1736, m. 1 June 1756, SARAH NUTTER.

Children, baptized at Newington:
- i. ANTHONY[6], of Newington, bapt. 8 May 1757, m. 12 Jan. 1787, ABIGAIL ROLLINS (11-i), dau. of Samuel[4] and Mary (Huntress), *q.v.* His will dated 5 Nov. 1814, proved 3 Apr. 1815, names only his wife, Abigail (*Rockingham Probate*).
- ii. WILLIAM, of Barnstead, sailor in the Revolution, bapt. 8 May 1757, b. 13 Dec. 1756, d. 15 Feb. 1811, m. 7 Nov. 1781, ANNA[5] NUTTER (8-vii), dau. of Maj. John[4] and Anna (Symmes), *q.v.*

  Children:
  1) Dorothy[7], m. Nathaniel Nutter.
  2) Anna Symmes, m. Samuel Perkins.
  3) Abigail, m. Charles Foster.
  4) William, m. Eleanor Pevey.

NUTTER (unconnected)

MARY NUTTER, m. 16 Jan. 1718, JAMES PICKERING.

ROSAMOND NUTTER, communion, 20 Sept. 1724.

ROSAMOND NUTTER, dau. of Rosamond, bapt. 31 Jan. 1725.

ELIZABETH NUTTER, covenant, 19 May 1728.

MARY NUTTER, covenant, 9 Apr. 1735.

Capt. JOHN NUTTER, covenant, 24 Sept. 1746.

CHILD OF ----- NUTTER, bapt. Apr. 1752, in North Church (*N.H. Gen. Rec.*, vol. 5, p. 90).

SARAH NUTTER, m. 27 Nov. 1760, JAMES MACDONALD, of Barrington.

PHEBE NUTTER, m. 8 Sept. 1761, WINTHROP PICKERING (3-v).

ARABELLA NUTTER, covenant, 27 Sept. 1761.

ANNA NUTTER, covenant, 25 Oct. 1761.

ELIZABETH NUTTER, covenant, 25 Oct. 1761.

GRAFTON NUTTER, of Portsmouth.
    Children, baptized in North Church, Portsmouth:
    i. JOTHAM, bapt. 30 Jan. 1763.
    ii. MARY, bapt. 16 June 1765.
    iii. GRAFTON, bapt. 16 Aug. 1767.
    iv. ANN, bapt. 4 Mar. 1770.

ARABELLA NUTTER, m. 16 July 1764, JOSEPH PEVEY, of Barrington.

ALICE NUTTER, m. 22 Oct. 1767, FRANCES MESERVY, of Portsmouth.

Maj. JOHN NUTTER, d. 1768, at Barnstead, *aet.* 80 (Jewett's *Barnstead*, p. 78).

HENRY NUTTER, son of Richard, of Rochester, covenant, 18 Feb. 1770.

MARY NUTTER, dau. of Jacob and Rebecca, bapt. 17 Nov. 1771, in North Church (*N.H. Gen. Rec.*, vol. 6, p. 43).

ALICE NUTTER, m. 10 Feb. 1774, JONATHAN DOWNING.

ANN NUTTER, covenant, 18 Sept. 1774.

HANNAH NUTTER, dau. of Ann, bapt. 18 Sept. 1774.

HENRY NUTTER, 1776, midshipman on *Raleigh* (*N.H. Gen. Rec.*, vol. 2, p. 181).

ABIGAIL NUTTER, m. 30 Jan. 1777, ISAAC WENTWORTH, both of Rochester (*N.H. Gen. Rec.*, vol. 4, p. 148).

ELIZABETH NUTTER, m. 7 Dec. 1778, JOSEPH BROWN, of Barnstead.

ZEBULON DOE NUTTER, son of Deborah, bapt. 17 Sept. 1780.

SAMUEL NUTTER, m. 15 Aug. 1784, MARY HUNTRESS (North Church rec.)

FRANCIS NUTTER, on confession, bapt. 26 Apr. 1791, at Rochester (*id.* 6-176).

JOHN NUTTER, m. 11 Oct. 1793, HANNAH HAYES, both of Rochester (*id.* 5-8).

RI.[3] NUTTER, m. 23 Apr. 1795, MARY WENTWORTH, both of Rochester (*id.* 5-50)

ALICE NUTTER, of New Durham, m. 25 Sept. 1798, MARK REED, of Rochester (*id.* 5-53).

SAM. NELSON NUTTER, m. 4 Dec. 1800, SARAH COOLBROTH, both of Farmington (*id.* 5-55).

CHRISTOPHER NUTTER, d. 21 Oct. 1830, *aet.* 55 yrs. (*Register*, vol. 73, p. 197).

Wid. **DEBORAH NUTTER**, d. 18 Dec. 1831, *aet.* 75 (*ibid.*).

JOHN NUTTER, d. 20 Mar. 1860, *aet.* 90-11, at Rochester (*Register*, vol. 80, p. 310).

HANNAH NUTTER, wife of JOHN, d. 15 May 1855, *aet.* 83-9, at Rochester (*ibid.*).

OSBORN

GEORGE OSBORN, m. 13 May 1756, ALICE PICKERING, both of Portsmouth.

E. P. and L. C.

E. P., m. 17 Sept. 1757, L. C.

PARCHER

ELIAS PARCHER, m. 3 Dec. 1747, KATHARINE HUGH.

SAMUEL PARCHER, son of Elias and Katharine, bapt. 3 Mar. 1749.

PARSHLEY

JOHN PARSHLEY, m. 1 Feb. 1741, TAMSEN HUNTRESS, both of Portsmouth.

PATCH

BENJAMIN PATCH, son of Benjamin, bapt. 26 July 1724.

JOHN PATCH, son of Benjamin and Lydia, bapt. 18 Sept. 1726.

PAUL

ELIZABETH[5] PAUL (Amos[4], Daniel[3], Stephen[2], Daniel[1]) (Stackpole's *Kittery*, p. 645), m. 16 Dec. 1762, AZARIAH LIBBY, both of Kittery.

SARAH[5] PAUL (Jeremiah[4], Daniel[3], Stephen[2], Daniel[1]) (*ibid.*), m. 31 Oct. 1765, WILLIAM DENNETT, both of Kittery.

ABIGAIL[5] PAUL (Stephen[4], Daniel[3], Stephen[2], Daniel[1]) (*ibid.*), m. 31 Oct. 1765, TIMOTHY SPINNEY, both of Kittery.

PEARL

JOSEPH PEARL, of Rochester, m. 28 Nov. 1749, SARAH BICKFORD.

PEARSON

ELIZABETH PEARSON, of Hampton, m. 12 Sept. 1750, CHRISTOPHER HUNTRESS.

PEAVEY

1. ABEL[1] PEAVEY[+](? Edward), of Portsmouth, 1691, and Bloody Point, 1713, m. ----- HUDSON, dau. of John and Mary (Beard) Hudson (*Genealogical Dictionary of Maine and New Hampshire*, p. 85).

In the will of John Hudson, of Newington, dated 5 July 1717, proved Mar. 1723/4, he names his wife, Mary (Beard) (Stackpole's *Durham*, vol. 2, p. 12) and grandchildren Hudson, Thomas and "Able" Peavey (*N.H. State Pap.*, vol. 31, p. 803).

Children (*id.*, p. 804):

2 i. HUDSON[2], b. 11 Feb. 1711.
3 ii. THOMAS, b. 19 June 1714, bapt. 3 Sept. 1727.
4 iii. ABEL, b. 30 June 1716, bapt. 3 Sept. 1727.

2. HUDSON[2] PEAVEY (Abel[1]), of Newington, b. 11 Feb. 1711 (*N.H. State Pap.*, vol. 31, p. 804), m. 11 May 1736, MADELINE BROWN, b. in Conn.

Children, baptized at Newington:

5 i. JOSEPH, bapt. 15 Mar. 1740/1.
6 ii. DANIEL, bapt. 20 Nov. 1743.
   iii. MARY, bapt. 15 Apr. 1747.
7 iv. JAMES, bapt. 14 Feb. 1748/9.
   v. ELIZABETH, bapt. 3 Feb. 1750/1, m. 24 Nov. 1773, ISSACHER WIGGIN.
   vi. MERCY, bapt. 8 Apr. 1753, m. 29 Mar. 1777, EDWARD GOTHAM, soldier.

+In 1713, Abel and Edward Peavey were at Bloody Point (*Register*, vol. 58, p. 249). Edward had, in 1721, a wife, Mary (*id.*, vol. 30, p. 60)

vii. TEMPERANCE, bapt. 18 May 1753.
8   viii. JOHN, bapt. 13 Nov. 1757.

3. THOMAS² PEAVEY (Abel¹), of Newington and Rochester, b. 19 June 1714, bapt. 3 Sept. 1727, m. 13 Nov. 1740, MARY² STEVENS, bapt. at Newington, 27 July 1728, dau. of John and Sarah Stevens.

Children, the first three baptized at Newington, the others at Rochester:
  i. OLIVER³, bapt. 18 Apr. 1742.
  ii. TEMPERANCE, bapt. 14 Sept. 1745.
  iii. SARAH, bapt. 19 Nov. 1748.
  iv. WILLIAM, bapt. 25 Aug. 1753, d. in infancy.
  v. WILLIAM, bapt. 9 Feb. 1755.

4. ABEL² PEAVEY (Abel¹), of Newington, b. 30 June 1716, m. MARY -----.

Child, baptized at Newington:
  i. EZEKIEL³, bapt. 2 June 1734.

5. JOSEPH³ PEAVEY (Hudson², Abel¹), of Newington and Barrington, bapt. 15 Mar. 1740/1, m. 12 July 1764, ARABELLA⁵ NUTTER, b. at Newington, dau. ? of Samuel⁴ and Sarah (Hoyt) Nutter.

Child, born at Barrington:
  i. JAMES⁴, of Barrington, Newmarket and Epping, b. 1772.

6. DANIEL³ PEAVEY (Hudson², Abel¹), of Rochester, bapt. 20 Nov. 1743.

Children, baptized at Rochester (*N.H. Gen. Rec.*, vol. 6, p. 171):
  i. OLIVER⁴, of Rochester, bapt. 24 Oct. 1780, m. 15 Nov. 1795 (*id.*, vol. 5, p. 51), PATIENCE YOUNG.
  ii. DANIEL, bapt. 24 Oct. 1780.
  iii. JACOB, bapt. 24 Oct. 1780.
  iv. SARAH, bapt. 24 Oct. 1780.

7. JAMES³ PEAVEY (Hudson², Abel¹), of Newington, bapt. 14 Feb. 1748/9, d. 5 May 1811, m. 17 Feb. 1774, MARY⁵ NUTTER, bapt. at Newington, 26 Aug. 1750, dau. of Maj. John⁵ and Anna (Symmes) Nutter.

Children, baptized at Newington:
  i. ANNA⁴, bapt. 19 Nov. 1774.
  ii. MARY, bapt. 21 May 1776.
  iii. JOHN NUTTER (twin), bapt. 26 July 1778.
  iv. JAMES BOYD (twin), bapt. 26 July 1778.
  v. SARAH, bapt. 13 Aug. 1780.
  vi. ELIZABETH D. (twin), bapt. 4 July 1783.
  vii. HOPLEY (twin), bapt. 3 Aug. 1783.

viii. DANIEL NUTTER, bapt. 1 Nov. 1785, d. 13 Mar. 1789.
ix. CHARLES, bapt. 4 Dec. 1787, d. 18 Mar. 1788.
x. ELEANOR, bapt. 16 Sept. 1789.
xi. DOROTHY, bapt. 12 Oct. 1791.
xii. HANNAH, bapt. 5 Aug. 1795.
xiii. HUMPHREY, bapt. 20 Aug. 1796.

8. JOHN^3 PEAVEY (Hudson^2, Abel^1), bapt. 13 Nov. 1757, m. 17 Sept. 1777, LOIS COOLBROTH.

PEAVEY (unconnected)

NATHANIEL PEAVEY, of Greenland.
Children, baptized at Greenland (*Register*, vol. 28, p. 442):
  i. NATHANIEL, bapt. 1727.
  ii. SAMUEL, bapt. 1727.
  iii. JOSEPH, bapt. 1727.
  iv. MARY, bapt. 1727.
  v. DANIEL, bapt. 1727.
  vi. ANTHONY, bapt. 1728 (*id.*, vol. 29, p. 30).
  vii. JOHN, bapt. at Stratham, 10 Apr. 1731 (*N.H. Gen. Rec.*, vol. 2, p. 11).

PETER PEAVY, of Hampton, 1722, m. ESTHER -----. He had a half share in the estate of Thomas Robie (*N.H. State Pap.*, vol. 32, p. 99).
Children (Dow's *Hampton*, p. 907):
  i. HANNAH, b. 14 July 1721.
  ii. MARY, b. 22 Mar. 1723.
  iii. RACHEL, bapt. 23 May 1725.
  iv. ESTHER, bapt. 2 June 1728.

WILLIAM PEAVEY, of Portsmouth, 1713, d. 1731$^+$, m. SARAH -----, living 1751.

William Peavey and Sarah, his wife, were admitted to the North Church at Portsmouth, 15 Dec. 1715. (*N.H. Gen. Rec.*, vol. 4, p. 100).

Children, born at Portsmouth (deed of 1765) (*N.H. Colonial Deeds*, vol. 91, p. 417):
  i. WILLIAM, of Barrington, bapt. 15 Dec. 1715 (*N.H. Gen. Rec.*, vol. 4, p.

+His "estate" at Barrington was taxed 1731-5 (town rec.), had Widow Peavey at Portsmouth, 1731-5 (town rec.).

100), m. ANNA -----.

In his will dated 1800, proved 1819, he names his wife, Anna; son, Pomfret, executor; daughters, Hannah (Hall), Elizabeth, Susanna (Page), and Mary (Fernald); and Anna and John (children of his deceased son, William) (*Rockingham Probate*).

ii. MARY, bapt. 15 Dec. 1715 (*ibid.*), living in 1777, m. -----STUART, of Portsmouth.

iii. JOHN, of Portsmouth and Barnstead, living in 1765, ship carpenter, bapt. 23 Aug. 1719 (*id.*, p. 103), m. DORCAS -----.

iv. SARAH, d. living in 1777, m. 1 July 1736, STACY DALLING, of Portsmouth, b. at Portsmouth, 27 Sept. 1710, bapt. 8 July 1716, d. before 1735, son of Thomas and Elizabeth (Pitman) Dalling.

v. MEHITABLE, bapt. 18 Mar. 1721/2 (*N.H. Gen. Rec.*, vol. 5, p. 38), m. Capt. SAMUEL DALLING, of Portsmouth, master mariner, gent., b. at Portsmouth 1711, bapt. 8 July 1716, d. 15 Oct. 1788, *aet.* 77 (tombstone), son of Thomas and Elizabeth (Pitman) Dalling.

vi. ABIGAIL, m. WILLIAM CANO, of Portsmouth, goldsmith.

vii. ELIZABETH, d. Apr. 1799, m. 21 June 1757, BENJAMIN[4] SEWARD, of Portsmouth, mariner, b. there about 1735, d. about 1764, son of George[3] and Margaret (Pendexter) Seward.

On 28 July 1774, Samuel Dalling, Gent., and Mehitable, his wife; Sarah Dalling, widow; Elizabeth Seward, widow; and Mary Stuart, widow; all of Portsmouth, conveyed 60 acres at Barrington, part of Lot 173 in the fourth range (*Strafford Deeds*, vol. 132, p. 406).

On 31 Oct. 1765, Mary Stuart, widow; Sarah Dalling, widow; Samuel Dalling, mariner, and Mehitable, his wife; William Cano, goldsmith, and Abigail, his wife; and Elizabeth Seward, widow; all of Portsmouth, conveyed to John Peavey, carpenter, the premises on Pickering's Neck where the grantee now lives, formerly of William Peavey, father of the grantors (*N.H. Colonial Deeds*, vol. 91, p. 417).

On 20 May 1771, John Peavey, of Portsmouth, ship carpenter, and Dorcas, his wife; conveyed the foregoing premises bounded E on the main road leading to Pickering's mills to Elizabeth Seward, widow of Benjamin (*id.*, vol. 96, p. 390).

EDWARD PEAVEY, had a seat in the North Church, 1693 (*N.H. Gen. Rec.*, vol. 3, p. 174).

ABEL, EDWARD and NATHANIEL PEAVEY, at Newington, 1713 (*Register*, vol. 58, pp. 249-50).

DEBORAH PEAVEY, m. 9 Apr. 1717, JAMES ROLLINS.

SARAH PEAVEY, m. 12 Feb. 1719, RICHARD CARTER.

JANE PEAVEY, m. 31 Dec. 1719, EBENEZER PLACE.

RACHEL PEAVEY, SR., m. 19 Dec. 1720, SALATHIEL DENBOW.

RACHEL PEAVEY, m. 17 Jan. 1721, THOMAS ROWE.

ANNA PEAVEY, covenanted, 1727, at Greenland (*Register*, vol. 28, p. 422).

JOSEPH PEAVEY and his daugher, ESTHER, at Dover, 7 Apr. 1727 (*Register*, vol. 29, p. 263).

MARY PEAVEY, m. 14 Dec. 1727, at Portsmouth, SAMUEL HOLMES, both of Portsmouth (*id.*, vol. 24, p. 359).

MARY PEAVEY, m. 15 May 1728/9, at Portsmouth, EBENEZER MORSE, both of Portsmouth (*id.*, vol. 25, p. 117).

SARAH PEAVEY, dau. of John and Rebecca, bapt. 2 June 1734.

SARAH PEAVEY, m. 30 June 1736, STACY DARLING, at Greenland (*Register*, vol. 65, p. 355; *id.*, vol. 26, p. 377).

ROSAMOND PEAVEY, dau. of John, bapt. 4 July 1736.

ELIZABETH PEAVEY, dau. of William and Dorcas, b. ab. 1737, at Portsmouth, m. 21 June 1757, BENJAMIN[4] SEWARD.

SAMUEL PEAVEY'S CHILD, d. 20 Jan. 1748, at Stratham[+] (vol. 47, p. 20).

DANIEL PEAVEY, bapt. 2 Sept. 1753, (*N.H. Gen. Rec.*, vol. 6, p. 74).

SAMUEL PEAVEY'S CHILD, d. 8 Dec. 1753, at Stratham (vol. 47, p. 480).

TEMPERANCE PEAVEY, bapt. July 1757 (*N.H. Gen. Rec.*, vol. 6, p. 114)

SAMUEL PEAVEY'S CHILD, d. 27 Apr. 1758, at Stratham (vol. 48, p. 29).

+The Stratham items are from the *Register*.

NATHANIEL PEAVEY, d. 24 Apr. 1763, at Stratham (vol. 48, p. 338).

SAMUEL PEAVEY'S CHILD, d. 26 Jan. 1764, at Stratham (vol. 48, p. 338).

SAMUEL PEAVEY'S CHILD, d. 3 Apr. 1764, at Stratham (*ibid.*).

SAMUEL PEAVEY'S CHILD, d. 2 May 1767, at Stratham (vol. 48, p. 339)

SAMUEL PEAVEY'S CHILD, d. 27 July 1767, at Stratham (*ibid.*).

JOSHUA PEAVEY, m. at Rochester, 25 Nov. 1779, MARY BUZZELL, both of New Durham (*N.H. Gen. Rec.*, vol. 4, p. 149).

ANTHONY PEAVEY, m. at Rochester, 30 Sept. 1784, BETTY HAMMOND, both of Rochester (*id.*, vol. 4, p. 152).

SIMON PEAVEY, m. at Rochester, 28 Mar. 1808, MARY VARNEY, both of Rochester (*id.*, vol. 5, p. 118).

JOHN S. PEAVEY, m. 14 Nov. 1816, SARAH YORK, both of Tuftonboro (*Register*, vol. 59, p. 288).

ABIGAIL PEAVEY, m. at Rochester, 28 Jan. 1818, EDWARD LEAVITT, both of Tuftonboro (*N.H. Gen. Rec.*, vol. 5, p. 151).

JOHN PEAVEY, JR., m. at Rochester, 11 Mar. 1818, MARY CAVERLY, both of Barrington (*id.*, vol. 5, p. 151).

ABIGAIL PEAVEY, of Tuftonboro, m. 3 June 1819, NATHANIEL DEERING, of Waterboro (*Register*, vol. 59, p. 289).

LUCINDA PEAVEY, of Wolfeboro, m. at Lee, 13 Dec. 1824, CALVIN CARSON, of New Durham, then in Dover Jail (*N.H. Gen. Rec.*, vol. 4, p. 184).

GEORGE C. PEAVEY, of Strafford, m. 5 Oct. 1858, SARAH C. TEBBETTS, of Deering (*Register*, vol. 68, p. 203).

ESKAR PEAVEY, m. about 1860, ELIZABETH DAME (*id.*, vol. 65, p. 313).

JOHN PEAVEY, born at Barrington, an early settler of Barnstead, representative, militia captain, d. *aet.* 80. His only daughter married DANIEL BICKFORD

(Jewett's *Barnstead*, p. 82).

All **PEAVEY** items in *N.H. Gen. Rec.* and first 50 volumes of the *Register* are noted.

PEIRCE

GEORGE PEIRCE, of Portsmouth, m. 25 Mar. 1738, JERUSHA FURBER.

PERKINS

DAVID PERKINS, of Epping, m. 29 Oct. 1771, MEHITABLE SWETT.

PETTIGREW

THOMAS^3 PETTIGREW (Thomas^2, Frances^1) (Stackpole's *Kittery*, p. 651), m. 31 Aug. 1764, ELEANOR ADAMS, both of Kittery.

STEPHEN^3 PETTIGREW (John$^{2-1}$) (*ibid.*) m. 20 Dec. 1768, LUCY DIXON, both of Kittery.

PEVERLY

ABIGAIL PEVERLY, m. 26 Nov. 1747, JOHN CLARK, both of Portsmouth.

PEVERTON

A CHILD of ----- **PEVERTON**, bapt. 17 Dec. 1732.

DAVID PEVERTON, son of ----- and Mary Peverton, bapt. 2 May 1734.

PHICKETT

MARGARET PHICKETT, of Portsmouth, m. 16 Dec. 1733, THOMAS QUINT, of Newington (*Register*, vol. 25, p. 120).

PHILBROOK

SARAH PHILBROOK, of Greenland, m. 7 July 1766, JUDAH ALLEN, of Stratham.

----- **PHILBROOK**, of Rye, m. 27 Aug. 1766, MARY FOLSOM, of Newmarket.

PHILLIPS

SARAH PHILLIPS, of Portsmouth, m. 19 Mar. 1736, MOSES DOW.

SARAH PHILLIPS, m. 22 Nov. 1739, ----- RENOLDS, of Stratham.

MARY PHILLIPS, b. at Ipswich (*Register*, vol. 27, p. 8), m. 20 Mar. 1740, CHARLES RUNLETT, of Stratham.

PICKERING

1. JOHN^1 PICKERING, of Portsmouth, 1633, farmer, miller, b. in England, d. 18 Jan. 1668 (*Register*, vol. 7, p. 125).

His will dated 11 Nov. 1668, was found inperfect and administration was granted to his son John (*N.H. State Pap.*, vol. 31, p. 111).

His estate in Portsmouth included the present Point of Graves Cemetery and extended thence down the river including the mill privilege on the south mill pond where he had a mill. He owned also a farm of some 500 acres on Bloody Point on the Great Bay, which by his will he gave to his son, Thomas, and which came to him on the family settlement (Eddy's *John Pickering Family*, p. 6; *Brewster's Rambles*, p. 50).

Children, born at Portsmouth (as named in his will):

    i. JOHN^2, b. about 1644, whose issue in the male line is extinct. (See NOTE below).

2   ii. THOMAS^2

    iii. REBECCA

    iv. ABIGAIL

    v. MARY

    vi. SARAH

        NOTE: Capt. JOHN^2 PICKERING succeeded to the mill properties which his father had entailed to him and his eldest son. He became one of the leading men in the colony (*Brewster's Rambles*, p. 57), was lawyer, King's attorney, representative to both the Massachusetts and New Hampshire Assemblies, and speaker to the latter. He established the Point of Graves Cemetery as a public burying ground.

        He married 10 Jan. 1665, MARY STANIAN, dau. of Anthony, of Hampton.

        His only son to have issue was John^3, born 1 Dec. 1666, who married Elizabeth Mendum. Eddy says in his book that of the sons of John^3, the only one to have issue was Thomas^4, slain by the Indians at Casco Bay in 1746. His son, John^5 had sons, John^6, Thomas, and Daniel; all of whom died without issue; and the name thus became extinct in the line of John². Thomas⁶, commander of the ship, *Hampden*, was killed in battle in 1779.

2. THOMAS² PICKERING (John¹), of Bloody Point and Portsmouth, farmer, m. MARY GEE, dau. of John⁺ and Hazelponi² (Willis) Gee (Bell's *Exeter*, p. 40; *Register*, vol. 50, pp. 47-8; *id.*, vol. 68, pp. 81-2).

In his will dated 14 Aug. 1719, proved 20 Apr. 1720, he mentions his wife, Mary, and children as below (*N.H. State Pap.*, vol. 32, p. 87). He had, besides his farm at Bloody Point, a house at the "Bank."

Children, as mentioned in his will:

3   i. JAMES³
4   ii. JOSHUA
    iii. THOMAS
    iv. MARY, m. ? 25 Dec. 1702, JOHN² FABYAN (2), son of John¹ and Sarah, *q.v.*
    v. SARAH, m. ? 26 Sept. 1714, JOSEPH LEACH (*Register*, vol. 22, p 270), of Portsmouth.
      Children (surname *Leach*), born at Portsmouth (*id.*, vol. 24, pp. 360-1):
      1) Phebe, b. 16 Dec. 1717.
      2) George, b. 7 Dec. 1722.
    vi. REBECCA, m. HENRY JAQUES, of Portsmouth (*N.H. State Pap.*, vol. 32, p. 145).
    vii. ABIGAIL, m. 12 June 1718, JAMES SEAVEY, of Newcastle.
      Child, born at Rye:
      1) James⁴, b. 1 Mar. 1743 (Parson's *Rye*, p. 535).
    viii. HAZELPONI
    ix. HANNAH, b. 1695 (Statement of Mrs. Mary Bennett Morse, of Haverhill).
    x. ELIZABETH, m. 10 Dec. 1724, JOHN BRACKETT, of Greenland.
    xi. MEHITABLE, m. at Greenland, 19 Mar. 1726, Lieut. SAMUEL³ WEEKS (*Register*, vol. 39, p. 235), of Greenland, tanner, b. at Greenland, son of Capt. Samuel².

3. Lieut. JAMES³ PICKERING (Thomas², John¹), of Newington, m. 16 Jan. 1718, MARY NUTTER.

His will dated 6 June 1766, proved 31 Aug. 1768, mentions his children as

---

⁺He was drowned at Martha's Vineyard in 1669. His widow m. (2) Obediah Baker, of Ipswich, Mass., and d. 27 May 1714. See also Hoyt's *Salisbury and Amesbury*, p. 1091.

below, except Stephen (*N.H. Probate*, vol. --, p. --)

Children, baptized at Newington:

6   i. JOHN^4, covenant, 9 Mar. 1740.

7   ii. ANTHONY, covenant, 30 Mar. 1740.

8   iii. THOMAS, covenant, 30 Mar. 1740.

    iv. STEPHEN, of Barnstead, bapt. 1 Mar. 1740, d. 1825, m. MEHITABLE -----, b. 1840, d. 1811.

9   v. WINTHROP, bapt. 1 Mar. 1740.

    vi. ABIGAIL, bapt. 9 Mar. 1740, b. 6 June 1733, d. 30 Sept. 1781, m. 6 June 1751, Deac. BENJAMIN^5 ADAMS (4), son of Dr. Joseph^4 and Johanna (Gilman) Adams, *q.v.*

4. JOSHUA^3 PICKERING (Thomas^2, John^1), of Newington, b. 28 Nov. 1703, d. 9 Dec. 1768, m. (1) 18 June 1724, Mrs. DEBORAH (PICKERING) SMITHSON (*Register*, vol. 24, p. 17), b. at Portsmouth, dau. of John^3 Pickering, m. (2) MARY BRACKETT.

His will dated 4 May 1767, proved 25 May 1768, mentions his children as below, except Mary. Dower was set off to his widow, Mary (*N.H. Probate*, vol. --, p. --).

Children, born at Newington:

    i. JOSEPH^4, bapt. 15 May 1726.

10   ii. JOSHUA, b. about 1728.

    iii. DEBORAH, bapt. 27 May 1730.

    iv. SAMUEL, bapt. 13 Feb. 1732.

11   v. EPHRAIM, bapt. 13 Jan. 1734.

    vi. DANIEL, bapt. 26 Oct. 1735.

12   vii. JOHN, b. 1738.

    viii. MARY, bapt. 2 June 1739, not mentioned in her father's will.

    ix. ELIZABETH, m. 25 Apr. 1763, SAMUEL^4 DOE, son of Samuel^3 and Abigail (Wiggin) Doe (Stackpole's *Durham*, vol. 2, p. 133).

    x. SARAH

----- HUNTRESS, m. 25 Dec. 1760, MARY PICKERING (South Church Rec.)

5. THOMAS^3 PICKERING (Thomas^2, John^1), of Newington, b. 28 Nov. 1703, d. Dec. 1786, m. (1) 7 Feb. 1727, MARY^3 DOWNING (2-vi), dau. of Col. John Downing, *q.v.*, m. (2) 17 May 1743, MARY^2 JANVRIN (1-iii), dau. of John^1 and Elizabeth (Knight) Janvrin, *q.v.*

In his will, dated 4 Apr. 1742?, proved Jan. 1787, he names his children as below, except Nos. ii, iii, iv, viii, ix, x, and xi (*Rockingham Probate*, vol. --, p. --)

His children Nicholas, John Gee, James, and Temperance are named in the will of their grandfather, Col. John Downing.

Children, born at Newington:

13   i. NICHOLAS[4], b. 1727.
- ii. ELIZABETH, bapt. 26 Oct. 1729, b. 18 Oct. 1729, d. in infancy.
- iii. BENJAMIN, bapt. 23 Sept. 1733, d. in infancy.
- vi. DOROTHY, bapt. 21 Apr. 1734 (*Register*, vol. 81, p. 448).

14   v. JOHN GEE, bapt. 24 Aug. 1735.

15   vi. JAMES, bapt. Sept. 1737.
- vii. TEMPERENCE, m. 15 Mar. 1759, as his second wife Ensign JOHN[3] KNIGHT (2-i), son of Capt. John[2] and Elizabeth (Heard) Knight, *q.v.*
- viii. MARY, bapt. 10 Dec. 1739, b. Oct. 1739, d. in infancy.
- ix. LYDIA, bapt. 6 Apr. 1740 (*Register, ibid.*).
- x. ELIZABETH, bapt. 4 Oct. 1741 (*ibid.*).
- xi. MARTHA, bapt. 11 Dec. 1743 (*ibid.*).

Children by his second wife, born at Newington:
- xii. ELIZABETH, bapt. 1 Apr. 1744, b. 24 Mar. 1744, m. 12 Mar. 1767, TIMOTHY[5] DAME (5- vii), son of Richard[4] and Elizabeth (Leighton) Dame, *q.v.*

16   xiii. WILLIAM, b. 17 July 1745.
- xiv. MARY, bapt. 19 Feb. 1748/9, b. 7 Feb. 1748/9, d. 8 Feb. 1802, m. 15 Oct. 1778, WILLIAM LANGDON, of Portsmouth, tanner, b. at Portsmouth, 1748, d. 30 Sept. 1820, son of William[3] and Sarah Langdon (Parson's *Rye*, p. 407).
- xv. BENJAMIN, bapt. 26 May 1751, b. 13 May 1751, m. MARY PICKERING.
- xvi. SARAH, bapt. 20 Jan. 1754, b. 5 Jan. 1754, m. 2 May 1782, Maj. GEORGE GAINES, of Portsmouth.
- xvii. RICHARD, of Newington, bapt. 4 May 1755, b. 15 Apr. 1755, d. 1 Dec. 1831 (*Register*, vol. 73, p. 197), m. 7 Nov. 1787, MARY[5] THOMPSON, b. at Durham, 11 Apr. 1767, d. 10 Oct. 1837, dau. of Ebenezer[4] and Mary (Torr) Thompson (Stackpole's *Durham*, vol. 2, p. 363).

  Child, born at Newington:
  1) Temperance[5], b. 22 Aug. 1788, d. 29 Jan. 1864, m. Joseph[7] Coe, of Durham, merchant, shipbuilder, b. at Durham, 1 June 1782, d. 22 Apr. 1852, son of Rev. Curtis and Anne (Thompson) Coe (Stackpole's *Durham*, vol. 2, p. 79).

- xviii. ALICE, bapt. 20 Feb. 1757, b. 6 Feb. 1757, m. 22 Nov. 1781, JOSHUA BRACKETT.
- xix. PATIENCE, bapt. 29 Apr. 1759, b. 21 Aug. 1758, m. 9 Dec. 1790, Rev. JOSEPH[5] LANGDON, of Rye, clergyman, b. at Portsmouth, 12 Mar. 1758, d. 27 June 1824, son of Capt. Samuel[4] and Hannah (Storer) Langdon (Parson's *Rye*, P. 141).

6. JOHN[4] PICKERING (James[3], Thomas[2], John[1]), covenant, 9 Mar. 1740, d. 1790, ? m. 28 Aug. 1740, MARY[4] NUTTER (4-v), dau. of Henry[3] and Mary[2] (Shackford) Nutter, *q.v.*

His will dated 4 Jan. 1790, proved 17 Mar. 1790, names his children as below (*Rockingham Probate*).

Children:
  i. JOHN[5], b. 1792, d. 10 Oct. 1834, *aet.* 42 yrs. (*Register*, vol. 73, p. 198).
  ii. WILLIAM PEPPERELL, of Portsmouth, b. 1759, d. 5 Jan. 1833 (*Register*, vol. 73, p. 197), m. MARY NELSON.
    Child, baptized at Portsmouth:
      1) Isaac[6], bapt. 23 Feb. 1787 (*Register*, vol. 82, p. 52).
  iii. STEPHEN, m. SARAH GROVE.
  iv. JAMES
  v. JOHN
  vi. TEMPERENCE
  vii. MARY
  viii. ABIGAIL, m. 25 Dec. 1760, NOAH[4] HUNTRESS (3-viii), son of Christopher[3] and Mary (Chick) Huntress, *q.v.*

7. ANTHONY[4] PICKERING (James[3], Thomas[2], John[1]), of Newington, b. 1725, m. (1) ELIZABETH (SMART) TUFTS, m. (2) ABIGAIL[4] (MESERVE) DURRELL, b. at Durham, 27 Aug. 1745, dau. of Daniel[3] and Abigail (Ham) Meserve, and wid. of NICHOLAS[3] DURRELL (Stackpole's *Durham*, vol. 2, p. 286). She m. (3) BENJAMIN GERRISH (*id.*, p. 168).

Children by first wife, born at Newington:
  i. ANTHONY[5], of Nottingham, bapt. 28 May 1749.
  ii. JAMES, of Newmarket, m. RACHEL WAKEFIELD DURRELL (Stackpole's *Durham*, vol. 2, p. 169). dau. of Nicholas[3] and Rachel (Wakefield) Durrell (*id.*, p. 168).
  iii. SAMUEL, of Newmarket, m. ELIZABETH BRACKETT.
  iv. WINTHROP, of Effingham, bapt. 12 Mar. 1751.
  v. LEVI, soldier and sailor in the Revolution (Parson's *Rye*, p. 260; *Register*, vol. 19, p. 138), bapt. 20 May 1753, d. unm.
    He was taken prisoner on the *General Sullivan's* prize and committed to Old Mill Prison (*ibid.*).

Children by second wife, born at Newington:
  vi. MARY
  vii. NICHOLAS, mariner, d. in Demarara.

8. THOMAS[4] PICKERING (James[3], Thomas[2], John[1]), of Newington, m. 10 July 1759, JERUSHA[5] FURBER (8-iii), dau. of Jeremiah[4] and Abigail (Leighton)

Furber, *q.v.*

Children, born at Newington:
- i. ABIGAIL[5], bapt. 15 June 1760, m. JAMES[5] BURNHAM, of Somersworth, soldier in the Revolution, b. 13 June 1754, d. 17 June 1845 (Stackpole's *Durham*, vol. 2, p. 43).
- ii. DEBORAH, bapt. 5 Sept. 1762, m. ----- KENNY.
- iii. NEHEMIAH, of Newington, bapt. 2 Dec. 1764, d. 12 Oct. 1843 (*Register*, vol. 73, p. 199), m. MEHITABLE -----, b. 1772, d. 26 Mar. 1832 (*id.*, p. 197).
- iv. LEVI, bapt. 24 May 1767.
- v. NICHOLAS, bapt. 4 Nov. 1770, m. ELEANOR MARSHALL.
- vi. MARY, bapt. 19 Sept. 1773, m. ----- GATES.

9. WINTHROP[4] PICKERING, (James[3], Thomas[2], John[1]), of Newington, bapt. 1 Mar. 1740, m. 8 Sept. 1761, PHEBE NUTTER.

His will dated 22 Jan. 1780, proved 5 Aug. 1783, names his children as below.
Children:
- i. ABSOLOM[5], of Newington, b. 1765, d. 4 Jan. 1835, *aet.* 70 yrs. 2 mos. (*Register*, vol. 73, p. 198).
- ii. JAMES, bapt. 13 Mar. 1768, d. 2 Sept. 1816, m. 16 Apr. 1798, NANCY[6] HOYT (3-iv-4), dau. of John[5] and Sarah (Furber) Hoyt, *q.v.*
- iii. GILBERT, of Newington, b. 1771, d. 10 June 1833, *aet.* 62 yrs. (*Register*, vol. 73, p. 197), m. SARAH -----, d. 17 Jan. 1859 (*id.*, p. 204)
- iv. TEMPERANCE, b. 1761, d. 31 Dec. 1847 (*id.*, p. 200).
- v. CHARLOTTE
- vi. MEHITABLE
- vii. HANNAH, b. 1777, m. (1) ----- DAME, m. ? (2) 22 Dec. 1812, THOMAS[4] LANG (*John Lang Family*, No. 34).
- viii. ELIZABETH
- ix. PHEBE BICKFORD
- x. ROSAMOND

10. JOSHUA[4] PICKERING (Joshua[3], Thomas[2], John[1]), of Newington, d. at Greenland, 5 June 1771 (*N.H. Gazette* of 7 June 1771), m. MARY BRACKETT (Eddy's *Pickering Family*, p. --). She m. (2) ----- JOHNSON.

Children:
- i. GEORGE[5], b. 1750, m. EUNICE BATCHELDER.
- ii. ELIZABETH, d. unm.
- iii. NANCY, m. EZRAH DREW, of Hampton.
- iv. MARY, m. SAMUEL HATCH.

11. Maj. EPHRAIM[4] PICKERING (Joshua[3], Thomas[2], John[1]), of Newington, officer in the Revolution, member of the Legislature, 1780-81, d. 1 Jan. 1803, m. LYDIA COLMAN (1-x), dau. of Eleazur³ and Ann (Nutter) Colman, *q.v.*

His will dated 27 Dec. 1802, proved 17 Jan. 1803, names his wife, Lydia, and children as below except Lydia, Joshua, and Olive (*Rockingham Probate*).

Children, born at Newington:
- i. ANN, bapt. 6 July 1760, d. 26 Dec. 1833 (*Register*, vol. 73, p. 197), m. 18 Oct. 1778, SAMUEL⁴ FABYAN (6), son of Samuel³ and Elizabeth (Huntress) Fabyan, *q.v.*
- ii. SARAH TOPPAN, bapt. 6 July 1763, m. ? VALENTINE PICKERING (See unconnected).
- iii. DEBORAH, bapt. 31 Jan. 1762, m. 10 Apr. 1778, PAUL ROLLINS.
- iv. LYDIA, bapt. 5 Aug. 1764, d. in infancy.
- v. JOSHUA, of Northampton, bapt. 12 June 1768, m. ELIZABETH⁵ FABYAN (6-iii), dau. of John⁴ and Mehitable (Berry) Fabyan, *q.v.*
- vi. OLIVE RING, bapt. 12 June 1766, d. unm. 16 Sept. 1840.
- vii. JAMES COLMAN, bapt. 18 Apr. 1772, m. ABIGAIL PICKERING FURBER.
- viii. JOSEPH WARREN, of Portsmouth, bapt. 1 Sept. 1776, d. 19 May 1850 (*Register*, vol. 70, p. 201), m. HANNAH⁶ NUTTER (17-v), dau. of Matthias⁵ and his first wife, Martha (Perkins) Nutter, *q.v.*
- ix. MARY, bapt. 1 Sept. 1776, m. JOSEPH PERKINS.
- x. LYDIA, bapt. 1 Sept. 1776, d. 3 Jan. 1842 (*Register*, vol. 73, p. 194, m. Capt. THEODORE FURBER, of Portsmouth.
- xi. ELIZABETH, m. JONATHAN STONE.
- xii. ABIGAIL, bapt. 12 Oct. 1777, m. MATTHEW B. PACKER.
- xiii. EPHRAIM, bapt. 20 Oct. 1774, m. SUSAN⁵ WEEKS, b. at Greenland, dau. of Dr. Ichabod and Abigail (March) Weeks (*Register*, vol. 39, p. 237).

EPHRAIM PICKERING, of Lincoln, Me., b. at Newington, 30 Apr. 1803, in 1844 with six children, m. 5 Feb. 1828, MARTHA MOULTON (Fellows' *Lincoln*, p. 388).

12. JOHN⁴ PICKERING (Joshua³, Thomas², John¹), of Portsmouth, lawyer, chief justice of the Supreme Court, justice of the U.S. District Court, Governor (*Brewster's Rambles*, p. 163), A.B. (Harvard, 1761), b. 1738, d. 11 Apr. 1805 (*Register*, vol. 10, p.52), m. ABIGAIL SHEAFE, b. at Portsmouth, 1743, d. 10 Dec. 1805, dau. of Jacob.

Children+, born at Portsmouth (*Register*, vol. 82, p. 52):
  i. ABIGAIL^5, bapt. 17 June 1770.
  ii. HANNAH, bapt. 28 Feb. 1773.
  iii. JEMIMA, bapt. 26 Aug. 1774.
  iv. DANIEL, bapt. 26 Aug. 1774, d. in infancy.
  v. SARAH, bapt. 17 Aug. 1776.
  vi. LUCRETIA, bapt. 6 Sept. 1778.
  vii. JOHN, bapt. 17 Jan. 1779.
  viii. JACOB SHEAFE, bapt. 10 Dec. 1780.
  ix. SUSAN, bapt. 9 Nov. 1783.
  x. SAMUEL, bapt. 21 Dec. 1783.
  xi. WILLIAM, bapt. 29 Sept. 1786.
  xii. HENRY, bapt. 26 Aug. 1787.
  xiii. DANIEL, bapt. 19 July 1789.
  xiv. BETSEY WENTWORTH, bapt. 7 July 1791.

13. NICHOLAS^4 PICKERING (Thomas$^{3-2}$, John^1), of Newington, b. 1727, m. (1) 7 Mar. 1758, HANNAH^3 BICKFORD (1-ix), dau. of Benjamin^2 and Deborah Bickford, *q.v.*, m. (2) MARY^4 LANGDON, b. at Portsmouth, d. Feb. 1783, dau. of William^3 and Sarah Langdon (Parson's *Rye*, p. 497).

His will dated 7 Nov. 1807, proved 16 Jan. 1809, names his son, Thomas, and daughters, Temperence Hodgdon, Polly Brackett, and Betsey Woodman (*Rockingham Probate*).

Children by first wife, born at Newington:
  i. TEMPERENCE^5, bapt. 24 Dec. 1758, d. 22 Dec. 1843 (*Register*, vol. 73, p. 199), m. 25 Feb. 1773, JOHN^5 HODGDON (8), son of John^4 and Mary (Decker) Hodgdon, *q.v.*
  ii. JOHN, bapt. 1 June 1760, not mentioned in his father's will.
  iii. HANNAH, bapt. 17 Oct. 1762, not mentioned in her father's will.

Children by second wife, born at Newington:
  iv. MARY, bapt. 29 Oct. 1775, m. ----- BRACKETT.
  v. ELIZABETH, bapt. 13 Apr. 1777, m. 19 Mar. 1797, JONATHAN^6 WOODMAN, of Durham, b. at Durham, 21 July 1774, son of Capt. Jonathan^5 and Martha (Davis) Woodman (Stackpole's *Durham*, vol. 2, p. 394).
  vi. NICHOLAS, bapt. 12 Feb. 1783, "the day his wife was buried" (*N.H. Gen. Rec.*, vol. 7, p. 14).

+Baptized as children of John Pickering. Perhaps some of them belong to another John.

BENJAMIN SMITH, of Durham, b. 1769, had a daughter who m. a NICHOLAS PICKERING (Stackpole's *Durham*, vol. 2, p. 315).

14. JOHN GEE[4] PICKERING (Thomas[3-2], John[1]), of Newington, bapt. 24 Aug. 1735, d. 15 Aug. 1795, m. 10 June 1773, DEBORAH[5] (FURBER) MILLS (i-vi), dau. of Nehemiah[4] and Abigail (Leighton) Furber and wid. of Luke[2] Mills, *q.v.*
Children, born at Newington:
- i. MARY[5], bapt. 17 June 1774, d. 1 Oct. 1849, m. 11 May 1794, BENJAMIN[5] THOMPSON, of Durham, clerk of the Common Pleas, b. at Durham, 31 Mar. 1765, d. 21 Jan. 1838, son of Ebenezer[4] and Mary (Torr) Thompson (Stackpole's *Durham*, vol. 2, p. 368).
- ii. TEMPERENCE, bapt. 17 Dec. 1775, m. SAMUEL HILL, of Biddeford, Me., carpenter, b. ? 25 May 1769, ? son of Robert[4] (or Samuel[4]) and Abigail (Hodgdon or Huckins) Hill (Stackpole's *Durham*, vol. 2, p. 211 and 212).
- iii. JOHN GEE, of Newington and Greenland, husbandman, bapt. 28 Sept. 1777, d. 14 Aug. 1858 (*Register*, vol. 73, p. 204), m. MARY[5] FABYAN (6-v), dau. of John[4] and Mehitable (Berry) Fabyan, *q.v.*
- iv. THOMAS, of Newington and Rochester, "Gentleman," bapt. 15 Aug. 1779, d. 8 Sept. 1825 (*Register*, vol. 73, p. 196), m. (1) ? ROSAMOND[5] FABYAN (6-ii), dau. of John[4] and Mehitable (Berry) Fabyan, *q.v.*, m. (2) LYDIA LOW.

    Child by first wife, born at Newington:
    1) Thomas[6], b. 1805, d. 9 Apr. 1834 (*Register*, vol. 73, p. 198).

    Child by second wife, born at Newington:
    2) Gee, of Newington, b. 30 May 1818, m. 1 July 1863, Sophia Antoinette de Rochemont, b. at Georgetown, Brit. Guiana, 28 July 1814, d. 15 Apr. 1871, dau. of George Washington and Henrietta Jacobs (de Wit) de Rochemont.
- v. SARAH, bapt. 23 Dec. 1781, d. at Groton, Mass., 14 Dec. 1858, m. 18 Dec. 1802, JAMES[6] JOY, of Durham, blacksmith, shipbuilder, b. at Durham, 4 Mar. 1778, d. at Groton, Mass., 14 July 1857, son of Jacob[5] and Hannah (Cram) Joy (Stackpole's *Durham*, vol. 2, p. 237).

    Children, born at Durham(*ibid.*);
    1) Maria, b. 25 Apr. 1804, m. 28 Nov. 1824, John L. Thorndike.
    2) John P., b. 17 May 1806, m. (1) Judith P. Batchelder, m. (2) Susan E. Parsons, m. (3) Jane Biggar.
    3) Caroline, b. 17 May 1806, d. in infancy.
    4) Charles, of Ill., b. 15 Sept. 1808, m. Georgianna Batchelder.
    5) James Frederick, of Detroit, Mich., lawyer, b. 2 Dec. 1810, at Durham, d. 24 Sept. 1896, in Detroit, m. (1) Martha A. Read, m. (2) Mary Bourne. (A.B. Dartmouth, 1833) (LLB. Harvard, 1836) (LLD. Harvard,

1869) (See Dartmouth General Catalogue).
6) Richard P., of Groton, Mass., b. 28 Mar. 1812, m. Mary M. Hartwell.
7) Henry B., b. 1814, d. 1827.
8) Calvin, b. 23 May 1816, d. 25 Dec. 1839.
9) Sarah Ann, b. 1820, m. 1854, Samuel D. Long.
10) Sylvester, of Ill., b. 5 Sept. 1822, m. 1846, Charlotte Pratt.
11) Mary, b. 21 Oct. 1823, m. John Pierce, of Bridgewater, Me.
12) Hannah, b. 1826, d. unm. 1875.

15. JAMES[4] PICKERING (Thomas[3-2], John[1]), of Newington and Exeter, b. Sept. 1737, d. 5 Dec. 1796, m. (1) 13 Dec. 1764, MARY[4] FABYAN (4-ii), dau. of Samuel[3] and Rosamond[4] (Nutter) Fabyan, *q.v.*, m. (2) at Newington, 16 Nov. 1773, MERCY GOWEN, ? dau. of Lemuel[3] and Mercy (Hammond) Gowen (Stackpole's *Kittery*, p. 469).

His will dated 12 Oct. 1791, codicil dated 26 Nov. 1796, proved 16 Dec. 1796, names his son, James and daughter, Mary, wife of Daniel Smith, of Meredith (*Rockingham Probate*).

Children, born at Newington:
    i. ABIGAIL LORD[5], bapt. 5 May 1776, not mentioned in her father's will.
    ii. ELIZABETH, bapt. 5 May 1776, not mentioned in her father's will.
    iii. JAMES
    iv. MARY, m. DANIEL SMITH, of Meredith.

16. WILLIAM[4] PICKERING (Thomas[3-2], John[1]), of Greenland, b. 27 July 1745, d. 16 May 1793(8?), m. 26 Jan. 1776, ABIGAIL[4] FABYAN (3-viii), dau. of Samuel[3] and Elizabeth (Huntress), *q.v.*

His estate was divided among his children John, Thomas, Stephen, Daniel, William, Sarah (Weeks) and Mary.

Children, born at Greenland:
    i. WILLIAM[5], of Portsmouth, state treasurer, collector of the port, (A.B., Harvard, ----) (*Register*, vol. 1, pp. 51, 141), b. 1778, d. 1 July 1850, m. Feb. 14, 1826, SUSAN BURBEEN WALKER, b. 24 Oct. 1801, d. 10 Apr. 1887, dau. of Charles, b. 25 Sept. 1765, d. 29 July 1834, and Hannah Pickering Walker, d. 12 Nov. 1821.
    ii. SARAH, b. 1780, m. BRACKETT[5] WEEKS, of Greenland, son of Dr. Ichabod[4] and Comfort (Johnson) Weeks (*Register*, vol. 39, p. 237).
    iii. JOHN, of Wolfeboro, b. 1782, d. *s.p.*, m. DEBORAH HOYT.
    iv. SAMUEL, b. 1784, m. MARTHA[5] WEEKS, b. at Greenland, dau. of Joshua[4] and Martha (Rust) Weeks (*Register*, vol. 39, p. 240).
    v. THOMAS, b. 1786, d. 1872, m. MARY ANN[5] WEEKS, b. at Greenland, dau. of Joshua[4] and Martha (Rust) Weeks (*Register*, vol. 39, p. 240).
    vi. MARY, b. 1788, m. Dr. STEPHEN HAINES, of Canterbury, physician.

vii. JAMES, b. 1790, d. 1796.
viii. RICHARD, b. 1791, d. 1796.
ix. Col. STEPHEN, of Wolfeboro, b. 3 Jan. 1793, d. 30 June 1844 (*Register*, vol. 73, p. 199), m. 4 July 1825, LYDIA FURBER, b. at Portsmouth, 28 Jan. 1799, d. 15 Apr. 1881.
x. DANIEL, of Wolfeboro, b. 22 Nov. 1795, d. 14 Feb. 1856, m. 26 June 1822, SARAH C. FARRAR, b. at Chelsea, Vt., 3 Mar. 1801, d. 12 Nov. 1867, dau. of Joseph.
Children:
1) Joseph W., d. in infancy.
2) Elizabeth A.
3) Caroline D., m. Chas. Rollins, of Boston (*Carroll County*, p. 382-3).

JOHN PICKERING, of Newington.
Children, baptized at Newington:
i. ROSE, bapt. 5 Nov. 1769.
ii. JOHN, bapt. 18 Feb. 1770.

JOHN PICKERING (John,----), of Newington, m. 26 July 1770, ELIZABETH VINCENT, wid. of Thomas (1), *q.v.*
Child, born at Newington:
i. SARAH FURBER, 27 Jan. 1772.

PICKERING (unconnected)

SARAH PICKERING, dau. ? of (John$^{3-1}$) m. 24 June 1722, WILLIAM HOOPER, both of Portsmouth (*Register*, vol. 7, p. 52).

ELIZABETH PICKERING, communion, 28 Jan. 1728.

SAMUEL PICKERING, minor son of SAMUEL, of Portsmouth, to guardianship of JOSHUA, of Newington, 31 Aug. 1748.

OLIVE PICKERING, m. 13 May 1756, GEORGE OSBORN, both of Portsmouth.

SARAH PICKERING, m. about 1760, BRACKETT^5 WEEKS, son of Dr. Ichabod^4 and Comfort (Johnson) (*Register*, vol. 39, p. 237).

----- PICKERING, m. int. 1762, MEHITABLE^4 WEEKS, dau. of Samuel^3, bapt. at Greenland, 1742 (*Register*, vol. 39, p. 237).

ELIZABETH PICKERING, m. 25 Apr. 1763, SAMUEL DOE, of Newmarket.

MOLLIE and EUNICE PICKERING, covenant, 5 Nov. 1769.

SARAH PICKERING, dau. of John, covenant, 5 May 1776.

TEMPERANCE and sister, CHARLOTTE PICKERING, covenant, 18 Oct. 1778.

BETSEY PICKERING, m. about 1775, JAMES³ WALDRON, son of Richard², had one child (*Register*, vol. 5, p. 206).

JNO. WRIGHT PICKERING, d. at Portsmouth, 21 Feb. 1859, *aet.* 66, b. at Newington, descendant of first John. His dau. m. ROBERT HENRY EDDY, who pub'd. 1884, an account of the Pickering family, and 1885, a supplement (*Register*, vol. 42, p. 214).

BETSEY PICKERING, d. 5 Aug. 1824, *aet.* 52 (*Register*, vol. 73, p. 196).

Wid. MARY PICKERING, d. 21 Feb. 1827, *aet.* 41 (*ibid.*)

Wid. POLLY PICKERING, d. 10 Oct. 1837, *aet.* 70 (*id.*, p. 198).

ABIGAIL PICKERING, wife of JOHN, dau. of Joshua Weeks, d. 27 Jan. 1847, *aet.* 33 (*id.*, p. 200).

DANIEL N. PICKERING, d. 5 Sept. 1848, *aet.* 62-7-12 (*id.*, p. 101).

JOSEPH PICKERING, JR., d. 12 Oct. 1848, *aet.* 44 (*ibid.*).

ROSAMOND PICKERING, wife of Capt. THOMAS, d. 22 Jan. 1849, *aet.* 61 (*ibid.*).

POLLY PICKERING, wife of JOSEPH, d. 21 Feb. 1849, *aet.* 70 (*ibid.*)

JAMES PICKERING, m. 10 Oct. 1826, RUTH MILLER (*id.*, p. 191).

VALENTINE PICKERING, m. 20 July 1827, RUTH CHASE (*id.*, p. 191).

THEODORE PICKERING, m. 13 July 1828, MARY HART (*ibid.*).

JOSEPH PICKERING, m. 20 June 1832, MARY J. GOSS (*id.*, p. 192).

EPHRAIM PICKERING, m. 5 Apr. 1837, LYDIA PILLSBURY (*ibid.*)

LORING PICKERING, m. 4 Aug. 1837, Wid. BEAN, of Lowell (*ibid.*).

THOS. L. PICKERING, m. 23 Mar. 1843, MARGARET WEEKS (*ibid.*).

RUTH PICKERING, wife of Judge JAMES PICKERING, d. 21 Apr. 1851, *aet.* 45 (*73 Reg. 202*).

JAMES JOSEPH PICKERING, d. at Barnstead, 1864, *aet.* 77 (*Jewett*, p. 241).

PILLSBURY

ABIGAIL PILLSBURY, dau. of Joseph and Mehitable (Weed) Pillsbury (Stackpole's *Kittery*, p. 664), m. 4 Oct. 1745, JOSEPH FIELD, both of Kittery.

PINDER (PINNER)

THOMAS⁴ PINDER (PINNER) (Joseph³, Benjamin², John¹) (Stackpole's *Durham*, vol. 2, p. 304), m. 4 Jan. 1779, ELIZABETH⁶ LEIGHTON, bapt. at Newington, 15 Feb. 1756, dau. of Thomas⁵ and Mary (Smithson) Leighton, *q.v.*

JAMES BICKFORD and JOSEPH PINDER (PINNER), sons of Elizabeth, bapt. 5 Aug. 1781.

PITMAN

MARY PITMAN, m. 17 Apr. 1748, ROBERT SAVERY, both of Portsmouth.

PLACE

1. **JOHN¹ PLACE**, of Bermuda, 1634, Portsmouth, 1678 (*Brewster's Rambles*, p. 62), Newington and Rochester, b. in Devonshire about 1612, m. (1) ----------, m. (2) ? PHEBE MUZEET, dau. of Thomas Muzeet (Rix's *Place Family*, MS in the Library of the N.E. Historical-Genealogical Society).

John Place, 22 yrs. old, was bound from London to St. Christopher, 6 Jan. 1684 (*Register*, vol. 14, p. 347).

Child by first wife:
2   i. RICHARD²

Child by second wife, born at Portsmouth:

  ii. ELEANOR, d. 23 Dec. 1748, m. (1) JOHN SACHEL, of Stratham, husbandman, m. (2) FRANCIS^2 DURGIN, of Newmarket, b. 1678, d. 9 June 1735, son of William^1 Durgin (Stackpole's *Durham*, vol. 2, p. 160).

    John Sachel, in his will without date, proved 8 Feb. 1725/6, names only his wife, Eleanor (*N.H. State Pap.*, vol. 32, p. 265).

    In her will, dated 17 Feb. 1747/8, proved 28 Dec. 1748, Eleanor Durgin, of Stratham, "laborer," names her brother, Richard Place, of Newington; Mary, wife of John Watson, of Greenland; and Eleanor, their daughter; and children of James Keniston, of Stratham (*N.H. Probate*, vol. 33, p. 537).

    Children (surname Sachel):

    1) Mary, m. John Watson, of Greenland.

    2) -----, m. James Keniston, of Stratham.

2. RICHARD^2 PLACE (John^1), of Newington, 1701, and Rochester, 1728, d. aet. 105, m. ----- LEIGHTON.

Administration on the estate of John Leighton was granted 3 July 1722 to his grandson, Ebenezer Place, of Newington (Stackpole's *Kittery*, p. 574).

  Children:

3   i. EBENEZER^3
4   ii. JOHN MUSSET
5   iii. JAMES
6   iv. SAMUEL

    v. SARAH, bapt. 7 Dec, 1728, m. (1) 20 Sept. 1724 (*Place Family*, MS, p. 7), MOSES ROBERTS, of Barrington, m. (2) NOAH THOMPSON, of Berwick.

    vi. ABIGAIL, m. 11 Dec. 1723, JOSEPH WALKER.

3. EBENEZER^3 PLACE (Richard^2, John^2), of Newington and Rochester, 1737, m. 31 Dec. 1719, JANE PEAVEY.

  Children, baptized at Newington:

7   i. ABRAHAM^4, bapt. 4 Oct. 1724.

    ii. ABIGAIL, bapt. 4 Oct. 1724, m. at Rochester, 22 July 1745 (*N.H. Gen. Rec.*, vol. 4, p. 145), WILLIAM RICHARDSON.

    iii. JANE, bapt. 26 June 1726.

    iv. JANE, bapt. 7 Apr. 1734.

8   v. EBENEZER

4. JOHN MUSSET^3 PLACE (Richard^2, John^1), of Newington and Rochester, 1740, m. (1) 5 Dec. 1716, EUNICE ROWE, m. (2) ELIZABETH -----.

Children by first wife, baptized at Newington:
9   i. JONATHAN⁴, bapt. 4 Oct. 1724.
10 ii. JOSEPH, bapt. 4 Oct. 1724.
    iii. EUNICE, bapt. 4 Oct. 1724, m. 9 Apr. 1741, DAVID² DECKER, bapt. at Newington, 4 Oct. 1719, son of John¹ Decker, q.v.

5. JAMES³ PLACE (Richard², John¹), of Newington and Rochester, 1740, m. (1) 9 Nov. 1727, MARY WALKER, m. (2) HANNAH -----.
Children by first wife, baptized at Newington:
11 i. JOHN⁴, bapt. 12 Jan. 1729.
    ii. ELEANOR, bapt. 13 Mar. 1737, m. ? 1760, EPHRAIM HAM, of Rochester, b. at Rochester, 1736, son of Eleazer³ and Elizabeth (Cave) Ham.
Children by second wife, baptized at Rochester:
12 iii. GEORGE, bapt. 24 Mar. 1734.
    iv. HANNAH, bapt. 6 Sept. 1741 (*N.H. Gen. Rec.*, vol. 6, p. 67).

6. SAMUEL³ PLACE (Richard², John¹), of Newington, m. 5 Jan. 1727, MARY ROWE (or RHODES⁺, *Register*, vol. 9, p. 104).
Children, baptized at Newington:
    i. JOHN⁴, bapt. 2 Sept. 1734.
    ii. RUTH, bapt. 7 Aug. 1737.
    iii. NICHOLAS ADAMS, bapt. 4 Mar. 1739.
    iv. OLIVE, bapt. 29 Sept. 1741.
    v. MIRIAM, bapt. 23 Oct. 1748, d. 9 Sept. 1822, m. 1772, JOHN KINGSBURY, of Pownalboro, Me., b. at Newbury.

7. ABRAHAM⁴ PLACE (Ebenezer³, Richard², John¹), of Rochester, bapt. 4 Oct. 1724, m. 12 Mar. 1745, MARY³ ROLLINS, bapt. at Newington, 26 Nov. 1727, dau. of James² (James¹) and Deborah (Peavey) Rollins, q.v.
Children, baptized at Rochester:
    i. EBENEZER⁵, bapt. 23 Mar. 1745/6 (*N.H. Gen. Rec.*, vol. 6, p. 69).
    ii. DOROTHY (DOLLY), bapt. 23 Nov. 1755 (*id.*, p. 113).
    iii. MARY, bapt. 23 Nov. 1755 (*ibid.*).

⁺A query in the *Register*, vol. 53, p. 450, says that Samuel Place, of Kittery, m. (1) Mary Rhodes, and (2) ----- Nash, and had children: 1) Nichodemus, who m. ----- Runlett, 3 children. 2) Mary, m. John Groves, 10 children. 3) -----, m. Thomas Parker, 6 children. 4) Miriam, youngest child, b. Sept. 1747, d. 9 Sept. 1822, *aet.* 75, m. John Kingsbury, of Pownalboro and Wiscasset, Me., b. at Newbury, Mass., July 1741, d. 9 Apr. 1791.

8. EBENEZER⁴ PLACE (Ebenezer³, Richard², John¹), of Rochester, m. LOVE -----.

Children, baptized at Rochester:
  i. MOSES⁵, bapt. 23 Sept. 1753 (*N.H. Gen. Rec.*, vol. 6, p. 74).
  ii. RACHEL, bapt. 27 July 1760 (*Register*, vol. 41, p. 279).
  iii. JACOB, bapt. 14 Sept. 1765 (*N.H. Gen. Rec.*, vol. 6, p. 115).
  iv. EBENEZER, bapt. 3 Dec. 1776 (*id.*, p. 119).
  v. ELIZABETH, bapt. 3 Dec. 1776 (*ibid.*).
  vi. MARTHA, bapt. 3 Dec. 1776 (*ibid.*).
  vii. SARAH, bapt. 3 Dec. 1776 (*ibid.*).

10. JOSEPH⁴ PLACE (John³, Richard², John¹), of Newington, bapt. 4 Oct. 1724, m. 17 July 1751, ALICE⁵ DAM, b. at Newington, 1733, dau. of John⁴ and Elizabeth (Bickford) Dam, *q.v.*

Children, baptized at Newington:
  i. ALICE⁵, bapt. 16 Nov. 1755.
  ii. ELIZABETH, bapt. 16 Nov. 1755.
  iii. SARAH, bapt. 20 May 1759.

12. GEORGE⁴ PLACE (James³, Richard², John¹), of Rochester, bapt. 24 Mar. 1734, m. 21 Aug. 1755 (*N.H. Gen. Rec.*, vol. 4, p. 147), KEZIA KNIGHT.

Children, baptized at Newington:
  i. SUSANNA⁵, bapt. 5 Nov. 1769 (*N.H. Gen. Rec.*, vol. 6, p. 117).
  ii. ELIZABETH, bapt. 1 Apr. 1770 (*ibid.*).
  iii. KEZIA, bapt. 27 Sept. 1772 (*id.*, p. 118).
  iv. OLIVE, bapt. 26 June 1774 (*ibid.*).

PLACE (unconnected)

JOHN PLACE (? Jonathan⁴, John M.³, Richard², John¹), of Rochester. He took the covenant with wife, LUCY, 16 June 1751 (*N.H. Gen. Rec.*, vol. 6, p. 72), b. ? 1724, m. LUCY -----.

Children, baptized at Rochester:
  i. MARY, bapt. 16 June 1751 (*N.H. Gen. Rec.*, vol. 6, p. 72).
  ii. SARAH, bapt. 8 Apr. 1753 (*id.*, p. 73).
  iii. HANNAH, bapt. 12 June 1757 (*id.*, p. 114).
  iv. JONATHAN, bapt. 10 June 1764 (*id.*, p. 115), m. 17 Jan. 1786, MARY DEERING (*id.*, vol. 5, p. 1).
  v. ABIGAIL, bapt. 13 May 1770 (*id.*, vol. 6, p. 117).

JAMES PLACE (? James³, Richard², John¹), of Rochester.
Children, baptized at Rochester:

i. RICHARD, bapt. on his deathbed, 7 June 1753 (*N.H. Gen. Rec.*, vol. 6, p. 73).
ii. JOSEPH, bapt. 11 June 1753 (*ibid.*).
iii. LYDIA, bapt. 14 June 1753 (*ibid.*).
iv. JONATHAN, bapt. 14 June 1753 (*ibid.*).

RICHARD PLACE (? John M.³, Richard², John¹), of Rochester, bapt. at Rochester, 16 May 1742 (*N.H. Gen. Rec.*, vol. 6, p. 68), d. 23 Oct. 1820 (*Register*, vol. 80, p. 310).

Children, baptized at Rochester:

i. JOHN MUSSET, of Rochester, bapt. 15 Nov. 1767 (*N.H. Gen. Rec.*, vol. 6, p. 116), d. 5 Feb. 1829 (*Register*, vol. 80, p. 310), m. 5 Jan. 1786 (*N.H. Gen. Rec.*, vol. 5, p. 1), SARAH TWOMBLEY, d. 28 Oct. 1843 (*Register*, vol. 80, p. 310).

Children, born at Rochester:

1) Elizabeth, bapt. 6 Sept. 1789 (*N.H. Gen. Rec.*, vol. 6, p. 115).
2) Phebe, bapt. 6 Sept. 1789 (*ibid.*).
3) Richard, b. 1795, d. 2 Aug. 1797 (*ibid.*).
4) John M., of Rochester, b. 1800, d. 1861, m. Pamela Bickford, d. 13 Sept. 1865 (*ibid.*), wid. of John Bickford.
5) Sarah, b. 1803, d. 12 July 1875 (*ibid.*).
6) William, b. 1807, d. 10 May 1826 (*ibid.*).

ii. PAUL, b. 23 Apr. 1769 (*N.H. Gen. Rec.*, vol. 6, p. 118).

Capt. DAVID PLACE, of Rochester, officer in the Revolution (*Register*, vol. 65, p. 258).

Children, baptized at Rochester:

i. JAMES, bapt. 3 May 1767 (*N.H. Gen. Rec.*, vol. 6, p. 115).
ii. STEPHEN, bapt. 3 June 1770 (*id.*, p. 116).
iii. MEHITABLE, bapt. 11 Mar. 1776 (*id.*, p. 118).
iv. ELIZABETH, bapt. 11 Mar. 1776 (*ibid.*).
v. DAVID, bapt. 20 July 1777 (*id.*, p. 120).
vi. SIMON, bapt. 6 June 1779 (*id.*, p. 121).
vii. SARAH, bapt. 1 July 1781 (*ibid.*).
viii. ISAAC, bapt. 13 July 1783 (*id.*, p. 173).

(Portsmouth and Alton)

SAMUEL PLACE, of Portsmouth, goldsmith, m. CHRISTIAN³ SEWARD, b. at Portsmouth, dau. of Capt. Giles² and Mary (Hodgdon) Seward (Queen's Chapel Rec.).

Children, born at Portsmouth:

i. JOSHUA, b. 19 May 1780, m. (1) at New Durham, 3 Apr. 1801, MEHITABLE ROBERTS, m. (2) 13 Mar. 1807, SARAH WILLEY.
Child by first wife:
1) Stephen, of Alton, b. 9 Aug. 1806, d. 30 June 1856 (Rix's *Place Family*, MS, p. 15).

Children by second wife (*ibid.*):
2) Joseph, b. 5 June 1809.
3) Amos, b. 2 Apr. 1812.
4) John, b. 1815.
5) Joseph, b. 1819.

(Wells, Me.)

AMOS PLACE, of Wells, Me., soldier in the Revolution, pensioner, b. 1756, m. POLLY -----, b. 1772.
Children (*Register*, vol. 65, p. 257):
i. HANNAH, b. 1805.
ii. SILAS, b. 1807.
iii. SIMEON, b. 1810.
iv. ENOS

(Dorchester, Mass., and Kingston, R.I.)

ENOCH PLACE, of Dorchester, Mass., and Rochester[+] (Kingston), R.I., m. ? (1) DINAH -----, d. at Dorchester, 28 May 1657 (*Register*, vol. 11, p. 332), m. (2) at Dorchester, 5 Sept. 1657, SARAH -----.
Child by second wife, born at Dorchester:
i. PETER^2, b. 16 Dec. 1660 (*id.*, vol. 16, p. 155).

(Boston)

PETER PLACE, of Boston, b. in England, 1615, m. ALICE -----.

[+]Enoch Sr. and Jr. were taxed there 6 Sept. 1687 (*Register*, vol. 35, p. 125). Enoch, Sr., was selectman (*id.*, p. 127). A Joseph was there (*id.*, p. 126).

It will be noticed that Enoch had a son, Peter, and Peter, of Boston, had a son, Enoch. This suggests that they were related, probably brothers, for Enoch could not have been a son of Peter.

A Thomas was freeman at Boston, 13 May 1640 (*Register*, vol. 3, p. 187). A Hannah was at North Kingstown, 15 May 1736 (*id.*, vol. 33, p. 313).

He came in the *Truelove*, 19 Sept. 1635 (*Register*, vol. 14, p. 323). He was freeman, 6 May 1646 (*id.*, vol. 3, p. 191).

He was executor 2 Oct. 1662, of JOHN LOVE, late of Plymouth, England(*id.*, vol. 11, p. 175).

Children, born at Boston:
- i. HANNAH[2], b. 20 Nov. 1642 (*id.*, vol. 2, p. 400).
- ii. ELIZABETH, b. 29 July 1644 (*id.*, vol. 8, p. 39).
- iii. JOSEPH, b. 19 Aug. 1646 (*id.*, vol. 9, p. 165).
- iv. ELIZABETH, b. 21 Oct. 1652 (*id.*, p. 250), d. 8 June 1654 (*id.*, vol. 10 p. 218).
- v. SARAH, b. 3 Sept. 1657 (*id.*, vol. 10, p. 70).
- vi. ENOCH, b. 18 July 1658 (*id.*, vol. 16, p. 155)

RICHARD PLACE, witness to will of THOMAS RICKER, of Newington, 1719 (*N.H. State Pap.*, vol. 32, p. 88).

RICHARD, JOHN, EBENEZER, MARY, and JANE PLACE, covenanted at Newington, 16 Aug. 1724.

MARY PLACE, m. 29 Apr. 1725, JOHN DAVIS.

SUSANNA PLACE, covenant at Newington, 7 Dec. 1728.

MARY PLACE, bapt. at Rochester, 25 Mar. 1739 (*N.H. Gen. Rec.*, vol. 6, p. 66).

ABIGAIL PLACE, covenant at Rochester, 7 Feb. 1741 (*ibid.*).

DAVID PLACE, bapt. at Rochester, 12 Sept. 1741 (*id.*, p. 67).

DEBORAH and DOLLY PLACE, bapt. at Rochester, 5 Aug. 1753 (*id.*, vol. 6, p. 73).

KEZIA PLACE, bapt. at Rochester, 13 Apr. 1755 (*id.*, p. 75).

JAMES PLACE, bapt. at Rochester, 20 Apr. 1755 (*ibid.*).

JOHN PLACE and wife, bapt. at Rochester, 3 May 1767 (*id.*, p. 116).

ABIGAIL and SAMUEL PLACE, children of Widow PLACE, bapt. at Rochester, 20 Oct. 1768 (*ibid.*).

ANNE PLACE, m. at Kittery, 22 Mar. 1774, NELSON PICKNAIL (*Register*, vol. 63, p. 173).

JAMES PLACE, m. at Rochester, 23 May 1776, ESTHER VARNEY (*N.H. Gen. Rec.*, vol. 4, p. 147).

HANNAH PLACE, m. at Rochester, 19 Nov. 1778, JOHN NUTE, JR. (*id.*, p. 148).

AMOS PLACE, m. at Rochester, 4 Nov. 1779, OLIVE KNIGHT, both of Rochester (*id.*, p. 149).

JOHN PLACE, JR., m. at Rochester, 11 Jan. 1781, PATIENCE DOWNING (*N.H. Gen. Rec.*, vol. 4, p. 150).

CHARITY PLACE, m. at Rochester, 15 Nov. 1781, DANIEL HORN, of Rochester (*id.*, p. 150).

MARY PLACE, m. at Rochester, 3 Aug. 1782, PHILIP JACKSON (*id.*, p. 151).

NOAH, ISAAC, and HANNAH PLACE, children of NOAH THOMPSON, adopted by JOHN PLACE, bapt. at Rochester, 31 Oct. 1784 (*id.*, vol. 6, p. 173).

JAMES PLACE, m. at Rochester, 3 June 1785, ABIGAIL HAYES (*id.*, vol. 5, p. 1).

LUCY PLACE, m. at Rochester, 8 Sept. 1786, JONATHAN LEIGHTON (*id.*, p. 2).

JOHN PLACE, JR., m. at Rochester, 2 Nov. 1787, LYDIA GARLAND (*id.*, p. 3).

PAUL PLACE, m. at Rochester, 29 Nov. 1787, JUDITH BROWN (*ibid.*).

SUSANNNA PLACE, m. at Rochester, 23 Mar. 1788, JOSIAH HALL, of Conway (*id.*, p. 3).

DOROTHY PLACE, m. at Rochester, 14 May 1789, RICHARD NUTTER, JR. (*id.*, p. 4).

MOSES PLACE, m. at Rochester, 23 July 1789, SUSANNA DOWNING (*id.*, p. 5).

ABNER PLACE, m. 1790, PHEBE ESTES, dau. of Henry and Sarah (Allen) Estes, b. at Berwick, 4 May 1770 (*N.H. Gen. Rec.*, vol. 4, p. 159).

ABIGAIL PLACE, m. at Rochester, 14 Apr. 1791, JOHN BREWSTER, JR. (*id.*, vol. 5, p. 6).

MARY PLACE, m. at Rochester, 21 July 1791, BARNABUS PALMER, JR. (*id.*, p. 6).

SARAH PLACE, dau. of Jonathan and Lydia Place, b. at Rochester, 2 Sept. 1794 (death rec.), d. 30 Dec. 1869, m. 20 Sept. 1824 (*N.H. Gen. Rec.*, vol. 1, p. 172), MOSES^6 ROBERTS, of Sandwich and Farmington, farmer, b. at Rochester, 11 Mar. 1795, d. 5 Apr. 1880, son of James^5 and Eunice (Varney) Roberts.

ELIZABETH PLACE, m. at Rochester, 9 Nov. 1794, BENJAMIN EVANS, JR. (*id.*, p. 50).

STEPHEN PLACE, m. at Rochester, 25 Dec. 1800, ELIZABETH CHESLEY (*id.*, p. 55).

POLLY PLACE, m. at Rochester, 16 Aug. 1801, PAUL HAM (*ibid.*).

SOLOMON PLACE, m. at Rochester, 2 July 1804, BELVIDERE CLAPPAM (*id.*, p. 146).

HANNAH PLACE, m. at Rochester, 13 June 1811, JAMES HANSON (*id.*, p. 145).

PHEBE PLACE, m. at Rochester, 12 Mar. 1812, JONATHAN TIBBETTS, JR. (*id.*, p. 146).

LUCY PLACE, m. at Rochester, 25 Oct. 1812, JOSEPH OTIS (*Register*, vol. 5, p. 221).

JENNY PLACE, m. at Rochester, 8 Oct. 1819, DANIEL COOK (*N.H. Gen. Rec.*, vol. 5, p. 51).

GEORGE PLACE, m. at Rochester, 15 Sept. 1821, PRUDENCE NUTTER (*Place Family*, MS p. 35).

BETSEY PLACE, m. at Rochester, 24 Dec. 1824, STEPHEN JACKSON (*id.*, vol. 6, p. 34).

SUSAN PLACE, m. at Rochester, 24 July 1825, NICHOLAS WHITEHOUSE (*id.*, p. 35).

JOHN PLACE, m. (2) 2 May 1826, ABIGAIL HENDERSON (*Place Family*, MS, p. 17).

OLIVE PLACE, m. about 1840, DAVID L.[6] EDGERLY, of New Durham and Alton, son of Jeremiah[5] and Betsey (Leighton) Edgerly (*Register*, vol. 34, p. 285).

ENOCH PLACE, was clergyman at Rochester, 1850 (*Register*, vol. 2, p. 267; *id.*, vol. 76, p. 28).

JOSEPH PLACE, soldier in the Revolution, d. at Barnstead, 1875, *aet.* 101, wife ANNA (Jewett's *Barnstead*).

All *N.H. Gen. Rec.* entries and all *Register* to vol. 72 noted.

PLUMMER

DANIEL PLUMMER, m. 28 Jan. 1720, SARAH WENTWORTH, both of Dover.

POMEROY

RICHARD POMEROY, at Newington, 1713 (*Register*, vol. 58, p. 249).

ELIZABETH POMEROY, dau. of Richard (Stackpole's *Kittery*, p. 740), m. 1 Mar. 1721, NATHAN SPINNEY, of Kittery, Me.

PRAY

ELIZABETH PRAY, m. 26 May 1727, SAMUEL WALTON.

PRYER

PATIENCE PRYER, m. 14 Mar. 1721, SAMUEL HAYNES, of Greenland.

QUINT

1. JOHN QUINT, of Newington, m. ANN ROWE, dau. of Thomas (*Dover Landmarks*, p. 97).
    Children, baptized at Newington:
    i. JOHN², bapt. 26 Sept. 1736.
    ii. ELIZABETH, bapt. 26 Sept. 1736.
    iii. ANN, bapt. 26 Sept. 1736, m. ? 1 Feb. 1741, EBENEZER³ BICKFORD, bapt. at Newington, son of Thomas² and Sarah (Simpson) Bickford, *q.v.*
    iv. JOSHUA, bapt. 26 Sept. 1736.
2   v. JONATHAN, bapt. 26 Sept. 1736.
    vi. MARTHA, bapt. 26 Sept. 1736.
    vii. SARAH, bapt. 24 July 1737.

2. JONATHAN² QUINT (John¹), of Newington, bapt. 26 Sept. 1736, m. ELIZA -----.
    Children, baptized at Newington:
    i. JOSEPH³, bapt. 29 July 1759.
    ii. BENJAMIN ROWE, bapt. 14 Sept. 1760.
    iii. MARY⁺, bapt. 27 Apr. 1765.
    iv. JOHN, bapt. 7 June 1765.
    v. JONATHAN, bapt. 28 May 1769.
    vi. ROSAMOND, bapt. 28 May 1769.
    vii. JOSHUA, bapt. 28 May 1769.

1. THOMAS QUINT, of Newington, m. at Greenland, 6 Dec. 1733 (*Register*, vol. 25, p. 120), MARGARET FICKETT⁺⁺, b. at Portsmouth.
    Children, baptized at Newington:
    i. A CHILD², bapt. 24 July 1737.
    ii. A CHILD, bapt. 24 July 1737.
    iii. ANNA, bapt. 29 Jan. 1738.
2   iv. THOMAS, bapt. 19 Sept. 1742.

+She and the following children were baptized as children of JONATHAN and ELIZABETH.

++Peter Ball, of Portsmouth, in his will made in 1719, recorded 28 Feb. 1725/6 names with other children, his daughter, Susanna, wife of John Fickett (*N.H. State Pap.*, vol. 32, p. 266). There is no other Fickett in the *N.H. State Pap.*, vols. 31-3.

2. THOMAS² QUINT (Thomas¹), of Newington, bapt. 19 Sept. 1742, m. 8 Nov. 1764, SARAH⁷ WALKER, bapt. at Newington, 9 Sept. 1744, dau. of Edward⁶ and Sarah⁴ (Nutter) Walker, *q.v.*

Children, baptized at Newington:
  i. MARTHA³, bapt. 12 Dec. 1773.
  ii. MARY, bapt. 12 Sept. 1784.
  iii. SARAH, bapt. 12 Sept. 1784.

QUINT (unconnected)

JOHN QUINT, was at Newington, 1713 (*Register*, vol. 58, p. 249).

THOMAS QUINT, bapt. 1 Dec. 1723, on Grandfather Rowe's account.

MARY QUINT, covenant, 1 July 1733.

MARY QUINT, m. 4 Apr. 1736, HENRY BENSON, of Portsmouth (*Register*, vol. 26, p. 376).

ESTHER QUINT, m. 4 Jan. 1778, JOHN GOODRIDGE, of Coxhall⁺.

DAVID QUINT, m. 5 Nov. 1778, MARY RYND.

HANNAH QUINT, m. 29 Sept. 1779, WILLIAM PEARCE.

DANIEL QUINT, m. 16 Sept. 1780, SARAH STILLINGS.

ELIZABETH QUINT, m. 18 Oct. 1780, JOHN GLASS.

JOHN QUINT, JR., m. 4 July 1781, MOLLY ABBOTT.

JOSHUA QUINT, JR., 1 Nov. 1783, int. with HANNAH FORD.

SARAH QUINT, 17 Mar. 1799, int. with JOSIAH MORRELL.

BETSEY QUINT, m. 1 July 1802, THOMAS ROBERTS.

POLLY QUINT, 1 Feb. 1807, int. with JOHN ROBERTS, JR.

+This and the following items are from Berwick, Me., town records.

POLLY QUINT, d. 28 Aug. 1824, *aet.* 53 (*Register*, vol. 73, p. 196).

JAMES QUINT, m. 17 Feb. 1825, ABIGAIL ROBERTS.

MARY QUINT, d. Apr. 1827, *aet.* 44 (*Register*, vol. 73, p. 196).

LEVI QUINT, m. 20 Sept. 1829, OLIVE ROBERTS.

GEORGE QUINT, of Dover, b. in the West Indies, m. SARAH[6] HALE. Their son, ALONZO HALE QUINT, of Dover, was the genealogist (*Hale Family*, p. 170).

RACKLETY (? RACKLIFF)

MARY RACKLETY (RACKLIFF), m. 14 Mar. 1755, PATRICK SHAFFEN, both of Newington.

RAITT

WILLIAM[2] RAITT (Alexander[1]) (Stackpole's *Kittery*, p. 673), m. 16 Dec. 1773, SARAH LEIGHTON, both of Kittery.

RANDALL

DANIEL RANDALL, m. 2 July 1767, CHARITY MEADER, both of Durham.

REED

JOSEPH REED, son of Andrew, bapt. 22 Nov. 1719.

REMICK

JOSHUA[2] REMICK (Christian[1]) (Stackpole's *Kittery*, p. 678), m. Sept. 1716, MARY HEPWROTH, of Portsmouth.

SUSANNA[4] REMICK (Joshua[3-2], Christian[1]), m. 19 Oct. 1768, THOMAS DIXON, both of Kittery.

STEPHEN[5] REMICK (Benjamin[4], Jacob[3-2], Christian[1]), m. 3 June 1773, as his second wife, HANNAH ROGERS.

REYNOLDS

----- **REYNOLDS**, of Stratham, m. 22 Nov. 1739, SARAH PHILIPS.

RICHARDS

BENJAMIN RICHARDS[+], of Newington, 1713, m. 19 Nov. 1702, ELIZABETH[3] (HODSDON) GALLOWAY, b. at Portsmouth, dau. of Jeremiah[2] and Ann (Thwaits) Hodgdon and wid. of BENJAMIN GALLOWAY (Stackpole's *Kittery*, p. 529.
Children, baptized at Newington:
  i. ABIGAIL, bapt. 10 July 1727.
  ii. ELIZABETH, bapt. 10 July 1727.
  iii. ESTHER, bapt. 10 July 1727, m. 13 May 1744, SAMUEL[4] ROLLINS, bapt. at Newington, 21 Sept. 1729, son of Samuel[3] and Alice (Dam) Rollins, *q.v.*
  iv. SARAH, bapt. 10 July 1727, m. 22 Jan. 1749, JOSHUA[4] NUTTER, of Newington, b. at Newington, son of Hatevil[3] and his second wife, Leah (Furber) Nutter, *q.v.*

JOSEPH RICHARDS, of Newington, planter, m. 2 May 1725 (*Register*, vol. 24, p. 357), ELIZABETH COOLBROTH.
Children, baptized at Newington:
  i. JOSEPH, bapt. 25 July 1727.
  ii. JANE, bapt. 15 June 1728.
  iii. SUSANNA, bapt. 19 Sept. 1731.

RICHARDS (unconnected)

JOSEPH RICHARDS, of Welshman's Cove, Newington, planter, and ABIGAIL, his wife, 20 Mar. 1702, conveyed 10 acres which his father had purchased of William Furber (*Dover Landmarks*, p. 97).

JOSEPH and BENJAMIN RICHARDS were at Newington, 1713 (*Register*, vol. 58, pp. 248-9).

REBECCA RICHARDS, m. 9 Aug. 1722, JOSEPH HEARD, of Dover.

[+]A Benjamin Richards was of Plaistow in 1755 (*N.H. State Pap.*, vol. 33, p. 568).

JOHN RICHARDS, m. 1 Dec. 1723, DORCAS HAM, dau. of John Ham (*N.H. State Pap.*, vol. 32, p. 409).

MARY RICHARDS, m. 2 Apr. 1734, THOMAS JACKSON, of Casco Bay.

SARAH RICHARDS, communion, 9 May 1732.

ESTHER RICHARDS, communion, 6 June 1742.

RICHARDSON

ABIGAIL RICHARDSON, m. 22 May 1760, TRISTRAM TUCKER, both of Kittery.

ELIZABETH RICHARDSON, m. 22 Feb. 1770, HUMPHRY SCAMMON, both of Kittery.

TIMOTHY RICHARDSON, m. 23 Feb. 1775, ANNA YOUNG, both of Kittery.

RING

Deac. SETH[3] RING, son of Joseph[2] (Hoyt's *Salisbury*, p. 385), and Mary (Brackett) (Whitcher) Ring[+], of Newington, yeoman, m. ELIZABETH LIBBY (*Libby Family*, p. 35).

Children, baptized at Newington:
  i. JOSEPH, bapt. 5 Jan. 1718.
  ii. BENJAMIN, bapt. 16 Feb. 1718.
  iii. JANE, bapt. 13 Dec. 1719, m. 14 Sept. 1740, JOSEPH[5] ALCOCK, of Portsmouth, merchant, b. at Portsmouth, 26 Feb. 1716/7 (*Register*, vol. 23, p. 393), *q.v.*
  iv. MARY, bapt. 4 Feb. 1722, m. 26 May 1743, GEORGE[3] HUNTRESS, of Portsmouth, bapt. at Newington, 15 Sept. 1717, *q.v.*
  v. SETH, bapt. 17 Apr. 1727.
  vi. ELIZABETH, bapt. 27 May 1733, m. 3 Nov. 1747, Capt. SAMUEL[4]

+Samuel B. Shackford notes that Keziah Mayhew of Boston, in her will, names her sister, Mary Whitcher; nephew, Seth Ring; and niece, Keziah Harvey; and that Boston records show John Harvey m. Keziah Ring.

SHACKFORD, of Newington, farmer, officer in the Revolution, *q.v.*
vii. ELIPHALET, bapt. 27 May 1733.
viii. DAVID, bapt. 24 Nov. 1734.

ROBERTS

TIMOTHY[5] **ROBERTS**, of Rochester, yeoman, soldier in the Revolution, b. ? 1740, m. 16 July 1761, MARY FURBER.

ROBINSON

MARY ROBINSON, of Portsmouth, m. 4 Jan. 1764, PAUL WAPLES.

ROGERS

MARY[4] **ROGERS** (John[3], Richard[2], George[1]) (Stackpole's *Kittery*, p. 706), m. 13 Sept. 1740, JOHN GODSO, both of Kittery, Me.

GEORGE[5] **ROGERS** (George[4], John[3], Richard[2], George[1]), m. 30 Aug. 1770, MARY FERNALD, both of Kittery.

HANNAH[5] **ROGERS** (George[4], John[3], Richard[2], George[1]), m. 3 June 1773, STEPHEN REMICK, both of Kittery.

ROLLINS

1. **JAMES**[2] **ROLLINS** (James[1]) (*Rawlins-Rollins Family*, p. 9), of Newington, yeoman, town officer, m. 9 Apr. 1717, DEBORAH PEVEY.

His will dated 12 Dec. 1743, proved 28 Mar. 1744, mentions his wife, Deborah, and children Edward, John, Ichabod, Abigail and Mary; son John, executor and residuary legatee (*N.H. State Pap.*, vol. 33, p. 191).

Children, baptized at Newington:
4   i. EDWARD[3], bapt. 26 Nov. 1727, b. 2 Mar. 1718.
    ii. JOHN, bapt. 26 Nov. 1727, b. 1720.
5   iii. ICHABOD, bapt. 26 Nov. 1727.
    iv. JAMES, bapt. 26 Nov. 1727, d. in infancy.
    v. ABIGAIL, bapt. 26 Nov. 1727, m. 21 Nov. 1748, PETER COOK, of Somersworth.
    vi. MARY, bapt. 26 Nov. 1727, m. 12 Mar. 1745, ABRAHAM[4] PLACE, son of Ebenezer[3] and Jane (Pevey), *q.v.*
    vii. BENJAMIN, bapt. 30 Sept. 1733, d. in infancy.

    viii. DEBORAH, bapt. 30 Sept. 1733, communion, 7 Feb. 1741/2, d. in infancy.
    ix. PARTHENIA, bapt. 24 Mar. 1734, d. in infancy.

2. JOSEPH² ROLLINS (James¹), of Newington, surveyor, town officer, m. SARAH -----, who m. (2) 18 Dec. 1760, EDWARD² WALKER.

His will dated 14 Feb. 1748/9, proved 30 May 1749, mentions his wife, Sarah, and children (*N.H. State Pap.*, vol. 33, p. 641).

Children, baptized at Newington (as mentioned in his will):

    i. JOSEPH³, bapt. 8 May 1727, m. 1 Feb. 1757, MARY CARTER (1-i), dau. of Richard and Sarah (Pevey), *q.v.* His estate was divided 16 Dec. 1783.

6   ii. SAMUEL

    iii. SARAH, bapt. 19 June 1727, m. 23 Apr. 1730, HENRY ALLARD, of Newington and Barnstead, *q.v.* Did she m. (2) EDWARD WALKER ?

    iv. MARY, bapt. 19 June 1727, m. ? ELNATHAN⁵ DAME (4-v), son of John⁴ and Elizabeth (Bickford), *q.v.*

7   v. NOAH, bapt. 21 June 1730.

    vi. DEBORAH, suspended from communion in Mar. 1765.

    vii. ELIZABETH, communion, 9 May 1742, m. ? JOSHUA³ DOWNING (9), son of Joshua² and Susannah (Dennett), *q.v.*

3. JOSEPH³ ROLLINS (Samuel², James¹), of Newington and Portsmouth, soldier in the French and Indian War, m. 10 May 1739, SUSANNA (COOLBROTH) FOLLETT, wid. of Thomas.

THOMAS FOLLETT, b. in the Island of Jersey, m. 1 Oct. 1730, SUSANNA COOLBROTH (*Register*, vol. 25, p. 117). She had by him, a son THOMAS, bapt. at Newington, 19 Nov. 1732.

Children, baptized at Newington:

    i. MARY⁴, bapt. 16 Mar. 1740.

    ii. VALENTINE, bapt. 24 Feb. 1744/5, b. 1739.

    iii. JOSEPH, bapt. 14 June 1747, b. 1742.

4. EDWARD³ ROLLINS (James²⁻¹), of Newington and Rochester, farmer, town officer, b. 2 Mar. 1718, d. 25 May 1756, m. 21 Nov. 1742, ELIZABETH⁴ NUTTER (3-viii), dau. of Hatevil³ and Leah (Furber), *q.v.*

Children, baptized at Newington (*Rawlins-Rollins Family*, p. 18):

    i. OLIVE⁴, bapt. 30 Oct. 1743, b. 1 Oct. 1743.

    ii. ALICE, bapt. 23 June 1745.

    iii. HANNAH, bapt. 30 Aug. 1747, m. ? 11 Oct. 1764, MOSES HORN, of Dover.

iv. ELIZABETH, bapt. 10 Sept. 1749, m. ? 14 Sept. 1796, WILLIAM CONNOR.
v. SAMUEL
vi. BENJAMIN, bapt. 26 Nov. 1758, as grandson of Mrs. Deborah.
vii. DEBORAH, b. 21 Jan. 1752.
viii. ANTHONY
ix. LEAH, b. 9 Sept. 1754.
x. JOSHUA NUTTER
xi. EDWARD, b. 16 Nov. 1756.
xii. SARAH, d. unm. 26 Sept. 1789.

5. ICHABOD^3 ROLLINS (James$^{2-1}$), of Newington, farmer, town officer, drummer in the Revolution, m. 6 Jan. 1749, OLIVE^4 NUTTER (3-ix), dau. of Hatevil^3 and Leah (Furber), *q.v.*

Children, baptized at Newington:
i. LEAH^4, bapt. near 1749/50.
ii. ABIGAIL, bapt. 17 Sept. 1752.
iii. ANNA, b. 10 Jan. 1754.
iv. JOHN, bapt. 20 Feb. 1757, b. 12 Feb. 1756.
v. ANTHONY NUTTER, bapt. 16 Dec. 1759.
vi. JOSHUA NUTTER, bapt. 8 Aug. 1762.
vii. OLIVE, bapt. 3 Nov. 1765, d. 1815, m. 8 Nov. 1787, STEPHEN WENTWORTH, of Rochester.
viii. TEMPERENCE, bapt. 18 Nov. 1768, m. 1792, STEPHEN WILLEY, of Rochester and Wheelock, Me.
ix. ICHABOD, bapt. 5 Jan. 1772.

6. SAMUEL^3 ROLLINS (Joseph^2, James^1), of Newington, b. about 1700, m. (1) 5 May 1720, ALICE^4 DAM (1-iv), dau. of John^3, *q.v.*, m. (2) 13 May 1744 (*Rawlins-Rollins Family*, p. --), ESTHER RICHARDS (1-iii), dau. of Benjamin and Elizabeth, *q.v.*

Children by first wife, baptized at Newington:
i. HANNAH^4, bapt. 6 Aug. 1721.
10 ii. JOHN, bapt. 10 Aug. 1723.
iii. ALICE, bapt. 1 Nov. 1724, d. unm. 1775.
iv. LYDIA, bapt. 28 Aug. 1726, m. NOAH ROLLINS.
11 v. SAMUEL, bapt. 21 Sept. 1729.
12 vi. JONATHAN, bapt. 13 Aug. 1732.
vii. HANNAH, bapt. 7 Oct. 1733.
viii. PAUL, bapt. 14 Sept. 1735.
ix. ELIZABETH, m. 8 Jan. 1755, THACHER CLARK, of Stratham.

Children by second wife, baptized at Newington:
- x. SARAH, bapt. 24 Feb. 1744/5.
- xi. LOUISA (or SALOME), bapt. 19 Apr. 1747, m. ANTHONY NUTTER.
- xii. AGNES, bapt. 2 Oct. 1748.
- xiii. A CHILD, bapt. near 1749/50.
- xiv. SUSANNA, bapt. 17 Mar. 1750/1, m. JOSEPH ROLLINS, of Albion, Me.
- xv. GEORGE, bapt. 1 Apr. 1753.
- xvi. SAMUEL, bapt. 8 June 1755.
- xvii. JOHANNA, bapt. 26 Sept. 1756, d. unm. 7 July 1829 (*Register*, vol. 73, p. 197).

The *Rawlins-Rollins Family* gives this second marriage and children by it to Samuel (6), but there may well be doubt of this.

7. NOAH^3 ROLLINS (Joseph^2, James^1), of Newington, d. 11 May 1804, m. ELIZABETH -----.

Children, baptized at Newington:
- i. ELIZABETH^4, bapt. 22 Nov. 1761, m. ? SAMUEL^6 DOWNING (19-iv), son of Josiah^5 and Elizabeth, *q.v.*
- ii. A CHILD, bapt. 22 Nov. 1761.
- iii. A CHILD, bapt. 22 Nov. 1761.
- iv. NOAH, bapt. 20 Oct. 1771.
- v. HANNAH, bapt. 20 Oct. 1771.
- vi. ALICE, bapt. 10 Oct. 1771.

11. SAMUEL^4 ROLLINS (Samuel^3, Joseph^2, James^1), of Newington, surveyor, town officer, d. 1799, m. 12 Apr. 1752, MARY^4 HUNTRESS (3-iv), dau. of Christopher^3 and Mary (Chick), *q.v.*

Children, baptized at Newington:
- i. JOANNA^5, bapt. 26 Sept 1756, d. unm. 7 July 1829.
- ii. ABIGAIL, bapt. 8 July 1759, d. 5 Feb. 1846 (*Register*, vol. 73, p. 200), m. (1) 12 June 1787, ANTHONY^5 NUTTER (7-viii), son of Anthony^4 and Sarah (Nutter), *q.v.*, m. (2) ----- PATTEN.
- iii. MARY, bapt. 8 Aug. 1762, m. BENJAMIN COOLBROTH, of Middleton.
- iv. ELIZABETH, bapt. 17 Nov. 1765, m. 1791, Deac. THOMAS^4 CAVERLY, son of Richard^3 and Sarah (Ham) (*Caverly Annals*, p. 67), of New Durham, farmer, b. at Portsmouth, 16 Aug. 1770, d. 5 Nov. 1825.
- v. SAMUEL, bapt. 13 Oct. 1771, of Barnstead, d. 5 Mar. 1845, m. 8 Nov. 1792, DEBORAH GODSO, b. 3 July 1769, d. ? 22 Mar. 1846 (*73 Reg. 200*).

    Only child, born at Barnstead:
    1) Samuel^6, b. 5 Sept. 1793.

ROLLINS (unconnected)

DEBORAH[2] ROLLINS (James[1]), m. 20 Mar. 1719, JAMES[2] (Henry[1]) BENSON, of Kittery, Me. (Stackpole's *Kittery*, p. 295).

ABIGAIL ROLLINS, dau. of John (1-ii), bapt. 22 Dec. 1745.

HANNAH ROLLINS, of Rochester, m. 11 Oct. 1764, MOSES HORN, of Dover.

HANNAH ROLLINS, covenant, 29 Dec. 1771.

PAUL ROLLINS, d. 22 Jan. 1824, aet. 59 (*Register*, vol. 73, p. 196).

SARAH ROLLINS, d. 5 Apr. 1829, aet. 83 (*id.*, p. 197).

ROWE

1. THOMAS[2] ROWE (Thomas[1]), of Newington, 1713, m. 17 Jan. 1721, RACHEL PEAVEY.
Children, baptized at Newington:
  i. MARY[3], bapt. 10 Aug. 1723, m. 1 Nov. 1742, EDWARD[4] AYRES (14-i), *q.v.*, son of Thomas[3] and Mary Ayres.
  ii. WILLIAM, bapt. 23 May 1725.
  iii. ELIZABETH, bapt. 30 Oct. 1726. She took the covenant, 19 May 1754.
    Child, baptized at Newington:
      1) James, bapt. 19 May 1754.
  iv. BENJAMIN, bapt. 20 Aug. 1732.
  v. JOSEPH, bapt. 7 Sept. 1735.
  vi. COMFORT, bapt. 12 June 1737.

1. SAMUEL ROWE, of Newington, m. 13 Apr. 1730, DEBORAH CANNEY.
Child, baptized at Newington:
  i. MOSES, bapt. 12 Jan. 1732.

ROWE (unconnected)

EDWARD and THOMAS ROWE, at Newington, 1713 (*Register*, vol. 58, pp. 248-9).

THOMAS ROWE, original member of the Church at Newington, 26 Oct. 1715.

EUNICE ROWE, m. 5 Dec. 1716, JOHN PLACE.

SUSANNA ROWE, m. 10 Aug. 1725, JAMES BENSON.

MARY ROWE, m. 5 Jan. 1727, SAMUEL PLACE.

ANNA ROWE, covenant, 18 Aug. 1728.

RUNLETT

CHARLES RUNLETT, of Stratham, m. 20 Mar. 1740, MARY PHILLIPS, b. at Ipswich, Mass. (*Register*, vol. 27, p. 8).

MERCY RUNLETT, dau. of Charles and Mary, bapt. 22 May 1743.

SARGENT

HANNAH SARGENT, m. 29 Apr. 1773, WILLIAM KENNARD, both of Kittery.

SAVERY

ROBERT SAVERY, m. 19 Apr. 1748, MARY PITMAN, both of Portsmouth.

EUNICE SAVERY, of Rye, m. 18 Feb. 1755, ROBERT SINNOTT.

SAYWARD

HANNAH SAYWARD, of Dover, m. 25 Feb. 1771, BENJAMIN HODGDON.

SCALES

JOHN SCALES, son of Matthew, bapt. 10 June 1716.

HANNAH SCALES, communion, 6 June 1742.

SCAMMAN

HUMPHREY[5] SCAMMAN (Humphrey[4-2], Richard[1]) (Stackpole's *Kittery*, p. 712), m. 22 Feb. 1770, ELIZABETH RICHARDSON, both of Kittery.

SEAVEY

JAMES[3] SEAVEY (William[2-1]) (Parson's *Rye*, p. 527), of New Castle, m. 12 June 1718, ABIGAIL PICKERING SEAWARD (See Leavers).

SHACKFORD[+]

1. **WILLIAM[1] SHACKFORD**, of Dover (Bloody Point), 1662, (*Register*, vol. 4, p. 249; *id.*, vol. 8, p. 66), housewright, constable, 1671/2, b. in England about 1641, d. 1720, m. DEBORAH[2] TRICKEY (1-i), dau. of Thomas[1] and Elizabeth, *q.v.*.

   Children, born at Bloody Point:
   2   i. SAMUEL[2], b. about 1674.
   3   ii. JOHN, b. about 1677.
   4   iii. JOSHUA
       iv. MARY, b. about 1683, m. 26 July 1703 (*N.H. Gen. Rec.*, vol. 4, p. 12), HENRY[3] NUTTER (4), son of Anthony[2] and Sarah (Langstaff), *q.v.*
       v. JANE, m. ALEXANDER[3] HODGDON (1), son of Jeremiah[2] (*Hodsdon-Hodgdon Family*, p.--), of Newington.
       v. JANE

2. **SAMUEL[2] SHACKFORD** (William[1]), of Portsmouth, blockmaker, b. about 1674, m. (1) in 1696, ABIGAIL RICHARDS, dau. of William and Mary[++] (Batchelder), m. (2) at Haverhill, Mass., 10 May 1716 (*Register*, vol. 23, p. 392), FRANCES (HOYT) PEABODY, dau. of John and Mary (Barnes) and wid. of

---

[+] I have had the advantage of examining an elaborate genealogy of this family in course of preparation by Samuel B. Shackford, Esq., Strafford Banks Bldg., Dover, N.H.; Samuel Shackford, of Chicago; and Mrs. Mary B. Morse, 24 Park Street, Haverhill, Mass.

[++] In 1702/3, administration on the estate of Mary Richards, wid. of William was granted to her son, Samuel, and his brother-in-law, Samuel Shackford, of Portsmouth, blockmaker (*N.H. State Pap.*, vol. 31, p. 499).

Administration on the estate of Stephen Batchelder was granted 26 Mar. 1673, to William Richards, husband of Mary Richards, dau. of the deceased (*id.*, p. 141).

NATHANIEL[2], b. at Andover, Mass., about 1670 (*Register*, vol. 2, p. 155), d. 25 Feb. 1749.

His will undated, proved 11 Mar. 1730/31, mentions his wife, Frances; brother, John; sons John, Joshua, William, Samuel (then dead), and his children and daughters; wives of Samuel Sherburn and Ezekiel Pitman; and Mary Hodgdon (*N.H. State Pap.*, vol. 32, p. 404).

Children, born at Bloody Point (in the order in which they are mentioned in the will, baptisms at North Church):

5   i. JOHN[3], bapt. Sept. 1716, b. 1698.

    ii. ABIGAIL, b. 1700, m. 11 June 1719 (*Register*, vol. 24, p. 13), SAMUEL[3] SHERBURN, son of Capt. John[2] and Mary (Cowell) (*Register*, vol. 58, p. 31), of Portsmouth, innholder, blacksmith, b. at Newcastle.

    iii. ELIZABETH, b. 1702, m. 23 May 1717 (*N.H. Gen. Rec.*, vol. 5, p. 88), Lieut. EZEKIEL[3] PITMAN, son of Ezekiel[2] and Elizabeth (Stackpole's *Durham*, vol. 2, p. 308), of Durham.

    Child, born at Durham:

    1) Ezekiel[4], m. 13 July 1740, Elizabeth[4] Peverly, dau. of Nathaniel[3] and Elizabeth[3] (Cotton), bapt. at Portsmouth, 11 Nov. 1716.

6   iv. JOSHUA, bapt. Sept. 1716.

7   v. WILLIAM, bapt. Sept. 1716.

    vi. SAMUEL, dead when his father's will was made leaving children who were given legacies "if they or any come here."

    vii. MARY, m. (1) 22 Nov. 1722, RICHARD[4] FURBER (6), son of William[3] and Sarah (Nute), *q.v.*, m. (2) at Greenland, 9 July 1727, ALEXANDER[4] HODGDON, son of Alexander[3] and Jane[2] (Shackford), *q.v.*

3. JOHN[2] SHACKFORD (William[1]), of Portsmouth, blockmaker, b. about 1678, d. 25 Oct. 1738 (*N.H. Gen. Rec.*, vol. 1, p. 19), m. about 1699, SARAH HUDSON.

His will dated 11 Sept. 1738, proved 25 Oct. 1738, mentions his children as below (*N.H. State Pap.*, vol. 32, p. 724).

8   i. JOHN[3], b. about 1708.

    ii. PAUL, of Newburyport, Mass., blockmaker, m. 29 Feb. 1728, REBECCA HUDSON, dau. ? of Eleazer and Deborah (Ford)

    iii. MARY, m. 28 July 1715 (*Register*, vol. 23, p. 272), Capt. WILLIAM[1] SEWARD, of Portsmouth, master mariner, officer at Louisburg 1744/5 (*Adj. Gen'l's Rep. 1866*, vol. 2, p. 69), b. at Devonshire, England.

    Children, born at Portsmouth (baptisms, except the last, in South Church):

    1) Giles[4], of Portsmouth, master mariner, b. 7 Mar. 1717 (town rec.), d. 4 Nov. 1797 (town rec.), m. 4 June 1738 (*Register*, vol. 26, p. 378) Mary Hodgdon, of Boston, b. about 1720, d. 30 Apr. 1783 *aet.* 63 (North Church rec.) *aet.* 66 (town rec.).

His will dated 22 Aug. 1789, was proved 21 Feb. 1798 (*Rockingham Probate*).

His daughter, Deborah, bapt. 25 Mar. 1739, m. 19 Dec. 1758 (Queens Chapel rec.), John Shackford, of Portsmouth.

2) John, of Portsmouth, master mariner, bapt. 6 Oct. 1723, m. 14 Nov. 1746 (Queen's Chapel rec.), Elizabeth Stoodly.

3) George, bapt. 12 Nov. 1727.

4) William, of Portsmouth, caulker, b. about 1728, d. in Sept. 1793 *aet.* 63 (*N.H. Gazette* of 8 Oct. 1793), m. Sarah -----, b. about 1730, d. in Sept. 1793 (*N.H. Gazette, loc. cit*).

5) Paul, bapt. 16 Aug. 1730.

6) Mary, bapt. 7 Nov. 1731, m. 24 June 1752 (Queen's Chapel rec.), Joseph Nelson, of Portsmouth.

7) Lieut. Shackford, of Portsmouth, officer in the Revolution (*Adj. Gen'l's Rep. 1866*, vol. 2, p. 291), b. about 1735, d. 8 July 1801 (St. John's Church rec.), m. 8 Dec. 1757 (Queen's Chapel rec.), Abigail Bennett, b. about 1736, d. 3 Mar. 1816 *aet.* 82 (St. John's Church rec.).

8) Ann, m. 6 Nov. 1760 (Queen's Chapel rec.), Henry Hilton.

9) Dorothy, bapt. 15 Oct. 1740 (Queen's Chapel rec.), m. 24 Sept. 1761 (*id*.), Caleb Currier.

iv. ELIZABETH, m. 12 Nov. 1730 (*Register*, vol. 25, p. 118), ANDREW TOMB, of Portsmouth, mariner, King's officer, b. at Minehead, Somerset, England.

v. SARAH, m. JOHN FLAGG, mariner.

vi. DEBORAH, m. (1) ISAAC SUMNER, of Portsmouth, merchant, m. (2) SAMUEL WATERHOUSE, of Portsmouth, master mariner, b. at 1707, d. 1 Jan. 1745, m. (3), JOHN[3] AYRES (12), son of Edward[2] and Alice, *q.v.*

Child by first husband, born at Portsmouth:

1) Mary[4] (mentioned in the will of John[2] Shackford).

4. JOSHUA[2] SHACKFORD (William[1]), m. (1) MARY -----, m. (2) 4 Dec. 1707 (*N.H. Gen. Rec.*, vol. 4, p. 13), ELIZABETH BARNES, ? dau. of Thomas and Mary[2] (Rand) (Parson's *Rye*, p. 499), who m. (2) 22 June 1760 (*Register*, vol. 27, p. 9) DANIEL QUICK, of Portsmouth.

Children by first wife, born at Newington:

i. SARAH[3]

ii. MARY, dau. of Joshua and Mary, owned the covenant and was baptized 8 Oct. 1732.

iii. LAZARUS, witness to documents.

Child by second wife, baptized at Newington:

iv. SAMUEL[3], of Newburyport, Mass., mariner, bapt. 8 July 1728, d. 10 Jan.

1796, m. at Newburyport, 9 July 1740, MARY COMBS, b. at Newburyport.

Children, born at Newburyport, Mass.:
1) Mary, b. 29 Mar. 1741.
2) Susanna
3) William
4) John, b. 28 Dec. 1753.
5) Sarah
6) Rebecca
7) Levi, b. 25 Dec. 1766.

v. PAUL, of Wells, Me., ship carpenter, bapt. 8 July 1728, m. 30 May 1744, SARAH DAY (*Register*, vol. 21, p. 217), dau. of Joseph and Patience, b. at Wells, 21 Oct. 1717.

vi. JOHN, bapt. 8 July 1728.

5. JOHN^3 SHACKFORD (Samuel^2, William^1), of Andover, 1731, and Chester, 1750, cordwainer, d. 2 Nov. 1786, m. (1) 26 Oct. 1727, DORCAS LOVEJOY (*Register*, vol. 24, p. 359), dau. of Nathaniel and Dorothy (Hoyt), b. about 1701, m. (2) at Methuen, Mass., 27 Nov. 1751, HANNAH LANCASTER.

Children (Chase's *Chester*, p. 588), the first one born probably at Portsmouth, the others at Andover, Mass.:

i. THEODORE^4, of Chester, b. about 1728, m. 14 Feb. 1754, MARY BARTLETT, d. 1 Apr. 1807.

ii. SAMUEL, of Haverhill, Mass., b. 4 Feb. 1732, m. ? at Haverhill, 13 June 1758, ANN FRINK.

iii. JOHN, of Chester, b. 9 Sept. 1735, d. 15 Apr. 1779, m. SARAH DEARBORN, dau. of Lieut. Ebenezer and Huldah (Nason) (*Register*, vol. 2, p. 302), b. 29 Jan. 1734, d. 20 Aug. 1814.

iv. DORCAS, b. 22 Oct. 1742, m. SIMON FRENCH, son of Joseph and Ruth (Knowles), of Candia, b. at Salisbury, Mass., 27 Oct. 1740, d. 3 Aug. 1823.

6. JOSHUA^3 SHACKFORD (Samuel^2, William^1), of Newington and Andover, Mass., 1738, cordwainer, m. at Andover, 24 Dec. 1735, LYDIA LOVEJOY, dau. of Joseph and Sarah (Pritchard), b. at Andover, 2 June 1697.

Children, born at Andover, Mass.:

i. JOSHUA, b. 16 Sept. 1736, d. 17 Oct. 1736.

ii. LYDIA, b. 23 Apr. 1738, d. 22 Feb. 1827 (*Register*, vol. 80, p. 307), m. her cousin, ALEXANDER^5 HODGDON (3-vi), son of Alexander^4 and Mary^3 (Shackford) (Furber), *q.v.*

7. Capt. WILLIAM³ SHACKFORD (Samuel², William¹), of Portsmouth and Newington, 1743, Dover and Portsmouth, 1763, farmer, captain in the French and Indian War (*Register*, vol. 32, p. 298), deacon, J.P., 1763, d. 1773, m. (1) 5 Oct. 1727 (*Register*, vol. 24, p. 359), SUSANNA³ DOWNING (2-ii), dau. of Col. John² and Elizabeth (Harrison), *q.v.*, m. (2) 7 May 1752 (*Register*, vol. 26, p. 389), PATIENCE (HAM) DOWNING, dau. of Lieut. John and Elizabeth, and wid. of John² (2-iv), *q.v.*, m. (3) after 22 Dec. 1749 (*N.H. State Pap.*, vol. 33, p. 753), ELEANOR⁴ (MENDUM) (SHERBURN) MARSHALL, dau. of Capt. Nathaniel² and Frances (Stackpole's *Kittery*, p. 606), and wid. of JOHN⁴ SHERBURN, first husband, and SAMUEL MARSHALL, second husband (*Register*, vol. 58, p. 234), b. at Kittery, Me., about 1714, d. 4 Feb. 1804 *aet.* 90 yrs. (tombstone) (*N.H. Gen. Rec.*, vol. 2, p. 21).

By his father's will, he had the farm at Newington, and half the shop warehouse and tools at Portsmouth.

Children, baptized at Newington:

9   i. SAMUEL⁴, b. 21 Aug. 1728.

    ii. ABIGAIL HARRISON DOWNING, bapt. 10 Mar. 1744, d. 27 Feb. 1793, m. (1) 1756, REUBEN HAYES, son of Peter and Sarah (Wingate), b. at Dover, 8 May 1720, d. 1762, m. (2) 23 May 1765, NATHANIEL COOPER, son of Walter and Martha (Goddard), of Dover, town clerk, baptized at Cambridge, Mass., 18 Apr. 1742, d. 4 Mar. 1795.

    iii. Capt. JOSIAH, of Portsmouth, master mariner, lieutenant on the frigate *Raleigh* in the Revolution, master of the privateersman *Diana* (*N.H. Gen. Rec.*, vol. 5, p. 163), founder of Portsmouth, Ohio (*History of Scioto County*, p. 825), bapt. 7 Feb. 1745/6, d. *s.p.* 26 July 1829, m. 21 Feb. 1771, DEBORAH MARSHALL, dau. of Samuel and Eleanor (Mendum) (Sherburn), b. at Portsmouth, d. 16 Feb. 1826.

    iv. ELIZABETH, bapt. 29 July 1749.

Child by second wife, baptized at Newington:

    v. JOHN, bapt. 18 Jan. 1753.

Children, probably by third wife, baptized at Dover:

    vi. RICHARD, bapt. 25 May 1755 (*Register*, vol. 41, p. 190).

    vii. JOHN, bapt. 8 May 1757 (*id.*, p. 191).

    viii. DEBORAH, bapt. 13 May 1759 (*id.*, p. 279).

8. Maj. JOHN³ SHACKFORD (John², William¹), of Portsmouth, blockmaker, town officer, b. about 1708, d. 25 Oct. 1766 (tombstone), m. 20 Jan. 1731/2 (*Register*, vol. 25, p. 119), CATHERINE³ DENNETT, dau. of Ephraim² and Catherine (Stackpole's *Kittery*, p. 348), b. 15 Jan. 1715, d. 16 Dec. 1799.

Children, baptized in North Church, Portsmouth:

    i. CATHERINE⁴, b. 12 Oct. 1745, d. 19 Jan. 1812, m. 10 Sept. 1767, Dr. JOSEPH TILTON, son of Jonathan and Margaret (Shaw), physician, b.

at Hampton Falls, 25 Sept. 1744, d. 5 Dec. 1837.
ii. JOHN, bapt. 17 Jan. 1747/8.
iii. DOROTHY, bapt. 4 Mar. 1749/50, d. 25 Mar. 1788, m. 27 Dec. 1770, (*N.H. Gazette* of 4 Jan. 1771), JOSIAH MOULTON, son of Gen. Jonathan and Abigail (Smith), of Hampton, b. at Hampton, 11 Dec. 1749, d. 1 Sept. 1796.
iv. ELIZABETH, bapt. 17 May 1752, d. 1787, m. (1) SAMUEL LANGDON, son of Rev. Samuel and Elizabeth (Brown), of Portsmouth, master mariner, b. at Portsmouth, 19 Apr. 1748, d. Dec. 1772, m. (2) 18 May 1780, SAMUEL PAGE, son of Samuel and Elizabeth (Clark), of Salem, Mass., merchant, b. at Medford, Mass., 13 Dec. 1749, d. 24 June 1785.
v. MARY, bapt. 25 Aug. 1754, m. NATHANIEL GOOKIN, son of Rev. Nathaniel and Ann (Fitch) of Portsmouth, b. 10 Jan. 1747, d. 1803.
vi. NATHANIEL, bapt. 5 Dec. 1756.

9. Capt. SAMUEL[4] SHACKFORD (William[3], Samuel[2], William[1]), of Newington, farmer, town officer, soldier in the Revolution, militia officer, b. 21 Aug. 1728, d. 12 Apr. 1812, m. (1) 3 Nov. 1747, ELIZABETH RING, dau. of Deac. Seth and Elizabeth (Libby), *q.v.*, m. (2) 1 Dec. 1782, ELEANOR MARSHALL, dau. of Samuel and Eleanor (Mendum) (Sherburn), b. at Portsmouth, 1746, d. 25 Feb. 1837 *aet.* 91 (*Register*, vol. 73, p. 198).

Children, born at Newington (family Bible in possession, 1920, of Francis A. Dorr, of Woburn, Mass.):
i. WILLIAM[5], b. 22 Mar. 1748, d. in infancy.
ii. JOHN, of Newington, Durham, 1797, Newmarket, 1804, farmer, b. 4 Dec. 1749, d. 26 Sept. 1816, m. 20 Apr. 1777, RUTH WEBB[6] ADAMS (4-iv), dau. of Deac. Benjamin[5] and Abigail (Pickering), *q.v.*
Children, baptized at Newington:
1) Elizabeth[6], bapt. 31 Jan. 1778, d. 1799, m. Apr. 1798, George Dennett, of Portsmouth.
2) Abigail, bapt. 14 Feb. 1779, d. at Durham, 10 July 1820, m. John[6] Leighton, son of Jonathan[5] and Mary (Bampton) (Stackpole's *Durham*, vol. 2, p. 261).
3) John, bapt. 12 Jan. 1781.
4) Seth Ring, of Newmarket, farmer, town officer, bapt. 3 Aug. 1783, d. 9 Apr. 1848, m. 1 June 1806, Martha Boardman, dau. of William and Martha (Lane).
5) Samuel, b. 8 May 1787.
6) Benjamin Adams, b. 7 Sept. 1791.
7) John Downing, b. 16 Jan. 1795.
iii. SAMUEL, of Dover and Barrington, farmer, b. 8 Jan. 1752, d. 21 Oct.

1843, m. 6 May 1779, NANCY⁶ WALKER (10-ii), dau. of Seth⁵ and Ann (Tripe), *q.v.*

Children:
1) Samuel⁶, of Barrington, farmer, J.P., b. at Dover, 28 Feb. 1782, d. 12 Oct. 1832, m. 28 Jan. 1806, Nancy Buzzell, dau. of Solomon and Elizabeth (Burnham).
2) Nancy, b. at Barrington (Strafford), 10 Oct. 1798, d. 25 May 1868, m. 12 Sept. 1826, as his first wife, Benning W. Jenness, son of Thomas and Deborah (Sanborn) (See *Huckins Family*, p. 61).

iv. SETH RING, soldier in the Revolution, b. 22 Sept. 1754, d. unm. 7 Oct. 1777, at Saratoga, N.Y. killed in action.

v. SUSANNA, b. 4 Dec. 1756, d. 13 Nov. 1848, m. 8 Mar. 1781, HATEVIL⁵ NUTTER (8-i), son of Maj. John⁴ and Anna (Symmes), *q.v.*

vi. MARY, b. 12 Apr. 1759, d. 12 Apr. 1825, m. 10 June 1779, MARK⁴ WALKER (2-v), son of Seth³ and Ann (Tripe).

vii. ELIZABETH, b. 7 Oct. 1761, d. Sept. 1843, m. WILLIAM⁶ WALKER (10-v), son of Seth⁵ and Ann (Tripe), *q.v.*

viii. ABIGAIL, b. 21 Apr. 1763.

ix. HANNAH, b. 18 Sept. 1764, m. (1) 2 Jan. 1791, BENJAMIN⁵ COLMAN (5-iii), son of John⁴ and Mary⁵ (Woodman), *q.v.*, m. (2) JETHRO⁶ FURBER, son ? of Jethro⁵ (7-iii) and Mary (Sherburn), d. 1 Mar. 1811.

x. JOSIAH, of Barnstead, farmer, b. 21 Jan. 1767, d. 31 Dec. 1843, m. 22 Jan. 1796, LYDIA⁶ DENNETT, dau. of Jeremiah⁴ and Susanna⁵ (Peverly), b. at Newington, 19 June 1773, d. 5 July 1859.

Children, the first one born at Dover, the others at Barnstead:
1) Josiah Ring⁶, of Barnstead, farmer, town officer, b. 21 Dec. 1796, d. 19 Mar. 1874, m. 18 Sept. 1817, Mary Garland, dau. of Samuel and Abigail (Drew).
2) Lydia, b. 1798, d. May 1889, m. 1814, Joseph French, ? son of Joseph and Olive (Williams) (Stackpole's *Durham*, vol. 2, p. 391).
3) Susan, b. 9 June 1803, d. unm. 7 Feb. 1841.
4) William, of Barnstead, millwright, b. 24 Aug. 1806, d. 26 Dec. 1886, m. 30 Dec. 1830, Mary Dame, dau. of James C. and Phebe (Ayres).
5) Seth, of Barnstead, farmer, merchant, member of the Legislature, 1855/6, b. 31 Dec. 1811, d. 6 Dec. 1888, m. (1) 30 Dec. 1831, Harriet Hill, dau. of Samuel and Hannah (Dow), m. (2) 12 Apr. 1865, Roxana A. Nute, dau. of Moses and Eunice (Varney), m. (3) 28 Oct. 1873, Pamela A. (Prendergast) Brown, dau. of Stephen and Ann (Ayres) and wid. of Nathaniel Green.

xi. NATHANIEL COOPER, of Newington and Wakefield, farmer, b. 11 Apr. 1769, d. 27 Apr. 1852, m. 15 Apr. 1798, PHEBE⁶ NUTTER (17-vii), dau. of Matthias⁵ and Martha (Perkins), *q.v.*

Children, born at Newington:
1) Elizabeth Ring[6], b. 1 Mar. 1799, d. *s.p.* at Quincy, Mass., 29 July 1881, m. 14 May 1829, Horatio G. Dearborn.
2) Nathaniel, b. 11 Aug. 1800, d. 17 Jan. 1873, m. 24 Nov. 1825, Abigail Colman, dau. of Joseph G. and Mary (Goodwin), b. at Newington, 15 Mar. 1800, d. 8 May 1895.
3) James Nutter, b. 3 Oct. 1802, m. (1) 26 Nov. 1826, Elizabeth Keniston, m. (2) 12 Oct. 1850, Charlotte Burnham, m. (3) 29 May 1855, Rebecca McDaniels.
4) William (twin), b. 25 Apr. 1805, d. 2 June 1843, m. 28 Jan. 1824, Sarah Dearborn, b. 15 Aug. 1805, d. Jan. 1879.
5) Mary (twin), b. 25 Apr. 1805, d. 5 Apr. 1891, m. (1) 14 May 1829, Phineas G. Hanson, m. (2) Charles Dorr.
6) Ephram F., b. 25 Feb. 1810, d. 28 Mar. 1849, m. Mary A. Yeaton.
7) Martha Ann, b. 19 Mar. 1812, d. 31 Oct. 18--, m. 10 Nov. 1839, David D. Smith.

xii. WILLIAM, b. 29 May 1771, d. unm. ?

Child by second wife, born at Newington:

xiii. TEMPERENCE KNIGHT, b. 25 Oct. 1786, d. unm. 31 Mar. 1876.

On her death, the Shackford name became extinct in Newington.

SHACKFORD (unconnected)

SARAH SHACKFORD, covenant, at Newington, 10 Dec. 1727.

SAMUEL SHACKFORD, bapt. in North Church, July 1716 (*N.H. Gen. Rec.*, vol. 4, p. 51).

ABIGAIL SHACKFORD, covenant, in North Church, 3 Mar. 1716/7 (*N.H. Gen. Rec.*, vol. 4, p. 104).

ABIGAIL SHACKFORD, m. about 1740, REUBEN[3] GREEN, son of John[2] and ----- (-----) (Thompson), b. at Dover, 8 May 1720 (*Register*, vol. 29, p. 181).

ANNA SHACKFORD, m. at Falmouth, Me., 21 May 1762, JOSEPH CONANT, JR. (*Register*, vol. 14, p. 225).

SAMUEL SHACKFORD, m. at Newmarket, 20 Mar. 1771, SARAH HANAFORD (*N.H. Gen. Rec.*, vol. 6, p. 139).

JOHN SHACKFORD, private in Capt. Ward's Co., 31 Dec. 1775, prisoner at Quebec (*Register*, vol. 6, p. 136)

Capt. SHACKFORD, at L'Orient, 1777, to whom Ezra Green, surgeon, of the Ranger writes (*Register*, vol. 29, p. 13).

JOHN SHACKFORD, of Portsmouth, m. at Kittery, 26 Dec. 1785, AMELIA MOORE (*Register*, vol. 63, p. 174).

WILLIAM M. SHACKFORD, m. about 1790, JOANNA CHAUNCEY MOORE, dau. of John and Sarah (Chauncey) (*Register*, vol. 24, p. 148), Their children *ibid*.

DELIVERANCE SHACKFORD, m. at Epping, 4 Sept. 1791, ABEL KENDALL (*N.H. Gen. Rec.*, vol. 4, p. 15).

SAMUEL SHACKFORD, of Portsmouth, m. about 1810, OLIVE LAMSON[5] DEANE, dau. of Eliphalet and Olive (Swasey) (*Register*, vol. 63, p. 174). Their children (*Register*, vol. 37, 294).

Rev. CHARLES C. SHACKFORD, m. about 1820, CHARLOTTE ----- (*Register*, vol. 24, p. 148). Their children *ibid*.

SUSAN SHACKFORD, d. at Newburyport, 18 Feb. 1868, *aet*. 67 (*Register*, vol. 22, p. 202).

SHAFFEN

PATRICK SHAFFEN, m. 14 Mar. 1755, MARY RACKLEBY, both of Newington.

SHAPLEIGH

NICHOLAS[5] SHAPLEIGH (Nicholas[4], John[3], Alexander[2-1]) (Stackpole's *Kittery*, p. 717), covenant, 14 Aug. 1720.

DEPENDENCE[5] SHAPLEIGH (John[4-3], Alexander[2-1]) (Stackpole *loc. cit.*), m. 17 Nov. 1768, CATHERINE LEIGHTON, both of Kittery, Me.

SHERBURN

JOB SHERBURN, covenant, 18 Oct. 1747.

THOMAS SHERBURN, of Portsmouth, m. 15 Feb. 1749, **SARAH JOHNSON**, of Greenland.

SIMPSON

ELIZABETH SIMPSON, m. 24 Oct. 1750, **HENRY ABBOTT**, both of Andover, Mass.

SINNOTT

ROBERT SINNOTT, m. 3 Feb. 1756, **MARY GROVE**, both of Newmarket.

SMITH

ABIGAIL SMITH, covenant, 18 Aug. 1728.

ABIGAIL SMITH, m. 1729, **TOBIAS FERNALD**, both of Kittery, Me.

JOHN³ SMITH (John², James¹) (Stackpole's *Kittery*, p. 735), of Berwick, m. 26 Nov. 1734, **ELIZABETH LIBBY**, of Portsmouth.

JOSEPH³ SMITH (John², James¹) (Stackpole's *Durham*, vol. 2, p. 332), m. 31 Oct. 1734, **ALICE TRICKEY**.

JAMES³ SMITH (John², James¹) (Stackpole's *Durham, loc. cit.*), of Durham, m. 13 Jan. 1737, **MARY TRICKEY**.

PATIENCE³ SMITH (Samuel², Joseph¹) (Stackpole's *Durham*, vol. 2, p. 234), m. 14 Apr. 1743, Ensign **JOHN WRIGHT**.

SMITHSON

DEBORAH SMITHSON, m. 18 June 1724, **JOSHUA PICKERING**, both of Portsmouth.

MARY SMITHSON, m. 28 Oct. 1742, **THOMAS⁵ LEIGHTON** (4), son of Thomas⁴, *q.v.*

SPENCER

POLLY SPENCER, covenant, 22 Oct. 1780.

SPINNEY

SARAH[3] **SPINNEY** (James[2], John[1]) (Stackpole's *Kittery*, p. 740), of Portsmouth, m. 21 June 1716, JOSEPH DOWNING[7], of Dover *Register*, vol. 23, p. 392).

NATHAN[3] **SPINNEY** (Samuel[2], Thomas[1]), (Stackpole's *loc. cit.*), m. 1 Mar. 1721, ELIZABETH POMEROY.

TIMOTHY[4] **SPINNEY** (John[3-2], Thomas[1]) (Stackpole's *Kittery*, p. 742), m. 31 Oct. 1765, ABIGAIL PAUL, both of Kittery.

MARY[4] **SPINNEY** (Andrew[3], John[2], Thomas[1]) (Stackpole's *Kittery*, p. 743), m. 2 June 1768, ISAAC MORRILL, both of Kittery, Me.

STAPLES

TOBIAS[4] **STAPLES** (Peter[3-1]) (Stackpole's *Kittery*, p. 753), m. 22 Oct. 1767, CATHERINE STAPLES, both of Kittery, Me.

CATHERINE[4] **STAPLES** (Joseph[3], James[2], Peter[1]) (Stackpole's *Kittery*, p. 755), m. 22 Oct. 1767, TOBIAS STAPLES, both of Kittery.

BENJAMIN[4] **STAPLES** (Joseph[3], James[2], Peter[1]) (Stackpole's *Kittery, loc. cit.*), m. 30 Nov. 1762, JERUSHA LIBBY, of Kittery, Me.

ROBERT[4] **STAPLES** (Enoch[3], Peter[2-1]), (Stackpole's *Kittery*, p. 754), m. 4 Dec. 1764, ELIZABETH KENNARD, of Kittery.

JOSIAH[4] **STAPLES** (Peter[3-1]) (Stackpole's *Kittery*, p. 753), m. 6 Oct. 1767, EUNICE FOGG, both of Kittery.

STEVENS

1. **JOHN**[1] **STEVENS**, m. (1) SARAH -----, m. (2) MARY -----.
Children by first wife, born at Newington:
  i. WILLIAM[2], bapt. 27 July 1728.
  ii. MARY, bapt. 27 July 1728, m. 13 Nov. 1740, THOMAS PEAVEY.
  iii. SARAH, bapt. 27 July 1728.
  iv. A DAUGHTER, bapt. 13 Oct. 1728.
Children by second wife, born at Newington:
  v. JOHN, bapt. 14 Oct. 1733.

vi. TIMOTHY, bapt. 4 July 1736.
vii. LUCRETIA, bapt. 10 Sept. 1743.

STEVENS (unconnected)

SARAH STEVENS, communion, 28 June 1747.

STEPHEN STEVENS, gr. son of wid. Sarah, bapt. 28 Feb. 1754.

NAOMI STEVENS, covenant, 5 Nov. 1769.

STOKES

BENJAMIN STOKES, bapt. 15 Aug. 1742.

STOODLEY

ELIZABETH STOODLEY, m. 11 Oct. 1737, BENJAMIN WELCH, both of Portsmouth (*Register*, vol. 26, p. 380).

ELIZABETH STOODLEY, m. 24 July 1776, JOSEPH BOYD, both of Portsmouth.

JAMES STOODLEY, Esq., communion, 6 June 1776.

JAMES STOODLEY, Esq., d. 6 June 1779 *aet.* 62 (*Register*, vol. 10, p. 51).

JONATHAN and JAMES STOODLEY, both of Portsmouth, mariners, administrators of their sister, MARY, of Portsmouth, 30 Mar. 1743 (*N.H. State Papers*, vol. 33, p. 152).

MARY STOODLEY, wife of W. STOODLEY, d. at Newington, Jan. 1786, *aet.* 26 (*N.H. Register*, 13 Jan. 1786).

SULLIVAN

EBENEZER SULLIVAN, of Berwick, Me., m. 18 Feb. 1773, ABIGAIL COTTON, of Portsmouth.

SWETT

MEHITABLE SWETT, m. 29 Oct. 1771, DAVID PERKINS, of Epping.

JONATHAN[5] SWETT, son of Jonathan[4] and Jane (Rowe), m. 9 Nov. 1774, LYDIA[4] HUNTRESS (4-1).

SYMMES

ANNA SYMMES, of Portsmouth, m. 17 Nov. 1747, JOHN NUTTER (14-ii).

TASKER

MERCY[4] TASKER (John[3-2], William[1]) (Stackpole's *Durham*, vol. 2, p. 355), m. 19 Dec. 1778, BENJAMIN NUTTER (15-vi).

THOMPSON

1. SAMUEL[2] THOMPSON (John[1]) (Stackpole's *Kittery*, p. 770), of Portsmouth and Newington, 1713, carpenter, m. (1) ELIZABETH COTTON, dau. of John, m. (2) 16 Apr. 1717, MARY CROCKETT.

Children by first wife, baptized at Newington:
    i. ELIZABETH[3], bapt. 6 May 1716.
2   ii. ? NOAH

Children by second wife, born at Portsmouth:
3   iii. ? WILLIAM
4   iv. ? SAMUEL

JOHN COTTON, of Portsmouth, his will dated 14 Sept. 1714, proved 9 Dec. 1714, mentions his daughter, ELIZABETH "TOMSON." (*N.H. State Pap.*, vol. 31, p. 737). The Cotton family says this was GEORGE[3] COTTON, son of John (*Register*, vol. 58, p. 295).

2. NOAH[3] THOMPSON (Samuel[2], John[1]), of Newington, m. SUSANNA -----.

Children, baptized at Newington:
    i. MARY, bapt. 7 Sept. 1735.
    ii. LYDIA, bapt. 19 June 1737.

3. WILLIAM[3] THOMPSON (Samuel[2], John[1]), of Newington, m. 4 May 1744, ANNA BARKER.

Children, baptized at Newington:
    i. ANTHONY[4], bapt. 26 May 1754.
    ii. WILLIAM, bapt. 26 May 1754.
    iii. JOHN, bapt. 26 May 1754.

  iv. SARAH, bapt. 26 May 1754, m. JAMES⁵ LEIGHTON (2-xii), son of John⁴ and Abigail (Ham), *q.v.*
  v. RACHEL, bapt. 26 May 1754.
  vi. ENOCH BARKER, bapt. 12 Oct. 1755.
  vii. SAMUEL, bapt. 16 Jan. 1757.
  viii. SOLOMON, bapt. 16 Jan. 1757.

4. SAMUEL⁵ THOMPSON (Samuel², John¹), of Newington, m. 4 Dec. 1755, SARAH DOWNING.
 Children, baptized at Newington:
  i. BENJAMIN⁴, bapt. 3 July 1757.
  ii. HANNAH, bapt. 8 July 1759 (bapt. as dau. of Samuel and Abigail).
  iii. AMY, bapt. 4 Oct. 1761.
  iv. ALICE, b. 1763, d. unm. living with her sister, Susanna, (in 1850) in the Stavers family. (*Exeter News Letter*, 3 Mar. 1856).
  v. SUSANNA, b. Sept. 1765, d. Feb. 1856, m. 31 Dec. 1795, WILLIAM⁴ HUNTRESS, son of Joseph³ (1-viii).

JOHN THOMPSON, of Newington, m. 21 Nov. 1776, ELIZABETH WALKER.
 Child, baptized at Newington:
  i. SAMUEL WALKER, bapt. 2 Aug. 1778.

THOMPSON (unconnected)

Administration on **JOHN THOMPSON**, of Portsmouth, husbandman, to widow, SARAH, 17 Oct. 1732, John Wiley and Hugh Montgomery, of Portsmouth, sureties (*N.H. State Papers*, vol. 32, p. 459).

BENJAMIN THOMPSON, covenant, 21 Dec. 1740.

SARAH THOMPSON, covenant, 21 Dec. 1740.

WILLIAM THOMPSON, covenant, 20 Dec. 1741.

SAMUEL THOMPSON, covenant, 20 Dec. 1741.

WILLIAM THOMPSON, communion, 9 May 1742.

SARAH THOMPSON, communion, 18 Apr. 1742.

SARAH THOMPSON, m. 28 Nov. 1744, NICHOLAS KNIGHT (?).

MARY THOMPSON, m. 1 Dec. 1746, JOHN YEATON, of Portsmouth.

RICHARD THOMPSON, m. 15 Apr. 1752, ALICE HUNTER, both of Portsmouth.

MARY THOMPSON, wife of SAMUEL, Sr., bapt. 18 Apr. 1757.

JOHN THOMPSON, m. 21 Nov. 1776, ELIZABETH WALKER, both of Portsmouth.

TOPPAN

ENOCH TOPPAN, of Newbury, Mass., m. 21 Oct. 1756, SARAH COLMAN (1-ix).

TRICKEY

FRANCIS^1 TRICKEY, of Dover, 1649 (*Register*, vol. 4, p. 242), and Portsmouth, 1653 (*N.H. Gen. Rec.*, vol. 2, p. 23), d. before 1 Apr. 1682 (*York Deeds*, vol. 5, p. 39), m. SARAH ----- (Stackpole's *Kittery*, vol. --, p. 811).
  Children (Statement of Samuel B. Shackford, Esq., of Dover:
   i. JOHN^2, d. by 1686 (*York Deeds*, vol. 5, p. 39). He is said to have been the only son and to have died *s.p.*
   ii. MARTHA, m. 10 Nov. 1674, ELIHU GUNNISON, son of Hugh and Sarah (Tilly) (See *Gunnison Genealogy*, p. --), of Kittery, Me., shipwright, b. at Boston, 12 Feb. 1760, d. 1729.
     Children (See Stackpole, *loc. cit.*):
     Children, born at Kittery, Me. (Stackpole's *Kittery*, p. 478):
       1) Elihu, b. about 1676.
       2) A Child, b. about 1677, killed by Indians.
       3) Priscilla, b. about 1679, m. 7 May 1700, Nicholas Weeks.
       4) Mary, b. about 1681, m. Joseph Weeks.
       5) Sarah, m. ? in Boston, 14 Mar. 1700, John Follett.
   iii. SARAH, m. 1684, SAMUEL WINKLEY (Stackpole's *Kittery*, p. 802), b. at Lancashire, England, 1666 ?, d. 1736.

1. THOMAS^1 TRICKEY, of Dover, 1655 (*Register*, vol. 4, p. 247), and Bloody Point, 1657 (*id.*, p. 248), innkeeper, b. probably in Devonshire, England, about 1616 (*N.H. Court Pap.*, vol. 1, p. 221), d. in Nov. 1675, m. ELIZABETH -----.

Administration on his estate was granted 27 June 1676 to his widow, Elizabeth (*N.H. State Pap.*, vol. 31, p. 169).

Children:
- i. DEBORAH[2], b. about 1645 (*N.H. State Pap.*, vol. 31, p. 544), m. WILLIAM[1] SHACKFORD, *q.v.*
- ii. LYDIA, b. about 1650, d. 30 Apr. 1721, m. RICHARD WEBBER, of Portsmouth, butcher, b. 1638, d. 25 May 1720.
- iii. SARAH, m. JOSHUA CROCKETT, of Kittery, Me., b. at York, Me., son of Thomas[1] and Ann Crockett (Stackpole's *Kittery*, p. 331).
- 2   iv. ZACHARIAH, b. about 1651 (N.H. Court File 15187).
- 3   v. ISAAC (*N.H. Deeds*, vol. 3, p. 174b).
- 4   vi. EPHRAIM (*id.*, p. 175a).
- 5   vii. JOSEPH (*id.*, vol. 5, p. 185).

2. ZACHARIAH[2] TRICKEY (Thomas[1]), b. about 1651, d. about 1720, m. ELIZABETH WHITTUM (*N.H. Deeds*, vol. 6, p. 120), dau. of Peter.

Children:
- i. ZACHARIAH[3]. He executed a release in 1709 (*N.H. Deeds*, vol. 8, p. 298).

3. ISAAC[2] TRICKEY (Thomas[1]), of Bloody Point, 1670 (*Register*, vol. 4, p. 250), constable there, 1686 (*N.H. Court Pap.*, vol. 9, p. 217).

Administration on his estate 13 Aug. 1712 to his son, John. He had also a son, Thomas (*N.H. State Pap.*, vol. 31, p. 690).

Children, born at Bloody Point:
- 6   i. JOHN[3]
- 7   ii. THOMAS

4. EPHRAIM[2] TRICKEY (Thomas[1]), of Bloody Point, m. MARY NASON, dau. of Richard, who m. (2) WILLIAM WITTAM, of Dover.

Administration on his estate 24 Sept. 1701, to his brother, Isaac, and John Pickering, of Portsmouth, who had the eldest son as apprentice (*N.H. State Pap.*, vol. 31, p. 482).

Child, born at Bloody Point:
- i. THOMAS[3]. He had a grant 23 Jan. 1701 (*Dover Records*, vol. 2, p. 52).

5. JOSEPH[2] TRICKEY (Thomas[1]), of Dover, shipwright, m. REBECCA (ROGERS), dau. of William and Rebecca (Mackworth) (Stackpole's *Kittery*, p. 362), who m. (2) JOSHUA[2] DOWNING, son of Dennis[1] (*Piscataqua Pioneers*, p. 66).

Administration on his estate, 1 Sept. 1713, to his widow, Rebecca. It appears that he had a deceased brother, Ephraim (*N.H. State Pap.*, vol. 31, p. 713).

As widow of Joseph, she was fined, 1695, for a bastard (*N.H. Court Pap.*, vol. --, p. --).

6. JOHN³ TRICKEY (Isaac², Thomas¹), of Newington, m. MARY WHITTAM.

His will dated 8 Jan. 1753, proved 1756 (*N.H. Probate*, vol. 19, p. 540) mentions (children i, iii, iv, v, vi, and viii).

Children, baptized at Newington:

8   i. JOHN⁴, bapt. 4 Apr. 1725.

    ii. EPHRAIM, bapt. 4 Apr. 1725, of Durham, m. CATHERINE ----- (*Rochester Deeds*, vol. 142, p. 357).

    iii. MARY, bapt. 4 Apr. 1725, m. 13 Jan. 1737, JAMES³ SMITH, son of John² and Elizabeth (Buss) (Stackpole's *Durham*, vol. 2, p. 332), of Durham.

Children, born at Durham (See Stackpole, *loc. cit.*):

    iv. ALICE, bapt. 4 Apr. 1725, m. 31 Oct. 1734, JOSEPH³ SMITH, brother of James³ above (Stackpole, *loc. cit.*).

    v. SARAH, bapt. 4 Apr. 1725, m. 17 Sept. 1743, THOMAS² LANGLEY, son of James¹ and Mary (Runnels) (Stackpole's *Durham*, vol. 2, p. 246), of Durham.

Children, born at Durham (See Stackpole, *loc. cit.*):

    vi. ELIHU, b. 7 Aug. 1726.

    vii. DEBORAH, b. 16 Sept. 1733.

9   viii. JOSHUA

7. Capt. THOMAS³ TRICKEY (Isaac², Thomas¹), of Newington, shipwright, d. 23 Dec. 1737, m. 28 Aug. 1712, MARY GAMBLE, who m. (2) 4 Apr. 1751, JOHN³ BICKFORD (2-vii), son of Benjamin² and Deborah, *q.v.*

Administration on his estate 27 Sept. 1738, to his widow, Mary (*N.H. State Pap.*, vol. 32, p. 731).

Children, baptized at Newington:

    i. ISAAC⁴, bapt. 18 Apr. 1725, m. 28 Oct. 1734 (*Register*, vol. 25, p. 121), ELIZABETH WILLS, b. at Portsmouth. He was beyond the seas *s.p.*, in 1747 (*N.H. State Pap., loc. cit.*). ELIZABETH TRICKEY, m. 28 July 1741, PETER MILLER, of Portsmouth (*Register*, vol. 27, p. 9).

Child, baptized at Newington:

    1) Sarah⁵, bapt. 12 Oct. 1735.

10   ii. JONATHAN, bapt. 18 Apr. 1725.

    iii. SARAH, bapt. 18 Apr. 1725, m. 7 Dec. 1732, HATEVIL⁵ LEIGHTON (3), son of Thomas⁴ and Deborah, *q.v.*

    iv. ABIGAIL, bapt. 18 Apr. 1725.

    v. ELIZABETH, bapt. 18 Apr. 1725, m. 23 Oct. 1737, THOMAS² TRIPE, son of Sylvanus[1] and Margaret (Diamond) (Stackpole's *Kittery*, p. 782), of Kittery, Me., b. 12 May 1706.

vi. MARY, bapt. 18 Apr. 1725, m. 16 May 1742, ABRAHAM[4] FERNALD, son of Thomas[3] and Mary (Thompson) (Stackpole's *Kittery*, p. 384), of Kittery, Me., b. at Kittery.

Children, born at Kittery, Me. (See Stackpole, *loc. cit.*):

11 vii. JOSEPH, b. 10 Apr. 1726.

viii. KETURAH, m. 25 Dec. 1745, JONATHAN[3] LEATHERS, son of William[2] and Margaret (Willey) (Stackpole's *Durham*, vol. 2, p. 256), of Durham.

12 ix. THOMAS, b. 19 July 1730.

13 x. LEMUEL, b. 29 July 1733.

Administration on Edward Cater, of Portsmouth, to THOMAS TRICKEY, of Newington, 24 May 1732, Samuel Hart and George Walton, sureties (*N.H. State Pap.*, vol. 32, p. 440).

8. JOHN[4] TRICKEY (John[3], Isaac[2], Thomas[1]), of Rochester, 1742 (*N.H. Gen. Rec.*, vol. 7, p. 91), husbandman, m. REBECCA CHAMBERLAIN, dau. of William and Mary (Tibbetts), b. at Dover, 28 Dec. 1722, d. 1815.

His will dated 3 Mar. 1779, proved Dec. 1781 (*Strafford Probate*, vol. 1, p. 468), mentions the following.

Children:

i. +WILLIAM[5], of Rochester, b. 20 Nov. 1742, d. 14 May 1817, m. DOROTHY[4] FURBISH, dau. of Benjamin[3] and Hannah (Hussey) (Stackpole's *Kittery*, p. 438), b. in Lebanon, Me., 17 Sept. 1742, d. 9 Dec. 1824.

ii. JOHN, of Rochester, 1790, 5 males under 16, 4 females in his family (Census).

iii. EPHRAIM, of Rochester, 1790, one male under 16, 3 females in his family (Census).

iv. REBECCA

v. ALICE

vi. MARY

JOHN TRICKEY, m. at Rochester, 9 Mar. 1780, LUCY COOK (*N.H. Gen. Rec.*, vol. 4, p. 150).

+He was of Rochester, 1790, 3 males over 16, one under; and 3 females in his family (Census). No other William in census. He had sons John, William, and Benjamin; daughters Sarah (Ricker), Hannah (Hanson), Rebecca (Langley).

9. JOSHUA⁴ TRICKEY (John³, Isaac², Thomas¹), of Newington, m. 27 Dec. 1753, ROSAMOND⁴ COLMAN (1-viii), dau. of Eleazer³ and Ann (Nutter).
Children, baptized at Newington:
- i. ⁺JOHN⁵, bapt. 1 Dec. 1754, m. ? 3 June 1778, BETHIAH⁶ DAM (7-vi), dau. of Joseph⁵ and Mehitable (Hale) (*Register*, vol. 65, p. 215), *q.v.*
- ii. ANNA, bapt. 2 May 1762, m. (1) ----- VINCENT (*N.H. Probate Files*, No. 211), m. (2) MATTHIAS⁵ NUTTER (17), son of Matthias⁴ and Hannah (Furber), *q.v.*

JOSHUA TRICKEY, m. 5 May 1776, REBECCA TIBBETTS.

10. JONATHAN⁴ TRICKEY (Thomas³, Isaac², Thomas¹), of Newington, shipwright, b. about 1720, m. (1) 9 Mar. 1742, ABIGAIL MILLER, dau. of Benjamin (*N.H. State Pap.*, vol. 33, p. 423), b. at Portsmouth, m. (2) SARAH⁵ (FURBER) HOYT, dau. of Moses⁴ and Anna (Bickford) (Walker), and wid. of John⁵, *q.v.* He had his father's homestead at Newington.
Children, baptized at Newington:
- i. LYDIA⁵, bapt. 14 Aug. 1743, m. ? 17 Oct. 1765, THOMAS CRATON (South Church rec.).
- ii. ABIGAIL, bapt. 11 Aug. 1745, d. in infancy.
- iii. ABIGAIL, bapt. 11 Nov. 1748, m. ? her cousin, CHARLES⁵ FERNALD, son of Abraham⁴ and Mary⁴ (Trickey) (Stackpole's *Kittery*, p. 384), of Northwood, b. at Kittery, Me., 12 Mar. 1752, d. 5 Apr. 1828.
- iv. BENJAMIN, bapt. 22 Feb. 1756, not in Census of 1790.

JONATHAN TRICKEY, m. at Greenland, 30 Dec. 1762, TEMPERENCE BICKFORD (N.H.V.S)

11. JOSEPH⁴ TRICKEY (Thomas³, Isaac², Thomas¹), of Newington, b. about 1725, m. 20 Mar. 1748, ELIZABETH⁵ DAM (4-vi), dau. of John⁴ and Elizabeth (Hilliard) (*Register*, vol. 65, p. 214), *q.v.*
Children, baptized at Newington:
- i. THOMAS⁵, bapt. 15 July 1749, m. ? 20 Dec. 1774, ELIZABETH TRIPE (South Church rec.)

+Of Dover, 1790, 2 males over 16, one under, and 2 females in his family (Census). A Joshua Trickey was of Nottingham, 1 male under 16, 2 females in his family (Census). No other Joshua's. A Samuel Trickey was of Nottingham, 1792, 2 males under 16, 3 females in his family (Census). No other Samuel's in the Census.

ii. ESTHER, bapt. 21 Apr. 1751, d. unm. at Portsmouth, Feb. 1832 (*Enquirer*, 7 Feb. 1832)
   iii. JOHN, bapt. 1 Oct. 1752, m. ? 25 Aug. 1770, MARY WELCH (South Church rec.).
   iv. ABIGAIL, bapt. 1 Sept. 1754.
   v. +JOSEPH, bapt. 15 Feb. 1756, m. ? 4 Apr. 1785, SUSANNA BALL, dau. of Peter and Mary (Wallis) (Parson's *Rye*, p. 294).
   vi. LEMUEL, bapt. 18 Sept. 1757.
   vii. JONATHAN, bapt. 11 Feb. 1759, m. ? 10 Oct. 1782, LYDIA PINKHAM (*Dover Hist. Col.*, vol. 1, p. 81). He was of Dover, 1790, 2 males under 16, 3 females in his family (Census).
   viii. JAMES, bapt. 13 May 1763.
   ix. CATHERINE, bapt. 15 June 1766.
   x. WILLIAM, bapt. 5 June 1768, m. ? 18 Oct. 1790, MARY RICKER, dau. of Jabez and Mary (Wentworth) (*Wentworth Genealogy*, vol. 1, p. 418).
   xi. SAMUEL GRIFFIN, bapt. 10 June 1770.

ELIZABETH TRICKEY, widow, communion, 19 July 1775.

12. THOMAS[4] TRICKEY (Thomas[3], Isaac[2], Thomas[1]), of Newington and Portsmouth, 1790, yeoman, bapt. 19 July 1730.

Administration on his estate 28 Oct. 1813 to Edward Cale, of Portsmouth, trader; Benjamin Trickey, of Durham, husbandman, and John Trickey, of Portsmouth, blacksmith, sureties. The petition shows that the intestate's wife died some years before, that he was perhaps a soldier in the Revolution and had the following children.

Children, born at Newington:
   i. BENJAMIN[5], of Durham, husbandman, eldest son, m. ? 12 July 1808, BETSEY APPLEBY (Stackpole's *Durham*, vol. 1, p. 387; *N.H. Gen. Rec.*, vol. 4, p. 79).
   ii. SAMUEL
   iii. JOSEPH
   iv. -----, m. JOHN C. FLOYD.
   v. ANN, m. Nov. 1799, JOHN TARLETON (*N.H. Gazette*, 20 Nov. 1799).
   vi. -----, m. MICHAEL PRIEST.
   vii. JOHN, of Portsmouth, blacksmith.
   viii. SOPHIA
   ix. -----, m. GEORGE OSBORN.

+Of Portsmouth, 1790, one male under 16, 2 females in his family (Census).

x. MARY, m. 16 Mar. 1797, JOHN AYRES (town rec.), of Portsmouth.
xi. THOMAS, of Newington, m. ? 1781, MARY[4] HUNTRESS, dau. of Joseph[3] and Sobriety (Tobey), b. at Newington.
xii. ELIZABETH
xiii. DANIEL

THOMAS TRICKEY, covenant, 15 Feb. 1749.

13. **LEMUEL[4] TRICKEY** (Thomas[3], Isaac[2], Thomas[1]), of Durham, bapt. 29 July 1733, m. 23 Nov. 1758, ALICE[5] NUTTER (7-i), dau. of Anthony[4] and Mary (Downing), *q.v.*

Children, baptized at Newington:
  i. TEMPERENCE[5], bapt. 27 Sept. 1761, m. ? 14 Feb. 1788, JOSEPH HOOK (Daw's *Hampton*, p. 1054).
  ii. LOIS, bapt. 27 Sept. 1761.

TRICKEY (unconnected)

MARY TRICKEY, covenant, 3 Mar. 1728.

JOHANNA TRICKEY, covenant, 10 Mar. 1728.

MIRIAM TRICKEY, m. 16 Aug. 1751, JOHN DEAN (DAM?), mariner.

SARAH TRICKEY, covenant, 30 Dec. 1770.

PATIENCE TRICKEY, covenant, 3 Dec. 1770 (*N.H. Gen. Rec.*, vol. 5, p. 73).

ELIZABETH TRICKEY, dau. of John and Ann, bapt. 13 May 1770 (*id.*, p. 89).

ELIZABETH TRICKEY, widow, communion, 19 July 1775.

TRIGGS

ROBERT TRIGGS, m. 12 May 1731, SARAH LEIGHTON, both of Portsmouth (*Register*, vol. 25, p. 118).

TRIPE

SYLVANUS[2] TRIPE (Sylvanus[1]) (Stackpole's *Kittery*, p. 78), m. 25 June

1724, LUCY BRIARD, of Portsmouth (*Register*, vol. 24, p. 18).

THOMAS² TRIPE (Sylvanus¹) (Stackpole, *loc. cit.*), m. 23 Oct. 1737, ELIZABETH TRICKEY (1-v).

ANNA TRIPE, m. 2 Apr. 1752, SETH WALKER.

LUCY TRIPE, m. 27 Oct. 1761, SAMUEL GREENOUGH.

TUCKER

JAMES³ TUCKER (Hugh², Lewis¹) (Stackpole's *Kittery*, p. 783), m. 15 July 1749, RUTH KENNARD, both of Kittery, Me.

TRISTAM TUCKER, m. 22 May 1760, ABIGAIL RICHARDSON, both of Kittery.

TUTTLE

JOHN TUTTLE, m. 23 May 1773, DOROTHY JACOBS, both of Durham.

TWEED

ELIZABETH LOIS TWEED, covenant, 5 Nov. 1769.

VINCENT

THOMAS VINCENT, of Newington, m. 16 July 1753 (*N.H. Gen. Rec.*, vol. 3), Mrs. ELIZABETH FURBUR, who m. (2) 9 Aug. 1770, JOHN PICKERING, III.

Children, baptized at Newington:
   i. ANTHONY, bapt. 15 June 1755, m. 31 Dec. 1785, BETSEY ROGERS (Durham rec.).
   ii. WILLIAM, bapt. 27 June 1756, m. 28 June 1781, ALICE COOLBROTH.
   iii. JOHN, bapt. 2 Apr. 1758.
   iv. THOMAS, bapt. 20 Apr. 1760.

VINCENT (unconnected)

WILLIAM and MARGARET VINCENT, of Newington, 7 Apr. 1731.

THOMAS VINCENT, m. 16 July 1753, SUSANNA BICKFORD.

The will of **JOHN VINCENT**, of Newington, proved 28 Nov. 1744, mentions his wife, Martha; daughter, Margaret; grandson, Thomas Vincent who was son of Margaret; brother, Robert, in Ireland. Administration to William Vincent Vincent of Brunswick, Me., cordwainer (*N.H. State Pap.*, vol. 33, p. 174).

WALKER[+]

1. Capt. RICHARD^1 WALKER, of Lynn, Mass.
Children:
2   i. RICHARD^2, b. 1611.
     ii. WILLIAM, of Lynn, Mass., b. 1620.

2. RICHARD^2 WALKER (Richard^1), of Lynn, Mass., b. 1611, m. (1) JANE TALMADGE, m. (2) SARAH -----.
Children by first wife:
3   i. RICHARD^3, b. 1638.
4   ii. JOHN, b. 1640.

3. RICHARD^3 WALKER (Richard$^{2-1}$), of Ipswich, Mass., b. 1638, m. 29 Oct. 1661, SARAH STOREY, b. at Ipswich, Mass., 1641, dau. of William and Sarah (Foster) Storey.
Children, born at Ipswich, Mass.:
5   i. JOHN^4
     ii. HANNAH, b. 10 Sept. 1662.
     iii. SARAH, b. 29 Nov. 1666.
     iv. Capt. RICHARD, of Newbury, Mass., b. 6 Feb. 1674, d. 2 July 1745, m. 12 Jan. 1739/40, SARAH -----.
        Children, born at Newbury, Mass.:
        1) Sarah^5, b. 17 Dec. 1697.
        2) Hannah, b. 1 Oct. 1699.
        3) Tabitha, b. 7 Oct. 1701.
        4) Rebecka, b. 10 June 1704.
        5) Richard, b. 2 Sept. 1706.

4. JOHN^3 WALKER (Richard$^{2-1}$), of Charlestown, Mass., and Newington, b. 1640, d. 1716, m. ANNA LEAGER.

+The account of the first five families was furnished by Robert Walker, Esq., of Boston, great great grandson of Seth^5 Walker, No. 10, who has examined the entire account of this family.

Children, born at Charlestown, Mass. (baptisms in the First Church):
  i. JOHN⁴, of Newington, 1715, glover, b. 13 May 1669, "eldest son of John Walker of Charlestown" (*Middlesex Probate*, vol. 14, p. 374 and see *Middlesex Deeds*, vol. 18, p. 589).
  ii. ANNA, bapt. 16 Feb. 1676.
  iii. BENJAMIN, bapt. 7 June 1681.
  iv. JOSEPH, bapt. 5 May 1691.

JOHN WALKER, m. at Eliot, Me., 4 Jan. 1712, ELIZABETH GUNNISON.

JOHN WALKER, m. at Newington, 24 Oct. 1717, MARY BICKFORD.

LYDIA WALKER, m. at Hamilton, Mass., 27 May 1718, BENJAMIN PATCH.

5. **JOHN⁴ WALKER** (Richard³⁻¹), of Chelmsford, Mass., and Newington, b. 1660, m. LYDIA COLBURN, b. at Ipswich, Mass., 20 Aug. 1666, dau. of Edward and Hannah (Rolfe) Colburn.

Children, born at Chelmsford (town rec.):
  i. JOHN⁵, b. 9 Aug. 1686.
6 ii. EDWARD, b. 9 Jan. 1688.
  iii. ANDREW, of Newington, b. 25 Nov. 1691, m. at Berwick, Me., 18 Dec. 1718, MARY GRANT.
  iv. LYDIA, b. 4 Feb. 1693/4.
  v. HANNAH, b. 11 Apr. 1696.
  vi. JOSEPH, of Rochester, b. 11 Aug. 1698, m. at Newington, 11 Dec. 1723, ABIGAIL PLACE.
    His will dated 1776, mentions the following children.
    Children:
    1) Joseph⁶, baptized at Newington, 1 Nov. 1724.
    2) Richard
    3) Abigail, m. ----- Wallingford.
    4) Lydia, m. ----- Downes.
  vii. SARAH, b. 23 Feb. 1701, m. at Newington, 4 July 1726, WILLIAM WATERHOUSE.
  viii. RICHARD, b. 14 June 1703.
  ix. ELIZABETH, b. 12 Sept. 1706, m. at Newington, 20 Dec. 1725, WILLIAM HOLDEN.

6. **EDWARD⁵ WALKER** (John⁴, Richard³⁻¹), of York, Me., Berwick, Me., 1713, and Newington, 1726, m. at Kittery, Me., 6 Sept. 1710, DELIVERANCE

GASKIN (Stackpole's *Kittery*, p. 784), dau. of John[2] (Daniel[1]) and Joanna+ (Crocker) (Williams) Gaskin.

Children, the first four born at Berwick, Me., the others at Newington (See also Quint's *Ancient Dover*, p. 319):

7   i. EDWARD[6], bapt. 25 Oct. 1713 (*Register*, vol. 82, p. 76).
8   ii. JOHN, bapt. 25 Oct. 1713 (*ibid.*).
    iii. ELIZABETH, m. 5 Feb. 1736, NATHANIEL GROVER, and had 12 children.
9   iv. GIDEON, bapt. 24 Mar. 1719/20 (*id.*, p. 80). Jonathan[3] Huntress in his deed of 15 May 1758 mentions his brother-in-law, Gideon Walker.
    v. LYDIA, bapt. 24 Mar. 1719/20 (*id.*, p. 80).
10 vi. SETH, b. Apr. 1725, bapt. 9 Oct. 1726.
    vii. DELIVERANCE, bapt. 9 Oct. 1726, m. 31 Dec. 1741, JOSEPH MELOON.
    viii. MARY, bapt. 27 Aug. 1727, m. 5 Feb. 1747, JONATHAN[3] HUNTRESS.
    ix. OLIVE, bapt. 20 July 1729.
    x. MARTHA, bapt. 8 Apr. 1733, m. WILLIAM BRASSBRIDGE.
    xi. EBENEZER, bapt. 6 May 1733, d. *aet.* 10 yrs.

7. EDWARD[6] WALKER (Edward[5], John[4], Richard[3-1]), of Newington, bapt. 25 Oct. 1713, m. at Greenland, 28 Dec. 1732, SARAH[4] NUTTER (3-iv), dau. of Hatevil[3] and Sarah Nutter, *q.v.*, m. (2) 18 Dec. 1760, SARAH (-----) ROLLINS, wid. of Joseph[2] Rollins.

A church committee was appointed 21 Mar. 1765 to adjust the difference between Edward Walker and Sarah, his wife, whereupon the wife and her daughter by her first husband, Deborah Rollins, were suspended.

Children by first wife, baptized at Newington:
11 i. JOSHUA[7], bapt. 4 Nov. 1733.
    ii. LYDIA, bapt. Dec. 1738, d. *aet.* 16 yrs.
12 iii. DANIEL, bapt. 1 Nov. 1741, m. 27 Sept. 1764, ELIZABETH NUTTER, b. 1741, d. 22 Apr. 1824 (*Register*, vol. 73, p. 196).
    iv. SARAH, bapt. 9 Sept. 1744, m. 8 Nov. 1764, THOMAS[2] QUINT (2), son of Thomas[1] and Margaret (Fickett) Quint, *q.v.*

+She was daughter of Daniel Crocker and widow of Paul Williams.

v. ELIZABETH, d. 3 Feb. 1843[+], m. 4 Sept. 1766, MARK AYRES.
vi. ELEANOR, b. 1750, d. 1831 *aet.* 81 yrs., m. 25 Nov. 1773, DEPENDENCE COLBATH, of Barnstead, b. 1748, d. 1838 *aet.* 90 (Jewett's *Barnstead*, p. --).
vii. OLIVE, bapt. 29 Feb. 1756, m. SAMUEL GREENOUGH.
Child, born at Newington:
1) Seth Walker[8], bapt. 11 Aug. 1774.

8. JOHN[6] WALKER (Edward[5], John[4], Richard[3-1]), of Newington, bapt. 25 Oct. 1713, m. DORCAS -----.
Children, baptized at Berwick, Me.:

13 i. EBENEZER[6], bapt. 24 Nov. 1743/4, d. *aet.* 10 yrs.
14 ii. JOHN, bapt. 4 Aug. 1746.
    iii. DORCAS, bapt. 21 Sept. 1748.
15 iv. GIDEON, bapt. 24 May 1751.
16 v. JONATHAN (twin), bapt. 3 July 1754.
    vi. ELIZABETH (twin), bapt. 3 July 1754.

9. GIDEON[5] WALKER (Edmond[4], John[3], Richard[2-1]), of Newington, bapt. 24 Mar. 1719/20, m. 4 June 1752, ELEANOR BICKFORD (3-xi), dau. of Thomas[2] and Sarah (Simpson) Bickford, *q.v.*
Children[++], born at Newington:

17 i. SAMUEL[6], bapt. 18 Jan. 1753.
18 ii. JOHN, bapt. 19 Jan. 1755.
    iii. ELIZABETH, bapt. 23 July 1758, m. 21 Nov. 1776, JOHN THOMPSON, of Portsmouth.
    iv. ANNA, bapt. 7 June 1762, m. 1779.
19 v. GIDEON, bapt. 3 Oct. 1764.
    vi. SETH, bapt. 31 May 1767.
20 vii. SETH, bapt. 9 Sept. 1770.

+Administration on the estate of Elizabeth Ayres, of Newington, widow, who died 3 Feb. 1843, was granted 9 Aug. 1848 to Mehitable F. Drown, of Newington, widow of Samuel Drown, who died 25 Feb. 1847, grandson of Elizabeth Ayres, who had supported her for several years (*Rockingham Probate*).

++His will dated 27 Apr. 1793, proved 16 Oct. 1793, names his sons Samuel, Mark, and Seth; children of his daughter, Elizabeth Thompson, deceased; children of his daughter, Nancy Williams, deceased; grandson John, son of John Walker, deceased; and his wife, Eleanor (*Rockingham Probate*).

21 viii. MARK (named in the will).

10. SETH[5] WALKER (Edward[4], John[3], Richard[2-1]), of Newington, b. Apr. 1725, d. 12 Dec. 1769, m. 2 Apr. 1752, ANN[3] TRIPE, b. at Kittery, Me., dau. of Sylvanus[2] (Sylvanus[1]) and Lucy (Lewis) (Briard) (note: She m. (1) Samuel Briard) Tripe (Stackpole's *Kittery*, p. 781), b. 12 Aug. 1728. She m. (2) 12 Jan. 1779, WILLIAM HAM.

Children, born at Newington:

21 i. MARK[6], of Newington, b. 5 Mar. 1753, bapt. 15 Apr. 1753, d. 30 Mar. 1825 (*Register*, vol. 73, p. 196), m. (1) MARY[5] SHACKFORD (9-vi), dau. of Capt. Samuel[4] and Elizabeth (Ring) Shackford, *q.v.*, m. (2) ABIGAIL (WALDRON) BOARDMAN.

   Child, baptized at Newington:
   1) Seth Shackford[5], bapt. 18 June 1780.

ii. NANCY, b. 6 Sept. 1754, d. 30 Oct. 1837, m. 6 May 1779, SAMUEL[5] SHACKFORD (7-iii), son of Capt. Samuel[4] and Elizabeth (Ring) Shackford, *q.v.*

iii. Col. SETH, of Portsmouth, register of deeds, officer in the Revolution, b. 29 Aug. 1756, d. at Derry, 8 Oct. 1838, m. 13 Jan. 1777, TEMPERENCE[5] PEVERLY, b. at Portsmouth, 29 Mar. 1758, d. at Exeter, 30 Mar. 1841, dau. of George[4] and Ann Peverly.

   Children, born at Portsmouth (family Bible in possession, 1920, of Alan H. Strong, Esq., of Philadelphia, grandson of Betsey Briard[6] (Walker) Hartwell):
   1) Seth[7], b. 10 July 1777, d. 21 Aug. 1777.
   2) Seth, master mariner, b. 14 Sept. 1778, d. 18 Jan. 1824 (lost at sea). He married and is said to have son, Seth.
   3) William, b. 13 July 1780, d. 10 June 1854, m. Margery Greenleaf Ward, b. 17 Mar. 1779, dau. of ----- and Elizabeth (Lunt) Ward (*Lunt Family*, p. 28). He had 10 children.
   4) Betsey Briard, b. 6 Jan. 1783, d. 21 Sept. 1783.
   5) Betsey Briard, b. 10 July 1784, d. 28 Mar. 1839, m. 2 Oct. 1808, Jonathan Hartwell, of Portsmouth, Boston, and Littleton, Mass., merchant, farmer, state senator, 1843, son of John and Mary (Dix) Hartwell. She had 12 children.
   6) Nancy, b. 28 July 1786, d. 31 Mar. 1798.
   7) Lucy Maria, b. 11 Dec. 1789, d. unm. 29 May 1841.
   8) Temperance, b. 20 May 1792, d. 31 Mar. 1798.
   9) Samuel, b. 4 Sept. 1794, d. 27 Mar. 1798.
   10) Harriet, b. 10 Mar. 1797, d. 9 Apr. 1815.
   11) Temperance, b. 8 Nov. 1800, d. unm.
   12) Martha, b. 26 Jan. 1804, d. 6 Sept 1863, m. at Exeter, in Apr. 1832,

  Charles C. P. Gale, of Derry, teacher. They had 3 children, all of
whom d. unm.
- iv. NICHOLAS, b. 8 Sept. 1754, d. 20 June 1758.
22 v. WILLIAM, of Barnstead, 1784, soldier in the Revolution, pensioner, b. 21 Nov. 1759, d. 3 Dec. 1832, m. 29 Feb. 1784, ELIZABETH SHACKFORD (9-vii), dau. of Capt. Samuel[4] and Elizabeth (Ring) Shackford, q.v.
23 vi. GIDEON, b. 13 Sept. 1763, bapt. 25 Sept. 1763, m. 11 Mar. 1789, LYDIA WATSON.
- vii. LUCY, b. 16 July 1765, bapt. 21 July 1765, d. 11 Oct. 1842, m. 20 Dec. 1790, NATHANIEL HAM, of Portsmouth.
24 viii. SAMUEL, bapt. 6 Sept. 1778, m. ? ELIZABETH PEVERLY.
- ix. ELIZABETH KINSMAN, bapt. 6 Sept. 1778.

15. SAMUEL[6] WALKER (Gideon[5], Edward[4], John[3], Richard[2,1]), of Newington, b. about 1742 (tombstone), bapt. 18 Jan. 1753, d. 15 Nov. 1829, m. at Greenland, 19 Jan. 1774, ELIZABETH PEVERLY, b. about 1752 (tombstone), d. 7 Dec. 1835 (*Peverly Family*, pp. 38-9).

 Children, born at Newington:
- i. SAMUEL[7], bapt. 6 Sept. 1778.
- ii. ELIZABETH KINSMAN, bapt. 6 Sept. 1778, m. 13 Nov. 1794, WILLIAM[4] LANG, of Rye, son of Mark[3] and Salome (Goss) Lang.
- iii. ANNA, bapt. 6 Sept. 1778.
- iv. WILLIAM, of Portsmouth, b. about 1778 (tombstone), bapt. 7 May 1780, d. 21 May 1862, m. (1) 21 Apr. 1804 (Parson's *Rye*, p. 563), ELIZABETH CATER, m. (2) at Portsmouth, 5 Sept. 1819 (town rec.), ELIZA K. PEVERLY, b. at Newington, 1787 (tombstone), d. 11 Jan. 1861 (*Peverly Family*, p. 38).

 Children by first wife, born at Portsmouth (baptisms in North Church):
1) William[8], bapt. 2 Aug. 1806.
2) Daniel Clark, bapt. 2 Aug. 1806.
3) Mary E., b. about 1818 (tombstone), d. unm. 22 July 1861.
4) Dwight, b. 21 Aug. 1818 (tombstone), d. ? unm. 1 Jan. 1855.

 Children by second wife, born at Portsmouth:
5) Augustus, soldier in the Civil War, b. about 1828 (tombstone), d. (killed in battle) ? unm. 3 June 1864.
6) Joseph C., of Portsmouth, m. Elizabeth L. -----, b. 6 Apr. 1827 (tombstone), d. 23 June 1911.
- v. LUCY, b. about 1780, d. 13 Apr. 1860, m. 31 Dec. 1798, RICHARD[4] LANG, of Rye, son of Mark[3] and Salome (Goss) Lang.

JOHN WALKER[3] (?John[2], Richard[1]), of Newington and Kittery, Me., 1694, d. 3 June 1745, m. (1) 24 Jan. 1714/5, ELIZABETH[3] GUNNISON, dau. of Elihu and Elizabeth, b. at Kittery, Me., 15 June 1694, d. 4 Dec. 1715 (Stackpole's *Kittery*, p. 478), m. (2) 24 Oct. 1717, MARY BICKFORD, dau. of John and Susannah (Furber) (2-iv), *q.v.*

Child by first wife, baptized at Newington:

    i. JOHN, bapt. 24 June 1716, b. 27 Nov. 1715, d. 26 June 1718 (Stackpole's *Kittery*, p. 785).

Children by second wife, born at Kittery, Me. (Stackpole's *Kittery, loc. cit.*):

    ii. ELIPHALET, b. 12 Aug. 1718, d. 5 Nov. 1718.
    iii. GIDEON, of Arundel, Me., b. 6 Oct. 1719, m. (1) 3 Feb. 1741, HANNAH PALMER, m. (2) Mrs. HANNAH LASSELL (Stackpole's *Kittery*, p. 785).
    iv. ELIPHALET, b. 21 Apr. 1722, d. 31 Aug. 1735.
    v. TEMPERENCE, b. 9 Sept. 1724, d. 21 Aug. 1735.
    vi. JOHN, b. 8 Sept. 1727, d. 14 June 1752. He had a son, Tobias, of Portsmouth.
    vii. MARY, b. 27 Aug. 1730, d. 10 Sept. 1735.
    viii. ELIZABETH, b. 21 Mar. 1732/3, m. 2 Feb. 1750, PELATIAH WHITTEMORE.
    ix. MARY, b. 18 Aug. 1736, m. JOSEPH PETTIGREW.

JOHN WALKER, then of Newington, formerly of Ipswich, 1723, husbandman (*Essex Deeds*, 47-267).

JOHN WALKER, late of Newington, then of Portsmouth; wife, ELIZABETH, 1727, sold lands in Scarboro to Eleazar Colman.

SAMUEL WALKER, of Newington, m. 4 Oct. 1724, ANNA BICKFORD (2-vi), dau. of John and Susanna (Furber), who m. (2) 31 July 1727 (*Register*, vol. 24, p. 359), Deac. MOSES[4] FURBER (6), son of William[3] and Sarah (Nute), *q.v.*

Child, baptized at Newington:

    i. BRIDGET, bapt. 1 Aug. 1725.

Wid. SUSAN WALKER, d. 25 Sept. 1842, *aet.* 73 (*Register*, vol. 73, p. 199).

WALKER (unconnected)

MARY WALKER, m. 9 Nov. 1727, JAMES PLACE.

LEMUEL WALKER, son of Joseph and Mary, bapt. 13 July 1729.

RICHARD WALKER, son of Joseph and Mary, bapt. 16 Nov. 1735.

MARY WALKER, communion, 19 Dec. 1742.

ELLE WALKER, covenant, 24 Dec. 1767.

GIDEON WALKER'S grandson, **JOHN AYRES**, bapt. 13 Oct. 1778.

HANNAH and ABIGAIL WALKER, sisters, covenant, 18 Oct. 1778.

SAMUEL WALKER, d. 1777, *aet.* 30, soldier for Portsmouth (16 *State Papers*, 94).

MARY WALKER, dau. of Samuel and Mary, bapt. 28 Sept. 1783.

Wid. BETSEY WALKER, d. 22 Apr. 1824, *aet.* 83 (73 *Reg.* 196).

WALLINGFORD

(See *Pope's Pioneers*, p. 476)

JOHN³ WALLINGFORD (John², Nicholas¹), of Newington, 1710, Somersworth, 1743, Rochester, 1747, b. at Bradford, Dec. 14, 1688, d. 1761/2, m. **CHARITY** -----.

Children, baptized at Newington:
  i. JOHN⁴, bapt. 30 Apr. 1724.
  ii. MARY, bapt. 30 Apr. 1724, m. 24 Apr. 1740, WILLIAM DORR, of Dover.
  iii. SARAH, bapt. 30 Apr. 1724.
  iv. PHEBE, bapt. 30 Apr. 1724, communion, 18 Apr. 1742.
  v. PATIENCE, bapt. 30 Apr. 1724.
  vi. PETER, bapt. 29 May 1726.
  vii. FRANCES, bapt. 1 Sept. 1728.
  viii. SUSANNA, bapt. 7 Sept. 1735.
  ix. JUDITH, bapt. 4 July 1736.

WALLINGFORD (unconnected)

Capt. SAM WALLINGFORD, son of Judge Thos., of Somersworth, m. 16 June 1775, **LYDIA BAKER**. He was lieut. of marines with Paul Jones, on the *Ranger*, killed in battle with the *Drake*, 24 Apr. 1778, had son, Geo. Wash. (*Register*, vol. 5, p. 206).

Hon. THOS. WALLINGFORD, d. at Portsmouth, 4 Aug. 1771, *aet.* 75 (*N.H. Gazette* of 9 Aug. 1771).

EBENEZER WALLINGFORD, of Dover, yeoman, will 19 Aug. 1721, proved 6 Sept. 1721, mentions his brothers John, Thomas, of Somersworth and James (Clements) to whom he gives his wearing apparel; everything else to Mrs. Susanna Cotton, of Portsmouth, to whom he was engaged (*N.H. State Papers*, vol. 32, p. 136).

WALTON

FRANCES WALTON, dau. of George and Frances, bapt. 22 Jan. 1716.

SAMUEL WALTON, communion, 23 Oct. 1726.

SAMUEL WALTON, m. 26 May 1727, ELIZABETH PRAY.

GEORGE WALTON, and wife, PATIENCE, communion, 29 Sept. 1728.

ELIZABETH WALTON, m. 24 Oct. 1734, WILLIAM HOYT (1-v).

FRANCES WALTON, communion, 5 Nov. 1738.

GEORGE WALTON, d. at Newington, 13 Dec. 1769, *aet.* 89 (*N.H. Gazette* of 29 Dec. 1769), (*Register*, vol. 74, p. 126).

WAPLES

PAUL WAPLES, m. 4 Jan. 1764, MARY ROBINSON, of Portsmouth.

WARREN

GEORGE WARREN, of Portsmouth, m. 14 Aug. 1754, ELIZABETH HODGDON.

ELIZABETH WARREN, communion, 19 Aug. 1770.

WATERHOUSE

WILLIAM WATERHOUSE, m. 4 July 1726, SARAH WALKER.

RUTH WATERHOUSE, of Portsmouth, m. 18 Jan. 1727/8, JOHN GAINES, at Ipswich, Mass. (*Register*, vol. 24, p. 360).

SARAH WATERHOUSE, dau. of William and Sarah, bapt. 23 Sept. 1729.

SARAH WATERHOUSE, of Portsmouth, m. 22 Aug. 1734, ZACHARIAH FOSS, of Newcastle.

LYDIA WATERHOUSE, m. 23 Aug. 1747, SPENCER COLBY, of Newbury, Mass.

WATERS

JOSEPH WATERS, covenant, 9 Mar. 1740.

WATSON

ALICE WATSON, m. 28 Dec. 1716, ELEAZER YOUNG, both of Durham.

WEBBER

JAMES WEBBER, of Kittery, Me., m. 18 Dec. 1719, ELIZABETH FURBER (2-iv).

WILLIAM WEBBER, son of James and Elizabeth, bapt. 23 Jan. 1721.

LYDIA WEBBER, m. 14 June 1770, ABNER WILLIAM, both of Kittery, Me.

WELCH

JOSEPH WELCH, formerly of Ipswich, Mass., m. 8 Apr. 1733, SARAH SHACKFORD (*Register*, vol. 25, p. 120).

MARY WELCH, dau. of Joseph and Sarah, b. 26 Jan. 1733/4 (*Register*, vol. 25, p. 121).

JOSEPH WELCH, son of Joseph and Sarah, b. 2 Sept. 1735 (*Register*, vol. 26, p. 376).

BENJAMIN WELCH, m. 11 Oct. 1739, ELIZABETH STUDLEY, both of Portsmouth (*Register*, vol. 26, p. 380).

WELLS (WILLS)

HANNAH WELLS(WILLS), m. 9 Aug. 1722, HUGH BANFIELD, of Portsmouth.

ELIZABETH WELLS(WILLS), of Portsmouth, m. 24 Oct. 1734, ISAAC TRICKEY (2).

JOSEPH WELLS(WILLS), m. 13 Sept. 1752, ANNA MESERVY, both of Portsmouth.

WENTWORTH

SARAH WENTWORTH, m. 28 Jan. 1720, DANIEL PLUMMER, both of Dover.

PAUL WENTWORTH, of Kittery, Me., m. 24 Sept. 1724, DEBORAH JAQUES.

WHEELER

SARAH³ WHEELER (Joseph², John¹) (Stackpole's *Durham*, vol. 2, p. 379), m. 13 Oct. 1752, Rev. JOSEPH ADAMS, both of Durham.

WHIDDEN

SARAH WHIDDEN, of Greenland, m. 19 Feb. 1736, LAZARUS MOORE, of Portsmouth.

Capt. JAMES WHIDDEN, d. at Deerfield, 10 July 1844, *aet.* 83 (*Register*, vol. 73, p. 199).

WHITE

ELIZABETH WHITE, m. 4 Oct. 1745, JOHN MARSHALL, of Portsmouth.

WHITMORE

JOEL WHITMORE, son of Pelatiah and Margery (Pepperell) (Stackpole's *Kittery*, p. 649), m. 15 June 1739, ABISHA HOYT, both of Portsmouth.

WIGGIN

ISSACHAR WIGGIN, m. 24 Nov. 1773, ELIZABETH PEVEY.

WILLIAM WIGGIN, son of Issachar, bapt. 20 Oct. 1776.

ISSACHAR WIGGIN, son of Issachar, bapt. 29 June 1777.

OTIS WIGGIN, son of Issachar, bapt. 22 Aug. 1779.

WILKINSON

THOMAS WILKINSON, of London, Eng., m. Aug. 1715, ELIZABETH CAVERLY (*Register*, vol. 23, p. 272).

ANNA WILKINSON, dau. of James and Hannah, bapt. 16 June 1754.

JOSEPH WILKINSON, son of James and Hannah, bapt. 8 May 1757.

WILLEY

ZEBULON[1] WILLEY, b. 1748, of Newington, mariner, d. 2 Mar. 1825 (*Register*, vol. 73, p. 196), m. (1) MARY -----, m. (2) 1783, NANCY[4] HUNTRESS, dau. of Joseph[3] (1-viii) and Sobriety (Tobey), b. at Newington in 1755, d. 2 June 1835 (*Register*, vol. 73, p. 198).

Children by first wife, baptized at Newington:
    i. TEMPERENCE[2], bapt. 30 Dec. 1770.
    ii. JONATHAN, bapt. 13 Oct. 1771.
    iii. ABIGAIL, bapt. 22 Aug. 1773.
    iv. ZEBULON, of Kittery, Me., mariner, warehouseman, bapt. 19 July 1778.
    v. MATTHEW, bapt. 19 July 1778.
    vi. SARAH GARVIN, bapt. 2 July 1780.

WILLEY (unconnected)

JOHN WILLEY, m. 17 July 1755, SARAH FOX, of Newmarket.

WINTHROP WILLEY, covenant, 20 Dec. 1770.

WILLIAM

1. WILLIAM WILLIAM, of Newington, 1713, m. MARY NASON (Stackpole's *Kittery*, p. 804).
  Children:
   i. WILLIAM, covenant, 22 Dec. 1723.
   ii. ? PETER, covenant, 22 Dec. 1723.
   iii. ? JOSEPH

2. WILLIAM WILLIAM (William), of Newington, m. 21 Mar. 1717, ELIZABETH CARTER, dau. of ? John, *q.v.*

JOSEPH WILLIAM (William), of Newington, m. MERCY -----.
  Children, baptized at Newington:
   i. MARY, bapt. 29 Sept. 1736.
   ii. MARK, bapt. 24 Oct. 1736.
   iii. MERCY, bapt. 24 Oct. 1736.
   iv. HENRY, bapt. 19 Dec. 1736.

WILLIAM (unconnected)

EUNICE WILLIAM, m. 4 Oct. 1769, PELATIAH GREENOUGH, both of Kittery, Me.

ABNER WILLIAM, m. 14 June 1770, LYDIA WEBBER, both of Kittery, Me.

MARY WILLIAM, m. 2 June 1770, JACOB BREWER, both of Kittery, Me. (See further Stackpole's *Kittery*, p. 804).

WILLIAMS

BENJAMIN WILLIAMS, covenant, 30 Aug. 1741.

JOHN[5] WILLIAMS (John[4-3], William[2-1]) (Stackpole's *Durham*, vol. 2, p. 391), m. 2 July 1767, SARAH MEADER, both of Durham.

WOODEY

ELIZABETH WOODEY, covenant, 7 Dec. 1728.

WOODMAN

JOHN[4] WOODMAN (Jonathan[3], John[2], Edward[1]) (Stackpole's *Durham*, vol. 2, p. 393), of Oyster River, m. 11 Sept. 1732, MARY[2] FABIAN (1-v).

MARTHA (DAVIS) WOODMAN, dau. of Moses and Elizabeth (Davis) and wife of Capt. JONATHAN, bapt. 21 Dec. 1754 (Stackpole's *Durham*, vol. 2, p. 393).

JONATHAN[5] WOODMAN (Downing[4], Jonathan[3], John[2], Edward[1]) (Stackpole's *Durham*, vol. 2, p. 393), m. 5 Nov. 1766, CATHERINE FRY, both of Kittery, Me.

CATHERINE[5] WOODMAN (Downing[4], Jonathan[3], John[2], Edward[1]) (Stackpole's *Kittery*, p. 806), m. 15 Dec. 1771, JOSEPH JENKINS, both of Kittery, Me.

YEATON

JOHN YEATON, of Somersworth, m. 1 Oct. 1746, MARY THOMPSON.

MARY YEATON, m. 1 June 1759, JOSEPH BENSON.

YOUNG

ELEAZER YOUNG, m. 28 Dec. 1716, ALICE WATSON, both of Durham.

EBENEZER YOUNG, m. 21 Apr. 1749, ELIZABETH BICKFORD, both of Durham.

ANNA YOUNG, m. 22 Feb. 1775, TIMOTHY RICHARDSON, both of Kittery, Me.

ABBOTT, Elisha 116 Elizabeth 172 Henry 172 John 82 Mary 82 116 Molly 153 Ruth 17 Samuel 17

ADAMS, Abigail 36 96 118 132 168 Benjamin 118 132 168 Deborah 99 Ebenezer 37 56 90 Eleanor 129 Elizabeth 30 32 56 86 95 98 Esther 28 Ezekiel Gilman 86 87 90 James T 73 Jane 4 Joanna 95 96 Johanna 36 86 90 John 36 87 Joseph 30 36 47 56 86 90 95 96 98 195 Lois 37 56 Lydia 37 90 Mary 47 86 87 90 Mary Jane 73 Matthew 99 Muriel 32 99 Nancy 90 Nathaniel 86 99 Olive 86 Ruth Webb 168 Samuel 37 Sarah 87 195

ALCOCK, Hannah 63 Jane 156 Joseph 156

ALLARD, Henry 158 Sarah 158

ALLEN, Abigail 55 Judah 129 Sarah 129 150

AMEREDETH, Johanna 7 John 7

AMERIDETH, Joan 7 John 7

ANDERSON, Rebecca W 5

APPLEBY, Betsey 182

AVERY, Ann 20 Deborah 73

AYRES, Abigail 116 Alice 165 Ann 110 169 Anna 66 Deborah 165 Dependence 114 Edward 161 165 Elizabeth 114 188 George 116

AYRES (continued)
James 109 John 66 165 183 192 Mark 188 Mary 91 109 161 183 Nathaniel 17 66 67 91 Phebe 169 Rebecca 113 Ruth 91 Samuel 109 Sarah 86 Stephen 86 Susanna 116 Thomas 86 114 161

B, S 21 32

BABB, Deborah 25 Dorcas 82 Dorothy 89 John 25 Mary 84 Sampson 84 89 William 82

BAKER, Hazelponi 131 Lydia 192 Obediah 131

BALL, Mary 182 Peter 152 182 Susanna 152 182

BAMPTON, Mary 101 168

BANFIELD, Hannah 195 Hugh 195

BANKS, Elizabeth 7 Joseph 7 Richard 7

BARKER, Anna 101 175 Bridget 112 116 Enid 116

BARNES, Elizabeth 165 Mary 163 165 Thomas 165

BARTLETT, Dorcas 35 Mary 166

BASS, Comfort 17

BATCHELDER, Eunice 135 Georgianna 138 John 71 74 Judith P 138 Lucy 74 Mary 163 Mary Ann 72 Nathaniel 72 Olive 71 Samuel 74 Sarah 71 74 Stephen 163 Theodore

BATCHELDER (continued)
72 William 72 74
BEAN, Deborah 73 Elizabeth 33 72
James 72 Lydia 72 Samuel 72 73
BEARD, Mary 123
BECK, Mehitable 15
BELL, Andrew W 20 Elizabeth Bennett 20
BELLAMY, Elizabeth 5
BENNETT, Abigail 165
BENSON, Abigail 87 Christopher 87
Deborah 161 Henry 153 James 161
162 John 31 Joseph 198 Mary 153
198 Susanna 162
BERRY, Benjamin 28 James 100 Mary
58 103 Mehitable 59 100 136 138
Miriam 28 William 103
BICKFORD, Abigail 42 110 Alice 97
Ann 152 Anna 36 44 68 90 181
191 Benjamin 42 137 179 Bridget
65 Daniel 85 87 128 Deborah 21
137 179 Ebenezer 152 Eleanor 188
Elizabeth 42 67 81 85 87 145 158
198 Esther 6 100 Hannah 33 45 51
86 107 137 Jethro 51 John 50 51 52
65 68 87 115 146 179 191 Jonathan
31 Lemuel 50 52 Lydia 31 Mary 51
179 186 191 Miriam 23 Olive 54
Pamela 146 Percy 107 Sarah 19 42
87 115 123 152 188 Susanna 51 52
65 68 105 184 191 Susannah 191
Temperance 50 Temperence 52
181 Thomas 6 65 67 152 188
Winthrop 100
BIGGAR, Jane 138
BLACKBURN, Olive 96
BLAKE, Frances 27 Jonathan 27
BLUNT, John 69 Sarah Frost 69
BOARDMAN, Abigail 189 Martha 168
William 168
BOODY, Elizabeth 5
BOOTHBY, Hannah 53 Thomas 53

BORLAND, Anna 99 John 99
BOULTER, John 49 Martha 49
BOURNE, Joanna 49 John 49 Jonathan
70 Mary 70 138
BOWLES, Samuel 76
BOYD, Abigail 89 Elizabeth 174
George 89 Joseph 174
BOYNTON, John 87 Temperence 87
BRACKETT, Alice 133 Elizabeth 2
131 134 Frances I 118 John 58 131
Joshua 58 133 Mary 58 59 132 135
137 156 Polly 137 Sarah 59
Thomas 75
BRADFORD, Lewis 72 Olive 72
BRASSBRIDGE, Martha 187 William
187
BREWER, Jacob 197 Mary 197
BREWSTER, Abigail 110 150 Elizabeth 75 John 150 Samuel 110
Sarah 110
BRIARD, Betsey 189 Lucy 184 189
Samuel 189
BROWN, Abiah 50 Abigail 79 Benjamin 79 Elizabeth 67 91 121 168
Hannah 23 Joseph 121 Judith 149
Lydia 25 Madeline 114 123 Pamela
A 169 Susanna 3
BURLEIGH, Abigail 92 Dorothy 72 73
Eleanor 99 Jacob 92 Lucy 92
BURNHAM, Abigail 135 Charlotte
170 Elizabeth 6 70 71 169 Hannah
98 Jacob 71 James 135 Jeremiah 6
Lydia 71 Mary 118 Mehitable 37
Muriel 6 Winthrop 6
BURROUGHS, Mehitable 45
BUSBEE, Mabel 104 Richard 104
BUSS, Elizabeth 179
BUTLER, Dorcas 73 Jas 73
BUZZELL, Elizabeth 169 Mary 128
Nancy 169 Solomon 169
C, B 21 32 L 122
CAESAR, 112

CALDWELL, James 109 Lettice 109
CALE, Edward 182
CANE, David 49 Joanna 49
CANNEY, Deborah 161 Sarah 110 Thomas 110
CANO, Abigail 126 William 126
CARD, Dorothy 35 Phebe 35 Thomas 35
CARLETON, Mary 91 Theodore 91
CARR, Elizabeth 85
CARSON, Calvin 128 Lucinda 128
CARTER, Andrew 22 Elizabeth 197 Ezra 59 Hannah 28 Jerusha 22 John 28 Mary 158 Richard 127 158 Sarah 59 127 158
CATE, Edward 15
CATER, Edward 180 Elizabeth 190
CAVE, Elizabeth 144
CAVERLY, Azariah 5 Elizabeth 5 160 196 John 5 Mary 128 Richard 160 Sarah 5 160 Thomas 160
CHADBOURN, Bridget 98 James 98 Sarah 98
CHADBOURNE, Bridget 44 James 44 Knight 44 Patience 44
CHADBURN, Elizabeth 8 Humphrey 8 Lucy 8
CHAMBERLAIN, Dorothy 74 Mary 180 Rebecca 180 William 180
CHANDLER, Elizabeth 97
CHAPMAN, John 105 Susanna 105
CHASE, Hannah 48 John 48 Polly 96 Rachel 16 Ruth 141 Sarah 96
CHAUNCEY, Joanna 171 Sarah 171
CHESLEY, Abigail 75 Deborah 75 Elizabeth 75 150 Elizabeth Downing 75 George 99 Isaac Buzzell 75 Jacob 75 James 75 Mary 75 Nancy 75 Richard Furber 75 Sarah 75 99 Susanna 99 Thomas 75
CHICK, Lucy 83 Martha 24 92 Mary 84 92 134 160 Richard 24 92

CHICK (continued) Winifred 24
CHILD, Elizabeth 49 Henry 49 Richard 49 Sarah 49 William 49
CLAPPAM, Belvidere 150
CLARK, Abigail 129 Adam 53 Elizabeth 159 168 Hosea 77 John 129 Mary Buxsell 77 Mehitable 35 Sarah 53 Thacher 159
CLARKE, Apphia 21
CLEAVES, Sarah 53
CLEMENTS, James 193
COE, Anne 133 Curtis 133 Joseph 133 Temperance 133
COFFIN, Dorcas 22 Miriam F 28 Nathan 22
COGSWELL, John 65
COLBATH, Dependence 188 Eleanor 188 Elizabeth 38 118 Jane 39 Mary 86 Mehitable 31 Robert 39
COLBURN, Edward 186 Hannah 186 Lydia 186
COLBY, Lydia 194 Spencer 194
COLE, Amos 3 Benjamin 116 Elizabeth 3 Mary 3 Sarah 116
COLLINS, Deborah 101 William 101
COLMAN, Abigail 2 5 71 87 91 92 170 Alice 74 Ann 101 136 181 Anna 91 92 105 Benjamin 105 169 Eleazar 191 Eleazer 91 92 101 181 Eleazur 136 Elizabeth 91 Hannah 169 John 74 169 Joseph 5 Joseph G 170 Keziah 101 Lydia 5 60 75 118 136 Lydia Ann 96 Martha 118 Mary 71 74 91 169 170 Olive 65 Olive C 5 Phineas 2 71 87 91 92 Rosamond 4 45 87 181 Sarah 177
COMBS, Mary 166
CONANT, Anna 170 Joseph 170
CONNOR, Elizabeth 159 William 159
CONVERSE, Mary Ann 21
COOK, Abigail 157 Daniel 150 Jenny

COOK (continued)
150 Lucy 180 Peter 157
COOLBATH, Deborah 39 George 39 40 Hunking 39 James 39 Leighton 39 Lemuel 39 Marianna 40 Susanna 39
COOLBROTH, Alice 184 Benjamin 160 Deborah 102 Elizabeth 89 155 George 85 89 101 Hunking 99 James 99 101 102 Jane 85 Leighton 102 Lois 125 Mary 85 89 101 160 Olive 99 101 102 Pitman 85 Sarah 5 121 Susanna 99 158 Temperence 119
COOLBRUTH, Susanna 64
COOPER, Abigail Harrison Downing 167 Martha 167 Nathaniel 167 Walter 167
COTTON, Abigail 174 Bethia 70 Comfort 17 Elizabeth 164 175 George 175 Hannah 72 John 70 72 175 Joseph 16 76 Mary 11 Muriel 99 Oliver 72 Ruth 17 Susanna 193 Thomas 17 William 49
COUCH, Bridget 23 Joanna 23 Joseph 23 Roger 23
COVE, Jonathan 27 Sarah 27
COWELL, Agnes 13 66 Amy 13 66 Annie 66 Edward 13 66 Mary 164
CRAM, Hannah 138
CRATON, Lydia 181 Thomas 181
CRAWFORD, Benjamin 73 Elizabeth 79 John 73 Mary 73 Polly 71 William 73
CROCKER, Bethiah 80 Daniel 187 Hannah 106 Joanna 187 John 80 Timothy 106
CROCKETT, Ann 178 Elizabeth 112 Joshua 25 112 178 Mary 25 175 Sarah 178 Thomas 178
CROSS, Jesse 21 Mary 21
CRUMMEL, Abigail 46 Jacob 46

CURRIER, Caleb 165 Dorothy 165
CUTT, Bridget 82 John 12 Sarah 12 Susanna 12
DALLING, Elizabeth 126 Mehitable 126 Samuel 126 Sarah 126 Thomas 126
DAM, Abigail 41 104 112 114 Alice 145 155 159 Bethiah 181 Eliphalet 112 114 Elizabeth 65 68 83 89 101 114 119 145 181 Esther 117 119 Issachar 88 John 65 68 83 89 101 119 145 159 181 183 Joseph 117 181 June 101 Mary 114 Mehitable 117 181 Miriam 183 Moses 67 68 112 Olive 57 Richard 68 101 Sarah 88
DAME, Abigail 94 Eliphalet 94 Elizabeth 91 128 133 158 Elnathan 158 Hannah 135 James C 169 John 158 Mary 78 158 169 Phebe 169 Richard 133 Sarah 94 Theophilus 78 Timothy 133
DANA, Mary 42
DARLING, Sarah 127 Stacy 127
DAVIE, Alice 93
DAVIS, Abigail 25 Elizabeth 25 198 Hepzibah 102 Jane 25 John 25 Martha 137 Simon 75 Zebulon 25
DAY, James 10 Joseph 166 Patience 166 Robert 10 Sarah 166 Susanna 10
DEAN, John 183 Miriam 183
DEANE, Eliphalet 171 Olive 171 Olive Lamson 171
DEARBORN, Ebenezer 166 Edward 27 Elizabeth 27 Elizabeth Ring 170 Horatio G 170 Huldah 166 Sarah 166 170
DECKER, Abigail 104 David 144 Elizabeth 108 Eunice 144 Hannah 45 47 117 John 85 106 108 117 144 Mary 17 36 39 85 137

DECKER (continued)
Sarah 85 106 117
DEERING, Abigail 128 Dorothy 20 Ebenezer 20 Joanna 23 Mary 20 145 Nathaniel 128
DEMERITT, Elizabeth 72 Lydia 72 Moses 72
DENBOW, Rachel 127 Salathiel 127
DENEFORD, Elizabeth 81
DENMORE, Mary 83 Selathiel 83
DENNETT, Alexander 54 60 Ann Sherburn 60 Catherine 61 167 Charles 117 David 54 Dorothy 54 Elizabeth 107 168 Ephraim 11 167 George 168 Hannah 2 4 34 86 117 Jeremiah 60 61 169 Lydia 169 Mark 60 61 Mary 6 88 Mehitable 54 Olive 60 Sarah 122 Susanna 47 54 60 61 93 169 Susannah 158 William 122
DEROCHEMONT, George Washington 138 Henrietta Jacobs 138 Sophia Antoinette 138
DEWIT, Henrietta Jacobs 138
DIAMOND, Margaret 180
DITTY, Elizabeth 68 Francis 68
DIX, Mary 189
DIXON, Lucy 129 Susanna 154 Thomas 154
DOE, Abigail 132 Elizabeth 132 141 Martha 14 Mary 14 Sampson 14 Samuel 132 141
DONALD, Eunice 91 Thomas 91
DORR, Charles 170 Francis A 168 Mary 170 192 William 192
DOW, Abiah 31 Amos 60 Elizabeth 60 77 Frances I 118 Hannah 169 Henry 60 Isaac 118 Jeremiah 31 Lydia 60 76 77 Miriam 27 Miriam F 28 Moses 130 Nicholas 14 Philip 16 Phineas 28 Sarah 16
DOWNES, Lydia 186

DOWNING, Abigail 37 Alice 82 107 121 Benjamin 58 74 Dennis 178 Dorothy 47 Elizabeth 24 37 58 74 113 158 160 167 Hannah 24 John 11 24 58 59 90 109 112 113 132 133 167 Jonathan 109 113 121 Joseph 173 Joshua 47 93 158 178 Josiah 160 Lois 2 4 37 Mary 25 59 70 98 108 113 132 183 Mary Clark 59 Patience 90 113 149 167 Rebecca 178 Richard 107 Samuel 160 Sarah 90 98 173 176 Susanna 47 58 93 102 107 110 150 167 Susannah 158 Temperence 24
DOWNS, Abigail 111 Catherine 111 Thomas 111
DRAKE, Sarah 83
DREW, Abigail 169 Elizabeth 64 Ezrah 135 Lydia 36 105 Mary Elizabeth 77 Nancy 135 Wm 64
DROWN, Mehitable F 188 Samuel 188
DUDLEY, Sarah 2
DUMMER, Lydia 7 Shubael 7
DUNN, Joseph 73 Mary 73
DURGIN, Benjamin 28 Comfort 18 Ebenezer 116 Eleanor 143 Elizabeth 103 Francis 143 Olive 116 Susan 28 William 143
DURRELL, Abigail 134 Nicholas 134 Rachel 134 Rachel Wakefield 134
EARL, Etherington 93 Hannah 93 Love 93
EATON, Mary 111 Olive 96
EDDY, Robert Henry 141
EDGERLY, Betsey 151 Clara 18 David L 151 Elizabeth 43 Hannah 49 50 James 97 Jeremiah 151 John 43 Joseph 40 Moses 40 Olive 43 151 Polly 40 Rachel 97 Samuel 43 Sarah W 40
EDNEY, James 61
ELLIOTT, Mary 119

EMERSON, Dorothy 74 Elizabeth 5 Mary 74 Samuel 74 Solomon 5
EMERY, Ann 84 Daniel 84 Margaret 84 Martha 43 Meribah 43 Simon 43 Zachariah 84
ENGLISH, Mary Ann 20 Thomas Stanhope 20
ERRINGTON, Hannah 11
ESTES, Henry 150 Phebe 150 Sarah 150
EVANS, Benjamin 150 Edward 71 Elizabeth 150 Mary Jane 96 Tamsen 71 Wi 71
EVELETH, Hannah 13
EWER, Capt 3 Drusilla 3
FABIAN, Elizabeth 3 53 90 92 John 53 61 92 113 John S 61 Mary 53 90 92 113 198 Rosamond 61 113 Samuel 60 90 92 113
FABYAN, Abigail 139 Ann 136 Elizabeth 74 75 136 139 John 69 76 77 131 136 138 Mary 37 69 131 138 139 Mehitable 136 138 Phebe 69 Rosamond 75 138 139 Samuel 75 136 139 Sarah 131
FAIRFIELD, Mary 53
FARNISIDE, Hannah 63
FARNUM, Elizabeth 49 Paul 49
FARRAR, Joseph 140 Sarah C 140
FELING, Elizabeth 100 John 100
FELLOWS, Abigail 10 Hannah 13 Nathaniel 13 William 10
FERNALD, Abigail 172 181 Abraham 180 181 Charles 181 Diamond 34 Dorothy 37 Ebenezer 37 Elizabeth 34 Harriet 6 Lydia 5 Mary 96 126 157 180 181 Patience 37 Rebecca 5 Theodore 5 Thomas 180 Tobias 172
FERRIN, Elizabeth 18 Samuel 18
FICKETT, John 152 Margaret 152 187 Susanna 152

FIELD, Abigail 105 142 Agnes 111 Derby 111 Hannah 94 Joseph 142 Sarah 111 Zacharias 111
FITCH, Ann 168
FITZGERALD, Richard 106 Sarah 106
FLAGG, John 165 Sarah 165
FLOYD, John C 182
FOGG, Enoch 117 Eunice 173 Lois 117 Rachel 117 Samuel 117
FOLLETT, John 177 Sarah 177 Susanna 40 158 Thomas 40 158
FOLSOM, Mary 117 129
FORD, Deborah 164 Hannah 153
FOSS, Ann 87 Benjamin 87 Sarah 194 Zachariah 194
FOSTER, Abigail 119 Charles 119 John 12 Mary 12 Sarah 185
FOX, Sarah 196 Susan 27
FOYE, Ann Maria 76 Thomas M 76
FRANCH, Abigail 28
FREESE, Jacob 16 Jonathan 16 Rachel 16 Sarah 16
FRENCH, Dorcas 166 Ella F 78 George S 78 John 166 Joseph 169 Lydia 169 Olive 169 Ruth 166 Simon 166
FRINK, Abigail 114 Ann 166 Cyrus 114
FROST, Charles 19 Jane 19 Mary 14 20 Miriam 19 Sarah 69
FRY, Catherine 198
FURBER, Abigail 43 59 101 108 114 117 134 138 Abigail Pickering 136 Alice 37 Alice Coleman 37 Amy 13 Anna 24 36 44 90 181 191 Deborah 60 108 138 Dorothy 114 Elizabeth 37 44 48 53 194 Esther 28 103 Fabian 114 Hannah 91 116 169 181 Jeremiah 134 Jerusha 129 134 Jethro 13 58 111 112 116 117 169 Leah 44 111 116 117 155 158 Levi 59 Lydia 136 140 Mary 36 53

FURBER (continued)
    82 84 93 157 164 166 169 Moses
    24 36 44 90 91 181 191 Nehemiah
    59 82 101 108 114 138 Phebe 58
    Richard 37 53 84 164 Rosamond
    59 Samuel 84 Sarah 4 24 58 90 101
    135 164 191 Susanna 23 51 52 68
    191 Susannah 23 191 Temperence
    5 Theodore 136 William 23 24 36
    58 101 112 155 164 191
FURBISH, Benjamin 180 Dorothy 180
    Hannah 180
FURBUR, Elizabeth 184
GAINES, George 133 John 194 Ruth
    194 Sarah 133
GALE, Charles C P 190 Martha 189
GALLOWAY, Benjamin 155 Elizabeth
    155
GAMBLE, Mary 179
GAMMON, Mary 82 William 82
GARDNER, John 49 Mary 49
GARLAND, Abigail 169 Benjamin 74
    Clara 18 Comfort 18 Elizabeth 18
    Gideon 18 Hannah 18 Harriet 18
    James 18 John 18 Lucy Maria 74
    Lydia 149 Mary 18 169 Nathaniel
    18 Polly 18 Samuel 18 169 Sarah 4
    74 Thomas 74
GASKIN, Daniel 187 Deliverance 26
    30 80 93 112 186 187 Joanna 187
    John 187
GATES, Mary 135
GAULT, Dorothy Ann 77 Samuel 77
GEE, Hazelponi 131 John 131 Mary
    131
GERRISH, Abigail 31 134 Benjamin
    134 Richard 49
GIDDINGS, John 7 Sarah 7
GILMAN, Ezekiel 2 Joanna 3 95 96
    Johanna 2 36 86 90 Nicholas 52
    Sarah 2 25 51 52
GLASS, Elizabeth 153 John 153

GLEER, Elizabeth 41 Thomas 41
GODDARD, Martha 167
GODSO, Deborah 160 John 157 Mary
    157
GOLD, Hannah 14
GOODE, Mary 115
GOODRIDGE, Esther 153 John 153
GOODWIN, Hannah 93 Mary 170
    Susanna 53 Thomas 53
GOOKIN, Ann 168 Mary 168 Nathaniel 168
GOSS, Mary J 142 Salome 190 Sarah
    103
GOTHAM, Edward 123 Mercy 123
GOVE, Enoch 104 Hannah 104 Jonathan 28 Mary 28 Ruth 28
GOWEN, Lemuel 139 Margaret 84
    Mercy 139
GRANT, Mary 186
GRANVILLE, Ann 25
GRAY, Mary 104 Rev 2
GREELEY, Agnes 115
GREEN, Abigail 170 Bethiah 41 Ezra
    171 John 170 Nathaniel 169
    Reuben 170
GREENOUGH, Eunice 197 Lucy 184
    Olive 188 Pelatiah 197 Samuel 184
    188 Seth Walker 188
GRIFFITH, Caleb 12 Deborah 9
    Edward 12 Elizabeth 12 Gershom
    12 John 9 Joshua 12 Mary 9
    Nathaniel 9
GROVE, Hannah 109 Mary 172 Sarah
    134
GROVER, Elizabeth 187 Nathaniel
    187
GROVES, John 144 Mary 144
GUNNISON, Elihu 177 191 Elizabeth
    186 191 Hugh 177 Martha 177
    Mary 177 Priscilla 177 Sarah 177
HACKETT, Asa 19 Susanna 19
HAINES, Hannah 19 Mary 58 139

HAINES (continued)
Samuel 19 Stephen 139
HALE, Mehitable 181 Sarah 154
HALEY, Andrew 41 88 Deborah 41 88
Elizabeth 38 41 52 88 Sarah 73
HALL, Abigail 111 Hannah 126 John
111 Josiah 149 Mehitable 44 117
Sarah 57 Susanna 149
HALLIBURTON, Andrew 20 Ann 20
George 20 Sarah Ann 20
HAM, Abigail 36 54 58 91 101 134
176 Ann 189 Dorcas 156 Eleanor
144 Eleazer 144 Elizabeth 24 106
111 144 167 Ephraim 144 John 111
156 167 Lucy 190 Nathaniel 190
Patience 52 90 113 167 Paul 150
Polly 150 Samuel 24 101 Sarah
160 William 189
HAMMETT, Elizabeth 47 Thomas 47
HAMMOND, Betty 128 Elisha 103
Mercy 139 Sarah 103
HANAFORD, Sarah 170
HANSON, Hannah 150 180 James 150
Mary 170 Phineas G 170
HARN, Abigail 85 Eleazer 85 Elizabeth 85 William 85
HARRIS, Martha 5 Rebecca 5
HARRISON, Elizabeth 24 51 53 167
Mary 51 Nicholas 51
HART, Alice 54 Henry 54 Mary 69
141 Samuel 180
HARTWELL, Betsey 189 John 189
Jonathan 189 Mary 189 Mary M
139
HARVEY, John 156 Keziah 156
HASTY, Lettice 89
HATCH, Alice 98 Mary 135 Patience
51 Samuel 135 Sarah 98 Thomas
98
HAYES, Abigail 75 149 Abigail Harrison Downing 167 Daniel 75
Hannah 121 Peter 167 Reuben 167

HAYES (continued)
Sarah 167
HAYNES, Dorcas 21 Patience 151
Samuel 151
HEARD, Elizabeth 98 115 133 Joseph
155 Rebecca 155 Tristram 98 111
HENDERSON, Abigail 151 Elizabeth
90 Thomas 90
HEPWORTH, Mary 1 78
HEPWROTH, Mary 154
HERRICK, Henry 7 Sarah 7
HIGGINS, Mary 5
HILL, Abial 7 Abigail 69 70 138
Bradbury 72 Ebenezer 7 Elizabeth
72 Hannah 169 Harriet 169 John 34
Jonathan 72 98 Joshua 72 Mary 47
75 98 110 111 Nancy 71 72 Nathaniel 111 Noah 72 Pearl 72
Robert 138 Samuel 99 110 138 169
Sarah 99 111 Susannah 104
Temperance 138 Valentine 111
HILLIARD, Elizabeth 41 43 88 119
181 Nicholas 41 42 89
HILTON, Rebecca 111
HODGDON, Aaron 48 Abigail 93 138
Alexander 69 93 163 164 166 Ann
64 155 Benjamin 4 36 162 Charles
4 47 76 Elizabeth 4 29 193 Hannah
4 47 162 Jane 39 163 164 Jane
Shackford 69 Jeremiah 21 155 163
John 17 36 39 46 137 Lydia 166
Mary 17 36 39 46 48 69 93 137
146 164 Rosamond 4 36 Sarah 17
26 Sarah Ayres 4 Temperance 30
Temperence 137
HODGKINS, Sarah 45
HODGSON, Charles 2 Hannah 2 Olive
2
HODSDON, Elizabeth 155 Hannah 45
HOLDEN, Elizabeth 186 William 186
HOLMES, Mary 127 Samuel 127
Sarah Ann 20

HOOK, Joseph 183 Temperence 183
HOOPER, Sarah 140 William 140
HOPLEY, Elizabeth 14 111 Mary 13 14 Robert 14 111
HORN, Charity 149 Daniel 149 Hannah 158 161 James 75 Mary 75 Moses 158 161
HORNE, Rebecca 118
HOUSTON, James 49 Mary 49
HOYT, Abigail 29 Abisha 195 Anna 181 Benjamin 56 116 Daniel 31 Deborah 139 Dennis 3 59 Dorothy 21 166 Elizabeth 3 31 36 38 41 59 83 193 Enoch 36 Eunice 48 Frances 163 Hannah 74 Jackson 52 Jackson M 89 John 3 4 36 59 68 82 135 163 181 Lettice 82 Lydia 3 4 36 59 69 Mary 3 32 86 87 90 163 Moses 181 Nancy 3 135 Rebecca 116 Samuel Fabian 3 Sarah 4 56 68 102 115 124 135 181 William 38 41 83 193
HUCKINS, Abigail 138
HUDSON, Deborah 164 Eleazer 164 John 123 Mary 123 Rebecca 164 Sarah 164
HUGH, Katharine 122 Margaret 33
HULL, Elizabeth 66 Hannah 63 Mary 63 Reuben 63
HUNKING, Anna 43 Mark 43 Mary 15
HUNNEWELL, Elizabeth 51
HUNTER, Alice 177
HUNTRESS, Abigail 2 36 42 54 58 71 84 87 91 112 134 Alice 37 Ann Sherburn 60 Christopher 84 123 134 160 Deborah 75 113 Elizabeth 37 58 75 90 102 123 136 139 Enoch 113 George 36 42 156 James 37 John 75 John S 60 Jonathan 44 113 187 Joseph 176 183 196 Joseph Patterson 75 Lydia 175 Mark 75 Martha 104 Mary 36 42

HUNTRESS (continued) 44 84 105 113 119 121 134 156 160 183 187 Nancy 196 Noah 134 Samuel 36 37 54 58 Sarah 44 75 Seth 44 Sobriety 183 196 Solomon 91 Susanna 54 102 176 Tamsen 122 William 54 102 176
HURD, Elizabeth 66 John 66
HUSSEY, Hannah 62 180 Richard 62
INGRAHAM, Edward 12 Elizabeth 12 Moses 12
JACKSON, Betsey 151 Eleanor 11 John 11 Martha 49 Mary 15 149 156 Mary Hannah 14 Philip 149 Samuel 15 Stephen 151 Thomas 156
JACOBS, Dorothy 184 Hannah 3
JANVIN, Elizabeth 1 John 2
JANVRIN, Catherine 100 Elizabeth 2 56 132 John 2 98 100 132 Mary 43 59 98 132 William 2
JAQUES, Deborah 195 Henry 131 Rebecca 131
JENKINS, Catherine 198 Joseph 198 Mary 62 Miriam 119 William 62
JENNESS, Benning W 169 Deborah 169 Keturah 42 Nancy 169 Paul 42 Thomas 169
JEWETT, Dearborn 75 Mary 75
JOCE, Damaris 15 Richard 15
JOHNSON, Comfort 139 140 Hannah 19 21 114 Jotham 114 Mary 135 Olive 15 21 Sarah 172
JONES, Abigail 110 Alice 29 Elizabeth 106 Martha 107 Mary 13 Paul 192 Stephen 29 110
JOSE, Christopher 12 Hannah 12 Richard 12
JOY, Calvin 139 Caroline 138 Charles 138 Charlotte 139 Georgianna 138 Hannah 138 139 Henry B 139 Jacob 138 James 138 James Freder-

JOY (continued)
ick 138 Jane 138 John P 138 Maria 138 Martha A 138 Mary 138 139 Mary M 139 Richard P 139 Sarah 138 Sarah Ann 139 Susan E 138 Sylvester 139
JUDITH, P Joy 138
KELLEY, Abigail 101 John 101
KENDALL, Abel 171 Deliverance 171
KENISTON, Elizabeth 170 James 143
KENNARD, Edward 66 Elizabeth 66 68 173 Hannah 162 James 20 Mary Pierce 20 Ruth 184 William 162
KENNY, Deborah 135
KENT, Mary F 21 Rachel 57
KINGSBURY, John 144 Miriam 144
KIRKE, Eleanor 67
KITTS, Elizabeth 13
KNIGHT, Bridget 2 44 95 Elizabeth 1 56 95 132 133 John 2 95 133 Kezia 145 Mary 41 83 Nathan 41 Nicholas 39 176 Olive 149 Sarah 39 176 Susanna 39 Temperence 133
KNOWLES, Ruth 166
LAMB, Elizabeth 107
LANCASTER, Hannah 166
LANE, Hannah 72 Huldah 27 Martha 168
LANG, Benjamin 31 Catherine 95 Daniel 95 Deborah 9 Eleanor 11 31 Elizabeth 26 190 Hannah 108 135 John 86 Joseph 11 Lucy 190 Lydia 71 Mark 190 Martha 95 Mary 86 Mary J 86 Olive 86 Richard 190 Salome 190 Thomas 86 135 William 86 190
LANGDON, Elizabeth 168 Hannah 38 133 Joseph 133 Mary 133 137 Patience 133 Samuel 133 168 Sarah 133 137 William 133 137
LANGLEY, Esther 29 James 18 179 Mary 18 179 Rebecca 180 Sarah

LANGLEY (continued)
179 Thomas 179
LANGSTAFF, Henry 36 111 Mary 36 Sarah 67 111 163
LARY, Elizabeth 62
LASSELL, Hannah 191
LAVERS, Jacob 15 Mary 15
LEACH, Abigail 108 George 131 Joseph 108 131 Mehitable 23 Phebe 131 Sarah 131
LEAGER, Anna 185
LEATHERS, Jonathan 180 Keturah 180 Margaret 180 William 180
LEAVITT, Abigail 128 Edward 128 Martha 74 Mary F 73 Samuel 18 Samuel F 74 Sarah 18
LECOUTEUR, Elizabeth 95
LEIGHTON, Abigail 59 69 108 114 134 138 168 176 Betsey 151 Catherine 171 Deborah 35 37 39 43 69 179 Elizabeth 43 68 93 111 133 142 Hatevil 179 James 176 Joel 93 John 143 168 176 Jonathan 149 168 Keziah 37 Lucy 149 Mary 39 93 111 115 142 168 172 Olive 39 99 Sarah 154 176 179 183 Thomas 37 39 43 69 93 111 115 142 172 179
LEONARD, Elizabeth 57 John 57
LEVERITT, Elizabeth 82 Simon 82
LEWIS, Lucy 189
LIBBEY, Eleanor 67 James 67 John 67 Mary 67
LIBBY, Andrew 67 Azariah 122 Elizabeth 9 67 92 107 122 156 168 172 Esther 67 James 107 Jerusha 173 Lydia 103 Margaret 108 Mary 23 Matthew 67 Reuben 79 Samuel 103 Sarah 79 81 Stephen 108
LINCOLN, Drusilla 4 J L 4
LINN, Margaret A 73
LITTLE, Sarah 51 52

LITTLEFIELD, Hannah 7 Mabel 32
LOCKE, Anna 35 James 114 Love 114 Matilda 96
LONG, Samuel D 139 Sarah Ann 139
LORD, Abigail 76 Joseph 93 Martha 24 43 92 93 Mary 90 Sarah 106
LOUD, Abigail 42 47 John 47 Solomon 42
LOVE, John 148
LOVEJOY, Dorcas 166 Dorothy 166 Joseph 166 Lydia 84 166 Nathaniel 166 Sarah 166
LOVERING, Dorothy 96
LOW, Lydia 138
LUCY, Hannah 79
LUNT, Elizabeth 189
LYFORD, Anna 4 Deborah 63 Elizabeth 4 Francis 63 Jonathan 4 Joseph 4 Rebecca 63
LYON, Elizabeth 12 Henry 12
LYSSEN, John 83 Susanna 83
MACDONALD, James 120 Sarah 120
MACKWORTH, Rebecca 178
MANNING, Alice Sherburn 20 Edward Sherburn 20 Elizabeth Bennett 20 Mary 19 Mary Ann 20 Mary Pierce 20 Sarah Ann 20 Statira 19 20 Thomas 19 Thomas Augustus 20 William 20
MARCH, Abigail 136 Clement 116 Margaret 116 Mary 58 Peletiah 58
MARRINER, George 80 Mary 80 109
MARSH, Catherine 71 David 71 Elizabeth 71 James 71 Nancy 71 Samuel 71
MARSHALL, Deborah 167 Eleanor 135 167 168 Elizabeth 195 John 195 Rebecca 13 84 Samuel 167 168
MARSTON, Mary 109
MARTIN, Mary 92 Michael 92 Rebecca 106 William 92

MARTYN, Elizabeth 66 Hannah 12 Richard 12 66 Sarah 12
MASON, Lydia 49 Robt 28 Susanna 28
MATHES, Anna 36 Benjamin 36 Frances 36 Lydia 36
MATTHEWS, Francis 57 Lydia 57
MAYHEW, Keziah 156
MCDANIELS, Rebecca 170
MEAD, Sarah 62
MEADER, Abigail 63 Charity 115 154 John 63 Joseph 62 Sarah 63 197
MELCHER, Mary 15
MELOON, Deliverance 187 Joseph 187
MENDUM, Eleanor 167 168 Elizabeth 95 130 Frances 95 167 Nathaniel 95 167 Patience 37
MESERVE, Abigail 134 Daniel 134 Mehitable 35 Polly 35 Susanna 34
MESERVY, Alice 120 Anna 195 Clement 46 Elizabeth 46 103 Frances 120 Martha 97 Nathaniel 97 Sarah 46
MEZEET, Elizabeth 99 Isaac 99
MILLER, Abigail 100 181 Benjamin 89 181 Edward F 78 Elizabeth 179 Hannah 24 John 50 Joyce 13 Lydia 3 36 59 69 89 Margaret 103 Mark 54 Peter 179 Ruth 141 Sarah 78 Sarah F 78 Susanna 50 54 58 110
MILLS, Deborah 60 70 138 Hannah 70 Luke 70 138 Polly 18
MITCHELL, Bridget 23 Roger 23
MONTGOMERY, Hugh 176
MOODY, Elizabeth 46 Joseph 46 117 Mary 117
MOORE, Amelia 171 Joanna Chauncey 171 John 171 Lazarus 195 Sarah 171 195
MORISON, Elizabeth 18
MORRELL, Josiah 153 Sarah 153
MORRILL, Elisha 5 Elizabeth 70 Isaac

MORRILL (continued)
    173 Mary 173 Nancy 5 Nathan 4
    Nicholas 70 Rhoda 4
MORSE, Ebenezer 127 Mary 127
    Mary B 163 Mary Bennett 131
MOSES, Aaron 11 Anna 38 Benjamin
    38 Joseph 11 Martha 95 Mary 34
    Rebecca 11 Ruth 11 Theodore 16
MOULTON, Abigail 10 12 168 Alice
    10 12 Dorothy 168 John 10 12 105
    Jonathan 168 Joseph 10 12 Josiah
    168 Martha 136 Mary 105
MULLALY, Mary 104 William 104
MUNDY, Joseph 117 Mary 117
MURDOCH, Lettice 32
MURRAY, Hannah 80 Sarah 71 72 74
    William 80
MUZEET, Phebe 142 Thomas 142
NASON, Abigail 63 Benjamin 66
    Elizabeth 66 Huldah 166 Mary 178
    197 Richard 63 178 Sarah 49
NEAL, Hannah 15 Jeremiah H 71 Lucy
    71 Mary 10 Walter 10
NEALLEY, Alcey 73 Dorothy 72 73
    John 72 73 Joseph 73 Sarah 72
NELSON, Abigail 31 Elizabeth 38 41
    52-54 88 113 John 41 52 88 Joseph
    165 Leader 31 Mary 3 83 134 165
NEWMARCH, Elizabeth 8 John 8
NOBLE, Frances 27 Oliver 27
NOLE, Joanna 49 Stephen 49
NORRIS, Martha 57
NORTON, Nancy W 5
NORWOOD, Sarah 31
NUTE, Elizabeth 66 Eunice 169
    Hannah 149 James 66 67 John 149
    Leah 67 Moses 169 Roxana A 169
    Sarah 66 164 191
NUTTER, Abigail 3 43 44 45 67 94
    114 160 Alice 52 109 183 Ann 101
    114 136 181 Anna 36 44 70 91 92
    124 169 175 Anthony 52 56 67 114

NUTTER (continued)
    160 163 183 Arabella 124 Benja-
    min 175 Christopher 102 Deborah
    94 Dorothy 70 149 Ebenezer 40
    Elizabeth 17 31 41 44 52 56 158
    187 Esther 43 44 45 George 3
    Hannah 45 46 47 67 136 181
    Hatevil 44 45 46 47 52 66 67 155
    158 169 187 Henry 41 89 134 163
    James 43 67 Jethro 66 John 16 44
    46 58 67 70 124 169 175 Joshua 17
    155 Jotham 52 56 Leah 44 67 155
    158 Lois 63 Louisa 160 Martha 3
    136 169 Mary 3 41 52 56 69 89 93
    94 102 108 112 124 131 134 163
    183 Matthias 3 16 136 169 181
    Mattias 67 Mercy 175 Olive 159
    Phebe 90 135 169 Prudence 150
    Richard 149 Rosamond 58 139
    Salome 160 Samuel 89 94 102 124
    Sarah 17 52 67 89 102 104 114 124
    153 160 163 187 Susanna 16 169
    Temperence 40 William 114 Wil-
    liam G 77
ODELL, Lydia 72
OSBORN, George 140 182 Olive 140
OTIS, Joseph 150 Lucy 150
PACKER, Abigail 136 Matthew B 136
PAGE, Elizabeth 71 168 Samuel 168
    Susanna 126
PALMER, Barnabus 150 Hannah 191
    Mary 150
PARKER, Thomas 144
PARSHLEY, John 92 Tamsen 92
PARSONS, Susan E 138
PATCH, Benjamin 186 Lydia 186
PATTEN, Abigail 160
PAUL, Abigail 7 173 Daniel 7 Eliza-
    beth 7 103 Sarah 47
PEABODY, Frances 163 Nathaniel 164
PEARCE, Hannah 153 William 153
PEARL, John 26 Joseph 26 Mary 26

PEARL (continued)
  Sarah 26
PEARSON, Elizabeth 93
PEASE, Dudley 5 Hannah 28 Johanna
  Gilman 5 John 28
PEAVEY, Arabella 115 Deborah 144
  Jane 143 Joseph 115 Mary 173
  Rachel 161 Sarah 33 Thomas 173
PEELING, Belinda 96
PEIRCE, George 67 Jerusha 66 67
PENDEXTER, Margaret 126
PENHALLOW, Deborah 98
PEPPERELL, Jane 19 Margery 195
PERKINS, Abigail 16 116 Anna
  Symmes 119 David 174 Jonathan
  16 Joseph 136 Martha 3 117 136
  169 Mary 136 Mehitable 174
  Samuel 119 Sarah 16
PETTENGELL, Ansel 118 Augusta
  118 Joseph R 118 Lavina 118
PETTIGREW, Eleanor 6 Joseph 191
  Lucy 48 Mary 191 Stephen 48
  Thomas 6
PEVERLY, Abigail 34 Ann 87 189
  Eliza D 118 Eliza K 190 Elizabeth
  164 190 George 4 87 189 Harriet
  118 Jane 39 Joanna 118 Johanna 4
  118 Kinsman 118 Lois 4 Nathaniel
  164 Sarah 87 Susanna 60 61 169
  Temperence 189 William 4 118
PEVEY, Arabella 120 Deborah 112
  157 Eleanor 119 Elizabeth 196
  Hudson 31 114 James 114 John 40
  Joseph 120 Lois 40 Madeline 31
  114 Mary 114 Mercy 79 Rachel 17
  47 Sarah 158
PHILBRICK, Ruth 28 Sarah 74
PHILBROOK, Jonathan 64 Mary 64
  Sarah 9
PHILIPS, Sarah 155
PHILLIPS, Mary 162 Sarah 50
PHINNEY, Edmund 106 Elizabeth 106

PICKERING, Abby Frances 77 Abigail
  3 59 62 75 93 95 118 168 Alice 30
  122 Anna 60 90 Charlotte 90
  Deborah 36 60 69 108 172 Eliza
  Perkins 77 Elizabeth 30 43 48 60 69
  184 Ephraim 36 60 75 118 Hannah
  25 29 86 118 Harriet 18 Jacob S 77
  James 3 50 59 69 79 90 112 120
  James C 75 77 Jerusha 69 John 50
  93 112 178 184 John Gee 60 70
  108 Joseph 60 Joseph W 118
  Joshua 36 60 77 172 Lydia 36 60
  75 77 118 Lydia Furber 77 Mary 3
  25 43 50 52 53 58-60 69 70 92 93
  95 98 100 108 112 120 Maturin F
  77 Nancy 90 Nicholas 25 29 50 86
  Phebe 90 120 Rosamond 60 61
  Sarah 78 Stephen 77 Stephen Hale
  77 Temperance 50 Temperence 86
  98 Theodore F 77 Thomas 25 43 52
  58-60 69 70 95 98 108 William 59
  62 William Pepperell 3 Winthrop
  90 120
PICKNAIL, Anne 149 Nelson 149
PIERCE, John 139 Joshua 14 Mary 139
PIERREPONT, Alice Sherburn 20
  James H 20 Statira 20
PIKE, Robert 111
PILLSBURY, Abigail 62 Lydia 142
PINDER, Elizabeth 102 Hepzibah 102
  Joseph 102 Thomas 102
PINKHAM, Lydia 182
PITMAN, Elizabeth 126 164 Ezekiel
  164 Mary 162 Nancy 19
PLACE, Abigail 186 Abraham 157
  Alice 43 Dorothy 115 Ebenezer
  127 Elizabeth 75 Eunice 43 46 162
  James 191 Jane 127 John 46 162
  John M 43 Joseph 43 Mary 46 157
  162 191 Samuel 162 Stephen 75
PLAISTED, Hannah 65 Olive 65
  Roger 65

PLUMMER, Daniel 195 Sarah 195
POMEROY, Elizabeth 173
POMFRET, Elizabeth 65
POWERS, Mary 74
PRATT, Charlotte 139
PRAY, Elizabeth 193 John 15
PRENDERGAST, Ann 169 Pamela A 169 Stephen 169
PRIEST, Michael 182
PRITCHARD, Sarah 166
PRYOR, Patience 82
QUICK, Daniel 165 Elizabeth 165
QUINT, Ann 25 Margaret 129 187 Mary 23 Sarah 187 Thomas 129 187
RACKLEBY, Mary 171
RAITT, Sarah 103 William 103
RAND, David 2 Elizabeth 2 Mary 165
RANDALL, Charity 105 Daniel 105 Eleanor 14
READ, Martha A 138
REED, Alice 121 Mark 121
REMICK, Hannah 157 Joshua 82 Mary 82 Stephen 157 Susanna 48
RENOLDS, Sarah 130
RHODES, Mary 144
RICHARDS, Abigail 52 69 84 163 Alice 19 Benjamin 114 159 Dorcas 81 Elizabeth 40 114 159 Esther 159 George 19 55 John 81 Joseph 40 Mary 55 94 163 Rebecca 82 Samuel 163 Sarah 17 114 William 163
RICHARDSON, Abigail 184 Anna 198 Elizabeth 163 George 56 Mary 56 Timothy 198 William 143
RICKER, Jabez 182 Mary 182 Sarah 180 Thomas 148
RING, Elizabeth 3 9 37 72 92 114 118 168 189 190 Jane 9 John A 72 Mary 92 Seth 9 92 168
ROBERTS, Abigail 110 111 154 Anna

ROBERTS (continued) 70 Betsey 153 Elizabeth 14 111 Eunice 150 Hatevil 111 James 150 John 110 111 153 Joseph 111 Lydia 111 Mary 111 Mehitable 147 Moses 143 150 Olive 154 Polly 153 Rebecca 111 Sarah 69 70 111 143 Thomas 14 111 153 Timothy 70
ROBIE, Thomas 125
ROBINSON, Drusilla 4 George P 4 Mary 111 193 Timothy 111
ROGERS, Betsey 184 George 62 Hannah 154 Mary 79 Rebecca 178 William 178
ROLANS, Caleb 14 15 Ruth 14
ROLFE, Hannah 186
ROLLINS, Abigail 38 119 Alice 42 93 155 Benjamin 8 Caleb 14 15 Caroline D 140 Charles 77 Chas 140 Deborah 23 112 126 136 144 187 Dorothy 71 77 Edward 112 Elizabeth 34 54 55 112 Esther 155 Eunice 8 Hannah 88 Ichabod 112 James 77 112 126 144 Joseph 9 33 42 43 55 64 187 Keturah 8 Lydia 159 Lydia A 77 Mary 33 42 43 93 119 144 Mary B 77 Mary Elizabeth 77 Noah 55 Olive 112 Olive Pickering 77 Paul 136 Ruth 14 Samuel 42 93 119 155 Sarah 9 42 55 187 Susanna 64 Theodore Furber 77
ROSS, Jonathan 3 Mary 3
ROWE, Ann 152 Deborah 32 Eunice 43 46 143 Jane 25 41 93 June 101 Margaret 97 Mary 17 144 Rachel 17 127 Samuel 23 32 Susannah 22 Thomas 17 127 152
ROWSLEY, Abigail 7 Robert 7
RUNLETT, Charles 130 Mary 130
RUNNELS, Mary 179
RUST, Martha 139

RYND, Mary 153
SACHEL, Eleanor 143 John 143 Mary 143
SALTER, Abigail 20 Eliza 20 Henry 20 John 20 Lucy Maria 20 Richard 17 Sarah Ann 20
SAMPSON, Sarah 99
SANBORN, Deborah 169 John 21 Sarah 16 Sarah Peperell 21
SARGENT, Hannah 97
SAVERY, Mary 142 Robert 142
SAYWARD, Hannah 88 Nancy 86
SCALES, Susanna 11 William 11
SCAMMON, Elizabeth 156 Humphrey 156
SCHURMAN, Arthur 71
SEAVEY, Abigail 131 Eunice 46 James 131
SEAWARD, Abigail Pickering 163
SENTER, Abner 11 Mehitable 11
SENTLE, Johanna 7 John 7 William 7
SEWARD, Abigail 165 Ann 165 Benjamin 126 127 Christian 146 Deborah 165 Dorothy 165 Elizabeth 9 126 127 165 George 126 165 Giles 146 164 John 165 Margaret 126 Mary 146 164 165 Paul 165 Sarah 165 Shackford 165 William 164 165
SHACKFORD, Abigail 52 69 84 Deborah 15 83 112 178 Elizabeth 3 37 114 118 189 190 Hannah 37 Jane 83 164 John 3 Joshua 84 Lydia 84 Mary 41 53 69 84 89 93 112 134 166 189 Nancy 189 Nathaniel Cooper 118 Patience 81 Phebe 118 Ruth Webb 3 Samuel 3 37 52 69 84 114 118 156 157 189 190 Samuel B 156 177 Sarah 194 Susanna 50 52 114 William 50 52 83 112 178
SHAFFEN, Mary 154 Patrick 154
SHAPLEIGH, Catherine 103 Dependence 103 Johanna 7 Ruth 18 91
SHAW, Margaret 167 Mary Ann 20
SHEAFE, Abigail 136 Jacob 136
SHERBURN, Abigail 164 Alice 19 Edward 19 Eleanor 167 168 Elizabeth 18 Henry 13 Jane 39 John 14 164 167 Joseph 13 Mary 75 98 164 169 Mary Hannah 14 Mercy 75 Phebe 13 Ruth 11 14 Samuel 75 164 Sarah 13
SHERBURNE, Henry 18
SHERMAN, James 97 Margaret 97 Thomas 97
SIMPSON, Elizabeth 1 Jane 43 Sarah 25 152 188
SINGLES, Marie Downing 56
SINNOTT, Eunice 162 Mary 80 Robert 80 162
SLADE, Elizabeth 37
SLOPER, Bridget 2 95 97 Mary 98 Richard 97
SMALL, Olive Sanborn 74 William B 74
SMART, Elizabeth 134
SMITH, Abigail 62 168 Alice 179 Benjamin 138 Capt 3 Daniel 139 David D 170 Elizabeth 57 103 179 Hannah 98 James 3 179 John 73 103 179 Joseph 179 Martha Ann 170 Martha M 73 Mary 3 139 179 Patience 98 Samuel 98
SMITHSON, Deborah 36 132 Mary 39 93 102 115 142
SNELL, George 7 Hannah 7 John 7 Mary 116 Samuel 7
SOULE, Cornelius 11 Susanna 11
SPEED, Elsie 56 James 56
SPINNEY, Abigail 123 Elizabeth 151 Grace 53 James 53 Mary 108 Nathan 151 Sarah 53 Timothy 123
STANIAN, Anthony 130 Mary 130

STAPLES, Benjamin 103 Catherine 173 Elizabeth 97 Eunice 63 Jerusha 103 Joseph 63 Robert 97
STAVERS, 176
STEVENS, Abijah 49 Anna 4 Elizabeth 93 Jesse 19 John 124 Mary 14 124 Sarah 124 Susanna 19
STICKNEY, Elizabeth 2 95 Moses 95
STILLINGS, Sarah 153
STONE, Elizabeth 136 Jonathan 53 136 Phebe 53 Sarah 106
STOODLEY, Elizabeth 29 N D 87 Sarah 87
STOODLY, Elizabeth 165
STORER, Hannah 133
STOREY, Sarah 185
STOVER, Elizabeth 51 Sarah 51
STRONG, Alan H 189
STROUT, Sarah 106
STUART, Mary 126
STUDLEY, Elizabeth 194
SULLIVAN, Abigail 40 Ebenezer 40
SUMNER, Deborah 15 165 Isaac 165 Mary 165
SWASEY, Amy 13 Olive 171 Samuel 13
SWEATT, Sarah 27
SWETT, Jane 93 Jonathan 93 Lydia 93 Mehitable 129
SYMMES, Anna 44 70 114 119 124 169 John 114
SYMONDS, Anna 10 66 Joanna 10 Mark 10
TALMADGE, Jane 185
TALPEY, Elizabeth 3
TAPRILL, Grace 89 Robert 89
TARLETON, Ann 182 John 182
TASKER, John 117 Mary 117 Nathaniel 74
TEBBETTS, Sarah C 128
TETHERLY, Mehitable 54
THING, Bartholomew 52 Sarah 51 52

THOMAS, Sarah 25
THOMPSON, Ann 133 Anna 22 101 Benjamin 138 Ebenezer 133 138 Elizabeth 188 John 188 Mary 41 133 138 180 198 Noah 143 149 Polly 40 Samuel 41 56 Sarah 39 56 99 101 143 William 22 101
THORNDIKE, John L 138 Maria 138
THWAITS, Ann 155
TIBBETTS, Deborah 74 James 115 Jonathan 150 Mary 115 180 Phebe 150 Rebecca 181
TILLY, Sarah 177
TILTON, Catherine 167 Jonathan 167 Joseph 167 Margaret 167
TOBEY, Sobriety 183 196
TOMB, Andrew 165 Elizabeth 165
TOMSON, Elizabeth 175
TOOGOOD, Edward 11 Hannah 11
TOPPAN, Enoch 36 Sarah 36
TORR, Mary 133 138
TOWLE, Belinda 27
TOWNE, Augusta 118
TREFETHEN, Phebe 35
TREWORGY, Lucy 8
TRICKEY, Abigail 108 Alice 113 172 Anna 117 Bethiah 44 45 Deborah 112 163 Elizabeth 43 108 163 184 195 Isaac 195 John 36 45 108 Jonathan 52 68 90 108 Joseph 43 Joshua 36 45 Keturah 100 Lemuel 113 Mary 25 36 43 62 68 102 108 113 172 Miriam 46 Rosamond 36 45 Sarah 41 68 90 100 102 Thomas 25 41 43 68 102 113 163
TRIGGS, Sarah 102 Thomas 102
TRIPE, Ann 169 189 Elizabeth 179 181 Lucy 80 189 Margaret 180 Sylvanus 180 189 Thomas 179
TUCKER, Abigail 156 Elizabeth 14 111 James 97 John 14 111 Olive 114 Ruth 97 Samuel 114 Tristram

TUCKER (continued)
156 Ursala 14 Ursula 111
TUFTS, Elizabeth 134
TUTTLE, Abigail 63 Ann 101 Deborah 101 Dorothy 94 Ebenezer 101 John 94 Katharine 35 Sarah 12
TWISDEN, John 7 Mary 7
TWOMBLEY, Sarah 146
TWOMBLY, Nancy 75
VARNEY, Esther 149 Eunice 150 169 Hannah W 5 Mary 128 Mercy H 43
VAUGHAN, Mary 8
VAUGHN, Maj 51
VEASEY, George 13
VICKER, Johanna 4 118
VINCENT, Alice 40 Anna 117 181 Elizabeth 140 Thomas 140 William 40
WADLEIGH, Abigail 74 John 74
WAKEHAM, Elizabeth 43
WALDRON, Abigail 189 Anna 70 Betsey 141 James 141 Richard 141
WALFORD, Elizabeth 51 Jeremiah 51
WALKER, Abigail 7 143 Ann 169 Anna 23 24 36 44 68 81 90 181 184 Charles 139 Daniel 117 Deliverance 26 30 80 93 112 Edward 30 80 93 112 153 158 Eleanor 26 40 Elizabeth 88 117 176 177 Elizabeth Deliverance 80 Gideon 26 44 Hannah 139 John 24 Joseph 143 Lawrence 26 Mark 169 Martha 30 Mary 24 44 93 111 113 144 169 Mehitable 58 Nancy 169 Robert 7 Samuel 24 68 Sarah 2 4 52 112 153 158 193 Seth 169 184 Shadrack 111 Susan Burbeen 139 Susanna 68 William 24
WALLINGFORD, Abigail 186 Elizabeth 3 John 49 Mary 49 50
WALLIS, Mary 182
WALTER, Edward 20

WALTON, Elizabeth 89 151 Elizabeth A 96 George 180 John William 96 Samuel 151
WAPLES, Mary 157 Paul 157
WARD, Elizabeth 189 Margery Greenleaf 189
WARREN, Elizabeth 87 George 87
WATERHOUSE, Deborah 15 165 Elizabeth 68 Lydia 35 Richard 68 Ruth 78 Samuel 165 Sarah 64 186 William 186
WATSON, Alice 198 Eleanor 143 John 143 Lydia 27 190 Mary 143
WEBB, Henry 86 Mary 86 Mary J 86
WEBBER, Elizabeth 66 Francis 66 Lydia 31 178 197 Richard 178
WEED, Mehitable 142
WEEKS, Abigail 136 141 Brackett 139 140 Comfort 139 140 Ichabod 136 139 140 Joseph 177 Joshua 139 141 Margaret 142 Martha 139 Mary 86 177 Mary Ann 139 Mehitable 131 140 Nicholas 177 Priscilla 177 Samuel 131 140 Sarah 139 140 Susan 136
WELCH, Benjamin 174 Elizabeth 174 Mary 182
WELDON, Alcey Nealley 73 Vachel 73
WELLS, Anna 107 Hannah 22 Joseph 107
WELLWRIGHT, Mary 7
WENTWORTH, Abigail 121 Deborah 96 Isaac 121 John 118 Mary 121 182 Olive 159 Paul 96 Rebecca 118 Sarah 116 118 151 Stephen 116 159
WESCOTT, Margaret 106 William 106
WESTCOMBE, Elizabeth 26 John 26 Mary 26
WHEELER, Sarah 6
WHEELWRIGHT, Damaris 15 Eliza-

WHEELWRIGHT (continued)
beth 8 James 15 John 8 Mary 7 8
WHIDDEN, Abigail 113 Hannah 38 Michael 113 Samuel 38 Sarah 38 108
WHITCHER, Mary 156
WHITE, Eliza 28 Elizabeth 105 Mehitable 6
WHITEHOUSE, Nicholas 151 Susan 151
WHITMORE, Abisha 89 Joel 89
WHITTAM, Mary 179
WHITTEMORE, Elizabeth 191 Pelatiah 191
WHITTIER, Franklin 4 Sarah B 4
WHITTUM, Elizabeth 178 Mary 108 Peter 178
WIGGIN, Abigail 132 Andrew 13 Bradstreet 13 Elizabeth 123 Hannah 18 Issacher 123 Mary 49 Mercy 75 Nathan 18 Sarah 13
WILDES, Ephraim 53 Temperance 53
WILEY, John 176
WILKINSON, Elizabeth 33 Thomas 33
WILLEY, John 65 Margaret 180 Mary 26 Paul 26 Sarah 65 147 Stephen 159 Temperance 159
WILLIAM, Abner 194 Lydia 194 Mary 63 William 63
WILLIAMS, Joanna 187 John 105 Margaret 12 Nancy 188 Olive 169 Paul 187 Sarah 105
WILLIS, Hazelponi 131
WILLS, Elizabeth 179 Mary 115
WILSON, Deborah 41 George 13 Henry 40 Martha 13
WINGATE, Abigail 4 110 Ann 110 Caleb 110 John 4 110 Joshua 110 Mary 110 Moses 4 110 Sarah 4 110 167
WINKLEY, John 90 Lydia 90 Samuel 177 Sarah 177
WITHAM, Eunice 80 Mary 36 William 32
WITTAM, Mary 178 William 178
WOODMAN, Betsey 137 Catherine 65 Elizabeth 58 137 John 37 58 83 Jonathan 58 65 137 Katharine 97 Lydia Amanda 77 Martha 137 Mary 37 58 74 83 169
WORCESTER, Mary 106
WRIGHT, John 172 Patience 172
YEATON, John 177 Mary 22 106 177 Mary A 170
YORK, Sarah 128
YOUNG, Alice 194 Anna 156 Ebenezer 28 Eleazer 194 Elizabeth 28 Mary 117 Patience 124

www.ingramcontent.com/pod-product-compliance
Lightning Source LLC
Chambersburg PA
CBHW050144170426
43197CB00011B/1960